HOW
TO
SURVIVE
PARENTHOOD

HOW
TO
SURVIVE
PARENTHOOD

Eda J. LeShan

RANDOM HOUSE

New York

The author wishes to thank the authors and publishers for permission to reprint from the following copyrighted material:

Report on speech by Dr. William E. Martin, in April 1961 *Newsletter of the Association for Family Living.*

Article by Dr. Francis Bauer, entitled "The Plight of the Brand-New Parent," in the *New York Times Magazine,* April 7, 1963.

Article by Dr. Margaret Mead, entitled "Why Americans Must Limit Their Families," in *Redbook* magazine, August 1963.

Report by Susan Szekely in the *New York Post,* November 21, 1963. Copyright 1963, New York Post Corporation. Reprinted by permission of the *New York Post.*

The Widening World of Childhood, by Lois Murphy. Reprinted by permission of the publishers, Basic Books, Inc., New York.

Article by D. K. Winebrenner in *Today's Child,* December 1962.

Article by Selma Fraiberg, entitled "Life and Times with a Two-Year-Old," in *Parents' Magazine,* December 1963. Published by Parents' Magazine Enterprises, Inc., New York.

The Insider's Newsletter, September 9, 1963. © Copyright, 1963, by Cowles Magazines and Broadcasting, Inc.

Reprinted by permission from *The Book of the Dance,* by Agnes de Mille © Copyright, 1963, by Golden Press, Inc.

"The Pre-Teens," *Time* magazine, April 20, 1962.

Article by Harold Taylor, entitled "The Education of a Modern Girl," in *The PTA Magazine,* September 1963. Published by the National Congress of Parents and Teachers, Chicago, Illinois.

Anniversary Waltz. Copyright, 1954, by Jerome Chodorov and Joseph Fields. Reprinted by permission of Random House, Inc.

Material written by the author for the Eva Lawton Memorial Paper, published in the *Newsletter of the Association for Family Living,* 1963.

This book is respectfully dedicated
to the memory of a man who was absolutely
committed to his work, who affirmed life in every way,
who was utterly and completely himself—
and through these qualities could be
and was a joyous parent

JOHN FITZGERALD KENNEDY

Acknowledgments

The authorship of a book never truly reflects the full measure of those who have played a significant, indeed an essential, part in its creation. Let me first mention those who encouraged me from the beginning and who reflected in their lives, and made possible in mine, the wish to live creatively—my parents, Max and Jean Grossman. And also my daughter Wendy, who helped me to grow, to search for what is most human in myself, and who taught me so much about responding to life with honesty and wonder.

There have been so many friends, relatives and co-workers who have encouraged me that it would be impossible to name them all. However, to those who either read the manuscript and discussed the work with me or provided the inspiration of ideas and the challenge of disagreement, a special word of thanks: Dorothy Barclay, Catherine Chilman, Sarah Connell, Mildred Rabinow, Phyllis Shapiro and Myra Woodruff. I feel a very special indebtedness to a greatly loved teacher, the late Ernest G. Osborne. Also, a special word of deep appreciation to Dr. Marthe Gassmann and Dr. Pierre Rubé, who helped me to search out the deeper well-springs of my own thoughts and hopes.

I am grateful to Anne Einhorn, Joan Kassman and Naomi Rosenbloom for helping with preparation of the manuscript.

The source of most of my inspiration has been the hundreds of parents I have met and talked with during the past twenty years, who showed such wisdom and courage, humor and dedication, who worked so hard and tried so hard to make parenthood an honorable as well as a natural role in life. My grateful thanks to all of them, and especially to Mary Haslam, the director, and the parents and teachers of the Colonial Nursery School in New Rochelle, New York.

My thanks also to some of the many who helped me try learning to write: Mary Buchanan and her staff at *Parents' Magazine*; Frances DeArmand; Eva Grant, editor of *The PTA Magazine*; Freda Kehm, director of the Association for Family Living; and Edith Neisser.

As a working mother who knows the value of warmly and truly given service in helping with homemaking, may I also thank Mrs. Caroline Burke and Mrs. Ruby Hogans.

If it had not been for the encouragement and patient endurance of Murray Polner, who conceived the idea for this book and who made me work despite my protests, excuses and feelings of despair, this book would never have been completed.

And last, but far from least, to my co-worker in writing and in living, who sacrificed his own duties and time over and over again, to encourage and advise me, and without whom no accomplishment would have any meaning—to my husband, Lawrence LeShan, my love and gratitude.

EDA J. LeSHAN

New York, 1964

Contents

* *with apologies to Arthur Koppit*

The

EARLY
YEARS

The Guilty Parent and How He Grew

A very attractive and lively young mother walks into my office in a Westchester nursery school: "I suppose now you'll tell me all the things I've done wrong," she says wryly.

At parents' meetings in schools and community centers—in all parts of the country, and over many, many years—parents have asked:

My children fight—how can I make them stop?

My child is having nightmares—what have I done wrong?

My daughter is shy—how can I make her change?

My son said he hates me—where have I failed?

And in my own home—well, hardly a day goes by when I do not find myself feeling fearful and guilty because of my shortcomings as a parent.

As typical, normal, healthy, blamed, guilty, anxious American parents, we all worry much of the time. We feel guilty when we lose our tempers, we feel threatened and anxious when our children have problems. Many of us are self-conscious and inhibited with our children a lot of the time. Any self-respecting nineteenth-century parent would be horrified by the amount of time we spend *with* our children or worrying *about* our children. We are convinced that we will be judged by the world according to our children's behavior.

A recent cartoon, showing a picture of a mother and her small son in the psychiatrist's office, has her saying, "He makes me feel unwanted." *The New Yorker* magazine reports a conversation overheard in a crowded section of Macy's—a harried mother to a restless five-year-old: "You've got to behave, Arthur, because I have no time for psychology." And, as observant youngsters watch their parents, one five-year-old comments, "I don't ever want to be a mommy, it's too aggravating!"

A young father reported that he viewed the changing pattern of child-raising practices in terms of white-meat chicken. He went on to explain that when he was a child, his father had been the head of the house, with absolute authority. When the family sat down to Sunday dinner, Father stood at the head of the table and carved the chicken. Mother sat next to him, and was served first. Then Father served himself. The young man explained, "I was the youngest of five children, and by the time I was served, all the white meat was gone. It looked so delicious, but I never got to taste it. I swore to myself that when I grew up I would eat all the white meat I could. Now I'm grown-up and a father—and my children get first choice!"

At a child study meeting, one of the women brought her mother along to listen in on the discussion. Grandma was an old lady from the Old Country. All during the meeting she listened to the women complain about all their problems, their harassments, their anxieties. She kept shaking her head in sympathy, and after the meeting was over she said, "I enjoyed the meeting, but I tell you, young mothers today—the things they worry about! To listen to all of you, it sounds like you need a college degree to raise children. How did we do it —and without worrying so much? I'll tell you what I used to do when I got tired and wanted to get a little relaxation.

"I had eight children, and we lived in a tenement on the East Side, about half a mile from Central Park. On a nice spring day I would line up the children, each with a partner, and we would march to the park. When we got there I would find a nice hill with a tree on it, and some sun and a little shade, and I would tell my children to sit down in a big circle around me. I would lie down on the grass in the middle and say to the children, 'This is a special park for mothers to rest, but there are kidnapers here who steal mothers. You've got to sit here and guard me.' Then I would go to sleep." Then, shrugging her shoulders to show us how simple life could be if you just had good sense, she added, "They got the air, and I got my rest!"

This grandmother's story demonstrates so clearly the differences that have occurred in one generation. It is easy enough to imagine the guilt today's parents would feel about doing such a thing. What about the awful trauma that might result from telling children that Mother might be kidnaped? Why, we would be afraid that we would scar our children for life with such a tale!

Parents feel watched; as one father put it, "Every time I yell at my kids, I have the feeling that I'm being reported to some secret psychiatric police force!"

Parents blame the "child expert" for their feelings of unease and inadequacy. It isn't that simple: new knowledge brings new questions; rapid change brings uncertainties. Experts have been trying to answer parents' questions, and both have shared the confusion and disillusionment. Something has happened during the past fifty years which has tended to make many of us think that we could find simple answers to the most complicated questions. That "something" has been a dramatic revolution—the impact of psychiatry and psychology on our understanding of man. Many of us grew up in this era and started to raise our children in the belief that the research and new-found knowledge in these fields would provide us with a kind of perfect mastery over ourselves and our children.

It has taken us a long time to face the fact that nothing is that simple. The truth of the matter is that brothers and sisters will sometimes dislike each other and fight, in any home, under any kind of parental care; all children will have nightmares at some stage of growth—the psychoanalyst's child no less frequently than the grocery clerk's; some people stay shy all their lives—and may turn out to be among the nicest and kindest people we know; and parents who may be scored as "successes" or "failures" have been cordially hated by sons and daughters at one time or another.

A lot of us, parents and experts alike, are beginning to sense that something has gone wrong—things aren't working out the way we expected. We thought we could count on the magic power of science to make it possible for us to understand ourselves, to control our behavior, to become perfect parents raising children with perfect mental health (an illusive and uncertain goal, if ever there was one), and that we would accomplish all this as swiftly and efficiently as we are mastering the physical world through science.

Where did we get this sense of omnipotence? How did we become so presumptuous? How could we have believed that the human being, the whole miracle of life with its mysteries, its marvelous complexities, could be harnessed, tamed, molded and understood—or that this would even be a good idea, if we could do it?

Ever since the Renaissance, man has believed that he could change and control the physical world through reason and science. During the late nineteenth and early twentieth centuries, he began to apply this philosophy to human beings, considering them as objects in the universe, as "things" that could be studied and controlled in the same way as any other objects. If an engineer could discover the laws by which he could build a bridge that would not collapse, then the science of human engineering could produce blueprints for human development.

We have attempted, in the twentieth century, to bring human life under scientific scrutiny and control. Through the genius of Freud and the resultant development of a remarkable new body of valid and exciting knowledge, we thought we were on the threshold of utopia. While this was something of an exaggeration, a revolution in the understanding of man *has* taken place in our time. The last half-century of exploration in the fields of psychology and psychiatry *have* changed our most basic concepts of human development and experience. Every aspect of our lives has been modified and influenced by these remarkable breakthroughs in our understanding of human nature. There isn't a movie or a novel that doesn't reflect these changes. Our grade school youngsters speak of "unconscious feelings"; we accept as facts of life such radical concepts as "repression," "compulsion," psychosomatic illness and the idea that there are universal primitive needs and wishes shared by all human beings. The insights of the last fifty years have changed our entire frame of reference about human beings, and the impact on civilization staggers the imagination.

However, having brought science to the study of man, we made the mistaken assumption that this would solve all our problems. Where the great philosophies and religions of Western civilization had, for many people, left many questions unanswered, many problems unsolved, there was fallow soil for a new faith, a new hope. Fascinating new information was coming from research and clinical practice; through the study of pathology, of mental illness and maladjustment, we were learning that what happened to people when they grew up was influenced by childhood experiences. We thought that with the proper information about personality development and the right methods and techniques, all children could be well adjusted, mental illness would be cured—in fact, *prevented*; fears, anxieties, frustrations, hostilities—all these could be eliminated. A mother, a father and a baby, neurosis-free, could be the secret of man's salvation on earth! We stood in awe and wonder, as well we should, before our increasing knowledge—but we also lost our humility, our sense of proportion; we had tried to oversimplify the complex mystery of human beings.

Our unrealistic expectations were enhanced and reinforced by a secondary revolution going on simultaneously. Industrialization and urbanization were changing the pattern of family life, and along with woman suffrage, were causing swift and significant changes in the roles of men and women in society. The effects on women seemed most dramatic, and perhaps still are. An earlier and less complex society had made women partners with men in an economic struggle for survival. In an agricultural and nonindustrial society women were the manufacturers of the goods needed for living, they shared with their husbands a sense of personal importance in maintaining their own and their children's lives. If they didn't preserve vegetables and fruits, bake bread, smoke meat, weave cloth, manufacture soap and candles, their families could not live. Women had a sense of their importance, of the dignity and status of their role. The frozen food, the washing machine, the manufactured textile, the vacuum cleaner, as well as the urban dwelling and the corner bakery, meant a dramatic shift in women's sense of purpose and identity. While she might continue to bake homemade cakes and sew her own drapes, no woman could fool herself into believing that this was still an absolutely essential social function. And this reality, plus the new information about human personality, played a major role in the creation of the "professional parent."

With a loss of significance in so many aspects of homemaking, women brought a special fervor, a deep emotional investment, to the new frontier, to the arena in which they felt they could now make the greatest contribution of all—raising children scientifically. Parenthood could be the new source of gratification and self-esteem. Unfortunately, women who knew that if they measured the ingredients carefully and set the oven at an exact temperature, they could make a perfect cake over and over again, applied somewhat the same reasoning to child-raising, and the climate of public opinion (including many of the experts) tended to confirm this kind of thinking. They asked the specific question; they studied the theories of child development; they joined the PTA discussion group—and always there was that underlying assumption, "I will learn to do it right, and my children will be happy." Unfortunately, this frequently led to a subtle demand for perfection. A father said to me once, "I felt I was being pushed and pressured to go to college. My father had to go to work when he was fourteen years old, and he wanted me to have, and be, everything he wasn't. But you know, that wasn't half as bad as what *we* want from *our* children—and that is that they must be happy and well adjusted because we're so understanding!" It is true—there has been a covert, unconscious kind of demand we have made of our children, not open and direct like the old-fashioned kind. "Be better educated, be more successful than I was." Now the demand is: "Be a psychologically healthy person—mature, responsible, understanding, living without fear, and most of all, *love* us!" The strain on our children is increasingly clear!

The hope that "my children will be better adjusted because I will learn to avoid the pitfalls" just never happened that way—not for parents and not for experts. The "ingredients" could never be so clearly identified or understood, nor were they as constant as those in cake-baking! The most concerted efforts, quantities of understanding and unconditional love, assiduous efforts to maintain consistent disciplinary techniques, still produced children who refused to live up to our predictions, our formulas. Part of the problem was that we could not know everything about our children, we could not fathom the full scope and depth of human mystery. Insight in psychotherapy did not produce anxiety-free adults; security and love didn't eliminate the jealous sibling; identical child-raising practices had widely different results with different children. Marvelous things *were* happening; there is no question but that what we have learned has produced fantastic, positive changes in people and families—but we wanted much more. We were learning what emotional illness was and we were learning methods of healing. But some of us wanted to decide what *health* was and then produce it on a mass scale, and this is where we failed. And so, when we and our children have had to meet the necessary and normal frustrations of life, when we have needed to make peace with our special and inherent differences, when we should have celebrated and enjoyed the very things about personality that are still marvelously divergent and wondrously mysterious, we became disillusioned, we felt betrayed, for life had not been made tranquil, we and our children were not happy all the time, we could not seem to protect our children from the broad range of agony and ecstasy that is part of being human.

A few years ago, speaking at a meeting of the Association for Family Living in Chicago, Dr. Margaret Mead pointed out that just at a time when more and more was being demanded of parents in terms of knowledge and skills for parenthood, we were also making parents responsible for raising their children entirely alone. Fifty years ago, in small rural communities, almost every household included grandparents, often other relatives such as a maiden aunt or a widowed uncle. The small towns, which represented the majority of the population, were closely knit, and families were very dependent on each other and worked with and for each other. Young parents were rarely alone or totally responsible for child-raising. Now families are more mobile, they move from job to job, they live in small apartments or houses, quite alone, with fewer roots and ties to others. Dr. Mead's observations pointed up the fact that while we are demanding more of parents, we provide fewer sources of direct help and personal support.

In a speech given at a conference at the Merrill Palmer Institute in April, 1961, Dr. William E. Martin, chairman of the Department of Child Development and Family Life at Purdue University, talked about parenthood today:

> . . . The realization of their power has produced in parents self-consciousness, fear, anxiety, guilt, immobilization and suspension of judgment, sometimes resulting in paralysis and extreme permissiveness, and has impelled them to a search for authority and often a confessor . . .
>
> In the absence of clear evidence of success, the modern parent can never relax. He must be acutely sensitive, not only to what his child is doing, but also why he is doing it and the immediate and long-term consequences of that behavior. Being a parent must necessarily be a stressful, anxious, and often defeating experience under these circumstances.

In speaking several years ago at an annual conference for parent educators, sponsored by the Child Study Association, Dr. Benjamin Spock looked back over the last two decades of parent education and observed that the experts had overwhelmed parents by expecting superhuman virtues. He talked of the way in which we had listed what was good and what was bad, what was right and what was wrong in child-raising, and how we had warned parents of the unfortunate outcome, the possibly dire consequences of not doing it right. He said, "We scare and blame the wrong people—the ones who are listening to us!" He felt that much of parent education had discouraged parents from using their own initiative, intuition, judgment, and had created a great deal of guilt. He also talked about the psychiatrist's natural preoccupation with pathology, and the danger of this orientation in working with normal families. He hoped we would "see the need for trusting health more."

There seems to be an increasing awareness of parental distress, anxiety and disillusionment, as well as a need for a careful re-evaluation of some of the profound philosophical misconceptions and dangerous blind spots that have resulted from our first half-century of exploration of man's nature and needs.

When I meet and talk with parents I find that two central themes almost invariably appear in our discussion. The first is a constant hope that I will be able to give them simple formulas for raising their children, that I will be able to give them direct advice which will solve their problems. Usually the problems are very complicated. They have been going on for a long, long time, in one form or another. The parents are complicated people, and so are the children. The problems represent a myriad of connected causes and effects, many of which are normal and natural and necessary for growth, especially in as complicated a society as we live in. There isn't an answer in the world that could solve their questions easily, quickly, simply.

The other reaction is that nothing I say, or that anyone else says, can possibly help them. None of the books they've read, the speeches they've listened to, have made any difference at all. They feel betrayed and let down; they hoped for so much, and they haven't gotten any real help. They say, "I managed to grow up and my parents didn't know anything about child psychology. What was good enough for me will have to be good enough for my children."

When I talk to the experts, I find that there is no real difference. Many of us are horrified, we feel disillusioned when our children get into any trouble. When our children have learning difficulties, or lie to us, or we find that they have stolen something, or when a teen-ager wants to get married, we are filled with guilt and shock. How could this happen when we were understanding, patient—when we "did things right"?

I myself and all those experts whom I have admired were a lot harder on ourselves than on anybody else. We didn't scold or blame when we met with other parents, but for many years we did assume that we had to be better parents than anyone else, and so our failings were constantly accentuated.

Some of the most sensitive and perceptive experts in the mental health professions have children with problems. The "understood" son of a social worker leaves college to marry a waitress he has known for two weeks; the teen-age daughter of a minister who teaches pastoral counseling runs away from home; a psychologist's child stutters; a psychiatrist's child develops a school phobia.

Sex education by itself didn't guarantee happier marriages; kindly discipline didn't eliminate the bully; demand-feeding didn't create anxiety-free, stable young people. I know good, decent, intelligent parents who cared deeply, tried hard to learn the best new, modern ways to raise children, and who are horrified and ashamed because their children are not at all what they expected them to be. They are sometimes mean, unhappy, bratty kids; they are sometimes dishonest, irresponsible and unkind. They hate and distrust adults a lot of the time. And these are children around whom there has been love and understanding.

We have all known and thought about these facts, but we are all being *quietly* bothered and bewildered. *It is time we stopped the pretense.* Child-raising is more complicated than we dreamed and we have not found the magic key. What are the complexities we are dealing with?

One of our most difficult problems as parents is that we have been trying to do many things that don't "come naturally." New approaches to raising children have come about so rapidly that by the time our children came along, we were trying to use methods that we hadn't experienced ourselves. One of the revolutionary concepts of our generation has been that anger and hostility are normal and natural parts of being human, and that rebelliousness in our children is important for growth. We have been trying to accept the new idea that human beings have frequently paid a high price for keeping their less lovely feelings as secret as possible; that when it was considered evil or immoral or bad to feel hate or anger, people tried to keep it inside themselves and this interfered with their fullest development. Sometimes it led to finding a scapegoat —a socially acceptable way of expressing anger. Sometimes it could lead to such a blocking-off of feeling that people became too passive to be able to compete or work effectively. Sometimes anger got turned in on itself and could cause serious physical illnesses. In children, too much repression of anger could lead to learning problems, excessive fears and nightmares, stuttering, etc. Too much repression certainly seemed to play an important role in serious emotional problems. What we were learning was that we needed to help children understand and accept their feelings and learn to handle them.

A father told this story: One evening, when his daughter was a little over two years old, he had suggested in a quiet and friendly tone that Julie bring him her pajamas so he could help her get ready for bed. Julie looked up at him with a glint in her eye and said, "I will NOT, you big dope!" He said that for a moment he felt faint and nauseous. His heart started beating faster, and his hand was shaking as he reached for a cigarette. He couldn't understand what was happening to him; he had heard about two-year-olds getting negative, and he had heard about children trying to get a rise out of their parents, and he had been told it was normal for children to talk back as a way of proving they were growing up. Why this terrible feeling of danger and unease? He tried to understand: "I had read all the books, I knew she was just 'testing,' experimenting with her own power. And yet I felt sick, I wanted to murder her!" His wife, who had noticed her husband's shaking hand, asked, "What would have happened to you if you had ever talked to your parents that way?" Without a moment's hesitation he replied, "At the very least, I would have been struck dead by lightning."

In trying to be the reasonable, understanding modern parent, he was battling against all his own deep and half-forgotten childhood instincts. Reading books about the normality of aggressiveness in children didn't quite counterbalance those feelings and memories.

He was also taking a lot on faith. He had been raised differently; how could he be sure the new way was better? Was there any real proof? There were lots of different opinions in the new books on child-raising. How could you tell who was right—if anybody was?

I have been impressed by the parents who struggle to do things differently, to give their children experiences they never had themselves; mothers who were themselves rigidly and punitively toilet-trained at six months, trying desperately to be permissive and relaxed with a two-year-old still in diapers; mothers who were overstuffed as children, valiantly trying to listen to their pediatrician's advice that three-year-old children require very little food. I have talked to fathers who "got the strap" when they were fresh or naughty, now trying to control their wish to dominate, and to use other methods, such as reasoning or isolating a child, or responding with understanding instead of threats.

Sometimes, because what we have tried to do is so strange and new, we take ourselves too seriously, and try much too hard. In trying to help their children to be less frightened of their feelings, parents often become more afraid of their own feelings! What we haven't said often enough or clearly enough is that if recognizing and accepting feelings is good for children, it's also good for their parents! If acceptance of imperfection, of human frailty, of human failings, can help children to be more relaxed and to like themselves better, this is equally true for adults.

I remember a mother I met at a nursery school meeting who came up to me after everyone else had left, and told me she just had to unburden herself; she had done something really unforgivable to her children. The past winter had been a very trying one: her daughter was three and her son four and a half, and since this had been his first year in close contact with other children, he caught one cold and childhood disease after another, and passed them along to his little sister. As a result, and in combination with very bad weather, Mama had been stuck indoors with her two darling children for most of several months. She went on, "Then, one day about a week ago, when they were both still convalescing, I reached the end of my rope. They were crying and cranky and fighting with each other, and I think I went sort of crazy. I was shaking all over. I was afraid I might kill them. Even though they hadn't been out for weeks and there was snow on the ground, I put on their snowsuits and sent them outdoors. I told them they couldn't come back in until I let them. I locked the front and back doors! Then I sat down in the kitchen with a cup of coffee and the paper, and after about fifteen minutes I stopped shaking and began to calm down. Even after they started yelling I wouldn't let them in. I stayed alone for almost an hour, and then I opened the door. I was so ashamed of myself that I never even told my husband what I did. Do you think I did them some permanent damage?" I asked about the children. Did they have a relapse, did they seem upset? No, they were well now, and they had had a good lunch and nap after they came in. They seemed a little quiet and looked at her a little warily, but nothing else had happened. Did the older child seem at all fearful later? Oh no, he could hardly wait to go back to nursery school. If the children had cried or called for help, would she have let them in? *Of course.*

I started to laugh and soon this mother laughed too. At first she was quite startled by my reaction, but pretty soon she relaxed and joined me in seeing the funny side of this scene. I told her it would be a good story to tell her children when they had children of their own. I also told her that rather than being an unnatural and evil mother she was just exactly like all the rest of us, and that I hoped she'd enjoyed her stolen moment.—We sometimes reach a point where we have to be selfish and think of ourselves. Apparently her children had taken her need to be alone just for what it was: not total rejection, but human harassment and a need for relief.

At a meeting in a grade school, another mother told of an experience that was wonderfully therapeutic for all of us. She too had had a rough winter, with two boys, aged nine and eleven, out of school with a series of illnesses, and very much on each other's and her nerves.

"Every morning when I woke up I wondered what scene from an Edward Albee play would be enacted in my living room that day. Anybody who says some of these new writers exaggerate what goes on in families just never lived in one. Well, this day was the worst yet. Andy and Bill started picking on each other the minute they got up, and between their runny noses and droopy pajamas and the mess in their room, I was ready to give them away. They had about their fifth big fight early in the afternoon, when I decided I should try to pull myself together and be a good mother—even if it killed me! Yelling wasn't getting me anywhere. So, very sweetly I said, 'Come on, boys, let's have a party. I'll make some cocoa and we'll sit in the dining room and be very elegant.' They liked this idea, and I thought, 'Maybe there's something to all this psychology business after all.' I put out the good linen place mats, and the cocoa and a can of Redi-Whip. Just then the phone rang, and I told the boys not to touch anything until I got back. I made it as short as I could, knowing them, but not short enough. When I came back, they had tried to squirt the Redi-Whip into the cocoa, and there was cocoa on the rug, cocoa on the table . . . a real mess. Well, it was as if I suddenly blacked out—I really went berserk. It was the last straw, and a screw came loose. I took that can of Redi-Whip and I squirted it on the kids and I squirted it on the walls, and I ran around like a crazy nut with that thing, yelling the whole time. Suddenly I came to. My God, what was I doing? What a way for a mother to behave—what a terrible example to set—and I had probably scared them to death. I looked around, and at first I couldn't find them. Then I see they're in the living room, rolling on the floor, dying, they're laughing so hard! We had a marvelous time cleaning up, we laughed all afternoon, and got hysterical again telling my husband that night; and now, every time I start to get mad, the kids yell 'Redi-Whip' and duck. Do you think I scarred them for life?"

The audience listening to this story provided all the answer anyone needed. The uproar of laughter was cleansing and relaxing, and we agreed her sons had been given a hilarious lesson in human frailty.

It is because I have seen so much in my talks with parents that is marvelously human and refreshing, touchingly courageous, that I decided it was time to speak out. As a parent, I have been constantly watched by an expert—myself! This is known as double jeopardy! It had taken me a long time to realize how much I was expecting of myself, what enormous claims I was making: that knowledge and effort should make life smooth, easy and rewarding. I think, all in all, that I have been harder on myself than on other parents, although this was not always true. When I was in college, and during the years when I worked as a nursery school teacher and studied to become a child psychologist, I was as convinced as most other people that the new information that was coming to us from research centers all over the world was going to make it possible to solve all child-raising problems. At the age of twenty I knew with a burst of clarity that children were wonderful and could grow up to be perfect, except for one slight drawback: they had parents! If I worked hard, I might be able to undo some of the awful things those parents were doing.

My omnipotence lasted for quite a while. I became a fanatical and totally committed member of the religion of psychoanalysis. When I met my husband, a less rabid experimental psychologist, I used whatever resources I could muster to make him see the light, and we were married and lived by the Freudian tenet!

It might have gone on forever—exhorting parents to do what I said, blaming parents for their children's problems, enthusiastically instructing parents on "the right way" to raise children—but several factors intervened. I became a parent myself, and I began to look at reality with a little more candor. We discovered that our daughter, uncommitted to any school of psychiatry, wasn't going to fit any of our formulas; she was an unpredictable, mysterious, unknown quantity; she was *herself*. The whole thing came in a steady and continuing flow of shocks to our professional egos. In our work, we began to look with a jaundiced eye on the too-easy, pat explanations of human behavior. Clinical diagnoses failed to satisfactorily describe the marvelous quirks and fascinating peculiarities in people. It disturbed us mightily, but we began to admit to each other that diagnostic test reports all sounded alike; everybody went though an oral phase and an anal phase and an oedipal phase; but people who had the same labels were so markedly different—there just had to be more to the picture. We also began to observe that insight into their own unconscious problems wasn't curing patients receiving psychotherapy of all of their problems. Gradually our tools for understanding and solving human problems began to appear less magical and all-powerful. Humility set in; in fact, a new humility is abroad in the land. We are beginning to realize that it was a violation of the human spirit to treat it like a machine. No single theory or group of theories, none of the labels we created, however valid they may have been, in part, ever captured the essence of man. A diagnosis doesn't create a person or explain poetry or idealism or love. We are beginning to have a healthy respect for the unknown mysteries, the strange and special and still little understood human soul.

If we can accept and understand where we lost our way we can begin to move again, without that sense of having been betrayed, without cynicism and a sense of having failed. For we certainly did *not* fail at all. The new insights have contributed enormously in helping people to understand themselves and each other, to communicate, to express their needs, to release themselves from the paralyzing effects of serious emotional crippling. Our error lay only in expecting too much and in assuming that we could define and create the healthy personality, whereas this involves a range, a variety, a breadth of possibilities, before which we must still stand in awe and wonder.

Because I have felt deeply and struggled greatly to understand and to gain a new perspective on our problems and challenges, I want to share some of my thinking. In all my contacts with parents, my most intense and consistent impression has been that parents are, like any people, more often quite wonderful than not; that a very large number have worked gallantly to understand new ideas and to make use of new insights. Confusion has been coupled with courage; despite anxiety and uncertainty I have seen parents struggle tenaciously to learn, to adapt, to experiment. Because some of us demanded too much, we have felt disappointed and let down. Despite this, we really are making many wonderful and important gains, and we shouldn't be so discouraged. My hope is that we can regain a sense of perspective, and without rejecting new ideas, re-evaluate the use we make of our knowledge so that it may become more truly and individually ours. Rapid change has tended to make us feel uneasy, alienated from what is basic, true, instinctual, in ourselves. It seems to me that this need not continue. We need to find out what interferes most with the enjoyment of parenthood today, and what can be done about it.

My husband and I have had an opportunity to live with and become close friends with a French family living in a small town in the north of France. During one of our visits there, I tried to explain to the mother what it was that I did in America, what my job was. Despite my fractured French, she seemed to understand very well; in America there were people who studied all about children and then gave parents advice about raising them. She shrugged unhappily and said, "I am afraid we have nothing like that here. All we can do is raise them by the heart."

It seems to me that it should be possible to use new information, to go on learning, to use knowledge in such a way that instead of paralyzing us, it would free us to be more natural, to be more deeply and truly ourselves, to open ourselves to life, and to live by the heart as well.

We All Wanted *Babies*—but Did Any of Us Want *Children?*

My daughter and I were having lunch in a drugstore crowded with young mothers and their children. Four of the young women were very pregnant, and after my daughter had listened to them screaming at their nursery school age children for about fifteen minutes without letup, she asked a very perceptive and logical question, "If they hate their kids so much, why are they having more?"

A Dutch émigré, mother of four and grandmother of seven, asked me the same question recently when we were discussing the young families she was observing in the suburban community she had come to live in. "They complain so much— they have so many children, and they don't seem at all glad to have them. Is this an American trait?" Whether one could call it a trait or not, it does seem to me that in the last ten years I have met more young families with four to six children, usually one to two years apart, who seem to feel overwhelmed—after the fact. Millions of American couples are having larger families and enjoying it; we all know about them. What we don't talk about as often is the parents who are in serious conflict.

In an article in the *New York Times Magazine*, Dr. Francis Bauer, a psychiatrist, wrote of "The Plight of the Brand-New Parent." He reported on a study undertaken at the University of Michigan which had revealed some interesting facts:

> . . . Basically . . . many young parents are troubled because they are unable to reconcile their true, inner feelings with the way they think they ought to feel . . .
> . . . conflicts arise from an overemphasis on fulfilling the needs of the newborn. Ever since Sigmund Freud focused attention on the importance of early childhood . . . it has been open season on new mothers . . . It is not surprising that when the new mother leaves the hospital with her baby in one arm and three volumes on child care under the other, her thin smile often fails to mask her underlying sense of panic. She is in many instances terrified at the prospect of motherhood and has grave misgivings about proving equal to what has become the most formidable challenge of modern society—raising a healthy happy infant.

Most of us mothers who grew up twenty or thirty years ago, played with dolls and had lovely dreams of marrying a handsome prince and having several beautiful and charming children. This kind of fantasy has probably been true for most children over many generations. But our growing-up time was different and special in some ways. Many of us belong to the first generation to be told that dreams *do* come true and that we *would* live happily ever after. It was an era of hope, of increasing prosperity, of a sense of power about man's ability to conquer disease, poverty, unhappiness. The increasing power of mass media added fuel to a climate of "life can be beautiful." Advertisements teased us with easy answers and oversimplified solutions to complex problems: use the right deodorant and you will meet a rich and handsome man; buy the right set of sterling silver and the domestic scene will be forever blissful; feed your babies the only baby food guaranteed to be fortified with every vitamin and mineral and your baby will never be sick or cranky or funny-looking. Neither our parents nor the movies we saw nor the magazines we read ever suggested that life was more complicated, that happiness was a fortuitous by-product of living, not an end in itself. In truth, we had the least realistic preparation for the hardest job of all.

We knew about the joys and pleasures of marriage and parenthood, but no one ever really told us about the displeasures, the serious responsibilities, the plain drudgery.

I think most of us carry into marriage not only our childlike illusions, but we bring to it as well the demand that it *has* to be wonderful, because it's *supposed* to be. Of course the biggest illusion of all is that we are going to do the job of parenthood so well: it will all be fun and always deeply satisfying.

When we bring our babies home, we *do* feel proud and happy, and to the degree that our natural instincts are still permitted to operate, there is a strange and marvelous sense of having found one's destiny. But before we can really relax and let ourselves *feel*, we begin to get scared. First of all we get scared because we find we don't enjoy a baby every minute of the day and night. We feel uneasy because we begin to realize the utter helplessness of this baby, and the fact that we will belong to him and to his needs for a long, long time. Occasionally there is the feeling that we have unwittingly accepted life imprisonment! No man or woman I ever knew loved to spend half of every night feeding and walking and changing a baby. The large majority of perfectly decent, civilized adults simply do not enjoy a steady diet of having to wake from a deep sleep, move around in cold, dark rooms—especially while one's spouse snores peacefully—and know that even after the baby is clean and fed and happy, this whole operation is coming up again in a few hours, when, unbelievably, it will *still* be earlier than you ever got up before!

Discussing this with friends recently, one mother said, "My memory of those first few weeks is of a sense of utter chaos and of my being completely incompetent. I wasn't, but I felt that I was. Every time I made the formula I was sure something would go wrong, and I was absolutely certain I would never get the baby's clothes washed and dried in time. I could not imagine there was any possibility that I would ever again have time for such activities as reading a book, really talking to my husband or going to a movie. Shopping became a nightmare of anxiety—I couldn't leave the baby carriage outside the store, and of course the baby was too young to sit in the shopping cart. The whole business was so traumatizing that I can't remember what I finally *did* do!"

As parents, we all know and remember the joys and satisfactions: the attention we received, the pride in seeing other people's reactions to the baby, wheeling a carriage down the street, feeling this warm, tiny body snuggled against one, feeling that one has participated in the great miracle of life. With an easy, relaxed baby, it can be fun most of the time—but even under the best of circumstances it just has to be a nuisance sometimes. The isolation for the mother who now may lose contact with a job or with friends, being alone with a baby who certainly isn't much of a conversationalist, having to do the same routine things over and over again—all this is *not* completely compensated for because babies happen to be absolutely adorable. But we get frightened the very first time we think, "Why was I in such a hurry? Why didn't I wait another year? Why didn't we take a trip instead? Now I'm a prisoner forever—this baby owns me body and soul—I'm finished, all washed up!"

Wives feel trapped, husbands feel betrayed and neglected. Lack of sleep makes tempers short, and love which thrives on privacy is thwarted—and then that baby starts crying again! Nothing could be more normal. Life is never easy or fun all the time. Parenthood has wonderful attributes which hardly need explanation; it offers a special kind of fulfillment, it brings with it a keener sense of being alive, a renewed and re-awakened sense of wonder at life and at growth, and it is of course an affirmation of love—it makes the meaning of marriage more tangible and real. But even little babies can be big burdens, and why shouldn't we hate and resent them once in a while? Most of us feel overwhelmed with guilt if we are not delighted every single second.

We begin to come closer to a sane view of life and love when we begin to accept parenthood as a worthwhile but often difficult and trying job. I remember what a father told me, with a sheepish smile, when his four-month-old son started howling for the eighth time during a dinner party, "It's the funniest thing; I never used to notice how many people murdered their babies but when I read a newspaper now, that's all I seem to notice! Has there been a sudden epidemic of cases of infanticide, or do I just notice it more now?" If most of us were really honest with ourselves and each other, we would admit that there were moments——! One of the best-kept secrets is that almost every mother alive, at some time or other, has screamed at, shaken or even at times hit her baby. We work so hard to maintain the myth that changing diapers, worrying about fevers, cleaning up vomit and listening to crying are the most popular activities and the greatest privileges obtainable.

Another mother told me, "One day our very colicky and cranky three-month-old daughter just cried so much and made me feel so incompetent and helpless and miserable that I shook her hard and dumped her into the crib, ran out of the room, and sobbed and sobbed until my husband arrived home, found us both bawling, put his arms around us and said, 'There, there,' until we both stopped gulping hysterically and calmed down." That is as much part of the reality of becoming a parent as the blissful, wide-eyed wonder that one also feels the first time the baby smiles, rolls over, or says "Dadda."

. . .

People used to have children because (among other reasons!) they needed them: for farming the land, for settling new territories, for developing commerce on the seas—for keeping the human race going, in fact. Infant mortality was so high and death from childhood diseases so common that every living breathing child was a precious and necessary economic asset. Obviously things are quite the reverse now—we are made to feel guilty if we support the population explosion! While only four or five years ago birth control or population control were rarely if ever discussed publicly, a complete change has taken place. Magazines, newspapers—even politicians—are now discussing a real and grave concern: overpopulation. Margaret Mead, in *Redbook* magazine, stated openly and clearly "Why Americans Must Limit Their Families":

> . . . At the present rate of increase the population of the United States, now at some 189 million, is likely to reach 351 million in the year 2000 . . . Continuing at the same rate, the United States alone will pass the billion mark in 2050 A.D.

Whatever else all this may mean, one thing is sure: it does play a role in how we feel about children. Children are an economic drain on parents to such an extent that in all likelihood all those children who are brought into the world intentionally must have been conceived for reasons completely different from those of past civilizations. Even in earlier times the desire to have children was of course based on motives other than economic, but it makes a difference when society no longer needs so many children for survival. When we have children for emotional reasons, for love only, then our expectations are of an entirely dissimilar nature. This experience has to be more satisfying and rewarding, or we feel cheated.

To have children for reasons of emotional gratification and fulfillment and for fun may be perfectly reasonable, if we accept what this means. There will be no rewards for good behavior; children will not appreciate our selfless devotion and behave angelically just because we try so hard. We must not look forward to a time when our children will be an economic or a social asset; it will be a long, long drain on our resources of every kind. It can't be fun all the time; being human, children get sick, are often a nuisance, will have at least the normal range of problems that are simply part of growing up. We never get what we bargained for; there is no use in having prior claims and expectations, because these demands are a distortion of life and an impossibility. It is as foolish to say, "I will have a sweet, quiet child," as it is to say, "My child will look like his father."

To have children is no way to solve problems, whether it be a shaky marriage, a wish to quit working at a dull or tiring job, the next "right thing to do," a way to please one's parents, or a way to postpone the "menopause blues" when we don't quite know what to do with ourselves and feel less and less needed by our growing children. Most of us had mixed reasons for and mixed feelings about becoming parents; but all things considered, we will get on with the job at hand far more successfully if at the outset we try to gain some clarity on what we have been feeling and expecting.

Accepting reality—with its joys as well as its problems—makes it easier for us to plan, lest from the very beginning parenthood become the be-all and end-all for us; if it does, then our demands for satisfaction from it are just too awesome a burden for any child to carry. To keep one's sanity while raising an infant, one has to maintain a sense of proportion and perspective. That baby is not going to stay helpless and dependent forever, and he's not going to need us one hundred percent of the time, so we had better tend other gardens as well, such as seeing that our marriage is given time and attention, that we make opportunities for adult-centered activities, keeping up with friends and our own interests. Both husband and wife have a stake in the maintenance of a life apart from child-raising, and both must work at finding those outlets and opportunities that can keep their own communication and contact alive. One thing that we *have* to afford—it is as vital as the baby's regular visits to the doctor—is a long list of really reliable baby-sitters. Some of us may be lucky enough to have a number of volunteers, like grandparents, on our list, but it should also include several other older people who might be available when we need them. Such a list tends to make one feel less trapped—that there is, after all, an escape clause! Getting away for one afternoon a week to do something adult and refreshing or enriching is a necessity, not a luxury. Some women whine that it can't be done. It can. There is just no excuse for much of the self-pity we are sometimes inclined to wallow in.

Already with a tiny baby, parents feel the impact of the experts: the pediatrician; Dr. Spock; the lady in the park who's had seven children; the vaguely remembered pitfalls described in the psychology courses one took at college; the more than generous advice of grandparents. This is the time when one should begin thinking about how to make decisions, what "common sense" is; how to be discriminating and at the same time open-minded in learning to care for a child. Common sense is really the way in which we learn to combine information, experience, intuition and spontaneity. We never succeed completely, but there is simply no such thing as a perfect score where human relationships are concerned.

With all the realities of infant care that we may have been unprepared for, this is as nothing compared to our surprise at what *children* are like! They begin by saying "No," and we have the first inkling of the battles for power that lie ahead. We feel undermined, attacked; panic and anger set in. Then they begin to get into everything, nothing is sacred, and we have to change our entire household arrangements. Right after absolutely refusing to do what we tell them, they cling to us, won't let us out of their sight, and we find that we can't even go to the bathroom alone any more!

We begin to feel the pressures on us from grandparents and experts to toilet-train; we are instructed on how to encourage good eating habits; when to pick up a crying child, when not to. No two theories are very much alike, and none of the instructions seem to have much practical applicability to the crises we are facing. Nightmares may keep us sleepless, clinging and shyness embarrass us, as well as talking back, biting, selfishness with toys, aggressiveness with other children—this is just the beginning! At least they are still cute when all this starts. But they are no longer so cute when some of the most exasperating and frightening things begin to happen—lying, stealing, starting fires, not learning fast enough—and then, to add insult to injury, the final straw: they begin to show intense dislike for us from time to time. A mother said recently, "Sometimes I just look at Marian; who is this fresh, sloppy, unpleasant child? Can she really be that adorable baby I had twelve years ago?"

We feel guilty when we lose our patience, we worry about all the things we are doing wrong, we feel bored and discontented with the humdrum of daily routines. Survival doesn't seem a sure thing at all! We spend too much time worrying about our children and feel much too guilty about our failures; but ignoring the places where we get stuck, where we feel we are failing, won't help us to survive. What I'd like to do is talk about children for several chapters, with one central aim in mind: what seems to me to be some of the most common stumbling blocks, as I have learned about them from my own experience and from talking with other parents, and what ideas seem to me to be most helpful in relieving our sense of pressure and our concerns.

This is not a book about child development in general; there are now hundreds of books available if you want a broad picture of growth, and a discussion of all the aspects of growth. But it seems to me that there are a few quite specific aspects of each general stage of growth that, if they can be reassessed, might possibly ease some parental strain.

CHAPTER

❦ 3 ❦

If You Are a Parent It Helps
If You Are Grown-Up

I have met many parents who were not grownups. The immature parent wants life to be easy; consequently, every difficulty with children represents a threat to comfort and happiness. Partly because nowadays people get married very early, many of them are still intensely attached to their own parents, even when they have children of their own. Where parents are heavily subsidizing a marriage, this dependent tie is even more intense. During a period of prosperity, young people are often offered and accept help so that they may start out living on a scale their parents didn't achieve for many, many years. There is a street in Westchester called "Father-in-law Hill," and I remember my sense of shock on seeing very young families living in $40,000 to $60,000 homes, with parents paying for servants, nursery schools, camps, etc. These are usually not grown-up marriages—they are children playing house.

A nursery school mother once warned us in advance that she expected to have to stay with her child for many weeks. "Ronnie won't let me go," she said. She added, "That child controls me completely, he doesn't let me do anything. He won't go to bed, he won't take a bath, he hits me—what can I do?" I thought to myself, "Well, first of all, you could start acting like a mother."

One morning when I arrived at a nursery school the director said, "I have a new job now." She told me that a few minutes before, the phone rang and a childish voice said, "I'm Leslie. Are you making all the children wear boots today?" The director assured Leslie that that was the case. Apparently, Leslie's mother did not have enough authority or self-assurance to make the decision that it was boot-wearing weather.

The communities that have gone wildly enthusiastic over teen-age social codes represent the same kind of abdication of parental courage and conviction. Unable to impose the standards they want, they depend on external social pressures to take over their responsibilities for them.

I recently met a mother I knew coming out of a toy store in a great rush. She had an enormous toy box in her arms, and apologized for not stopping to talk. "I have a date to play golf and I'm an hour late already. Jerry wouldn't let me go until I said I'd get him this robot!" It was a fifteen-dollar toy. Jerry was four years old; as far as I know, he didn't have a loaded revolver or any other deadly weapon.

We once had a theater date with a group of friends and we planned to meet first for dinner. One couple didn't show up at all for dinner, nor were they at the theater when we got there. They came in, breathlessly, in the middle of the first act. "Danny wouldn't let us leave the house," they whispered. Danny was two and a half years old.

Many years ago, when I was working in a child guidance clinic, Patty, three years old, was referred to me because of her uncontrollable temper and malnutrition due to refusal to eat. When I went to meet her in the waiting room she had managed to disconnect the telephone switchboard lines and pull down the drapes. The desperate receptionist was glad to see me! Patty was told that she was to come into a playroom with me while her mommy talked to another lady in an office next door—we showed her where her mother would be. She began to kick and scream and bite, but I picked her up and carried her to the playroom, closed the door and stood against it. I explained just how long she would have to stay with me, but insisted firmly and quietly that she had to do what I said, even though I knew she was very angry at me. She tore the room apart, she cried, she tried to hit and kick, but I kept insisting I was in charge. After about fifteen minutes Patty stopped dead in her tracks, looked at me, heaved a deep, tired sigh, and said, "You *like* me, don't you?" She knew I liked her because I was the first adult who had ever said No to her! Of course, not all children who rebel or are fearful of being alone with a strange woman should be handled this way. But I knew about Patty before I ever saw her, since her mother had had several consultations with a social worker on our staff. We knew that Patty's mother was seventeen when Patty was born; that three weeks after her birth her nineteen-year-old soldier-father had been sent overseas, and that her mother had been a little girl herself, totally unable to cope with a healthy, robust, spirited youngster. She resented "being stuck with Patty," she wanted to be with her friends, to continue school and get a job. Because of her basic immaturity and her rejection of the responsibility of parenthood, she just gave in to Patty and never made any effort to control her; it was easier that way—at first. But at three, Patty was a holy terror, living on Coca-Cola, and behaving like a junior savage.

Patty felt that I cared for her because I set limits, I acted like a grownup. The day came, after several months, when her mother was able to say as they left the clinic, "No, you certainly may *not* have a candy bar; it's too near dinnertime."

Patty's relief was wonderful to behold. Her mother had grown up.

When my husband and I were graduate students we were invited to a psychology professor's home for a Saturday picnic. When we arrived, with the rest of our class, we discovered that this enterprising professor had invited us over for a leaf-raking party! The only compensation was the promise of a steak barbecue after we'd raked and burned the leaves. We worked hard and were good and hungry by the time his wife came out of the house with a tray of luscious, mouth-watering steaks. She put them on a table near the fireplace. Their two young children were playing in a sandbox nearby, and they began to sprinkle the steaks with sand. The professor spoke to them sweetly and calmly (but without protecting the steaks), "Now, I know you are pretending to salt the steaks, but I think that's enough." Turning to us—and most of us couldn't hide our speechless horror—he said, "Well, that's the price of encouraging creativity." I decided then and there that he had nothing further to teach me about child psychology!

Recently a friend told me about a birthday party she'd given for her four-year-old. One child looked awfully peculiar and puffy and didn't seem to be feeling too well, and she called the child's mother. "Oh yes," this mother responded cheerfully, "I just had her to the pediatrician before the party and he said she had the mumps and couldn't go, but she carried on so, I had to let her."

A friend of my husband's once called him on business and told him he was calling from a phone booth near his house. He went on to explain, "I can't make calls from home because Bobby keeps hanging up the receiver." Bobby was three.

These stories are in the category of "How to Make a Monster." They are all examples of child-adults who have become parents; adults who are too immature to act like grownups, and who have found the excuse of permissiveness to cover up the fact that they are really rejecting their children by refusing to be parents.

How grown-up are we? Can we stand a little discomfort in order to let our child know that we are there to protect him and to help him check impulses over which he has no control as yet? Children who can do whatever they want are cordially disliked by everyone, and are scared to death themselves; the abdication of responsibility that produces such results, under whatever foolish guise, is not love. Overpermissiveness has sometimes been the excuse, the rationalization, by some parents, for laziness and rejection; such permissiveness as this was never recommended by any experts I ever heard of. It is what Dr. Fritz Redl once called "the slimy swamp of total permissiveness."

Of course we want our children to be imaginative, to have a chance to explore the world, and to struggle for independence, because that's part of growth. But children must also feel protected and cared for; they can't be permitted to do things that are hazardous or antisocial; they can't be expected to control their normal, immature, childish impulses— that's where the grownups come in.

Another part of being grown-up is not expecting life to be easy or tranquil. Tranquillity is for cows, not for people! Once when I was sitting in a playground with my daughter, I saw a mother yelling loudly at her little boy to take turns on a slide. The mother returned to the bench, looking tense and unhappy, and said to the watching mothers, "I forgot to take my Miltown this morning; I'm a wreck!" This mother was hardly a candidate for tranquilizers, which may be very helpful to seriously disturbed people; I'd seen her on the playground for many months, and had talked to her. But she had a peculiar idea that raising a child was supposed to be a very calm and easy experience, and that if she took enough medication, nothing would faze her. What nonsense! Of course young children get into fights, and need to be taught to await their turn; of course growing up means learning to share, and not to bite; and it means all the other crises of normal life and growth. It takes work and involves getting tired; it means good days and cranky off-days; it means living, and working at living.

A young and harried mother who had been quite ill herself, and who had also been nursing two sick children, said to me, "I wish I could see what happens in other houses when a child gets sick. Are other people as terrible as I am? I felt so awful, and Elly had kept me up two nights and wouldn't take her medicine—and at two o'clock in the morning I began yelling at her like some kind of nut. I said she was a rotten kid, and if she didn't take her medicine I'd put her in a hospital where they'd give her injections—I even threatened to throw her out in the snow!" If this mother could look into other homes at such moments, she would find a lot of company in her depravity! All of us act like babies sometimes —each of us has a threshold of discomfort, fatigue, anxiety— and each of us has a breaking point. But if we are grown-up, we stop in our tracks and begin to pick up the pieces. It takes guts and energy and ingenuity to raise children and it is rarely a peaceful endeavor.

I think that one of the greatest tests of whether or not we are grown-up enough to be parents is being able to withstand the pressures on us to buy everything anybody wants to sell us, or to be trapped by the advertising propaganda into running a household that bears no relation to realistic needs. Countless advertisements in all media make it clear that if Mama will only provide her darling family with the right breakfast cereal, her husband will work hard and never look at another woman, and her children will never have a sick day in their lives. There is also an ad for monogrammed diapers —"Your assurance that Baby is completely protected"— which seems to me to be the absolute end in pressure to wage war on the germ. As any chemist will tell you, almost any of the bleaches or cleaning fluids now available do an admirable job of making things clean enough for human use. We're all glad Pasteur and Lister discovered our arch enemies, the germs, but if they could have envisioned the nonsense that we women are brain-washed with, they might have decided to keep those little beasts a deep dark secret. We are too often convinced that unless life is made germ-free, we are not good housewives, and the lengths we go to test for "sunshine whiteness" are extreme. Soap and water are great, and a reasonable degree of cleanliness is certainly aesthetic and healthy, but some of us have become slaves to antisepsis. Our homes are for people to *live* in. A little sloppiness goes a long way to make a house a home. It doesn't mean living in chaos —it means just stopping in our tracks and asking, *Why* do we have to work so hard to keep everything so shiny and in order?

We have to be grown-up enough to recognize how prosperity influences our choices: how easily we are drawn into a pattern of collecting things we don't need, buying more and more, replacing furniture that doesn't need replacing, drowning our children with toys they don't need, and substituting inanimate objects for genuine experiences. There is a kind of obscenity, an immorality, about our insatiability for material things. It is more difficult to be grown-up when things are easy and comfortable than when they are hard, as they were during the Depression of the thirties, or during wartime. The challenge to survive absorbs everyone; children and adults alike have to work at real issues, have to face life with courage despite uncertainty.

A mother told me that one day she heard some people talking, on her car radio, about the fact that now telephones covered by mink or ocelot were available. "I almost crashed the car when I heard that; I'd been feeling trapped for months in a big fancy house that I felt I had to redecorate—I still hadn't done anything much about drapes or rugs or lamps— and I felt the house owned me. This business about the telephones was the last straw. I went out and bought myself some clay and some sculpture tools, and I set up the sun porch as a studio for myself and the kids. I announced to my family, "This is some of the money we're *not* going to spend fixing up the house. We have chairs, beds, tables, everything we really need. The rest is going to be for things we want to *do*."

Being a grown-up parent also involves the question of our basic attitude toward growth: are we really deeply and genuinely *for* it; do we accept it; and can we adapt to it? Will we permit a child to grow at his own rate, and will we also be alert enough to recognize when he is ready to move on? I remember a nurse telling a group of parents who were very impatient with the length of time their babies would have to be in diapers and eat baby foods, "One thing you can't expect of a one-year-old is that he be two!" I'm sure that sounds logical enough, but considering all the available evidence that we push children too hard very often, it doesn't seem to be such an easy idea to accept. Nursery school parents always look surprised when I remind them that their three-year-olds have only been alive for thirty-six months! They seem less surprised when these children are reluctant to let them go, or when they are fearful or shy.

It is just as difficult not to hold children back as it is to push them too far ahead. A mother reported that she was getting her thirteen-year-old daughter's room ready for her return from camp. She started to put the sheet on the mattress cover, when she noticed that there was a rubber pad underneath. She was really shocked; that pad had been there all through her daughter's childhood—and yet, she hadn't wet the bed since she was about three years old! Why hadn't she ever thought of removing that thing? It had really never occurred to her before. Although it was unimportant and had never bothered anybody, it seemed to her that it represented a tendency to forget to look, and to take in with full awareness the changes that come with growing up. Of course, if this were something her daughter had been aware of and annoyed by, it would have been brought to her attention long since. When our children seem to rebel, or to become secretive, or when we begin to think that our home is turning into a battleground, it may be time to evaluate whether or not we have been holding the reins too tight and not allowed enough room for the necessary emancipation acrobatics, by which children test their increasing strength and struggle toward independence. It would be a terrible thing if this didn't happen; to move from helpless babyhood to the point where you are grown-up enough to marry, work at a job, take care of children, be a responsible citizen, is quite a long and strenuous task. It has to happen in small doses, and there must be room for change, for increasingly independent decisions and for self-determination.

Growth is so uneven—it seesaws back and forth, and it is so hard to judge correctly whether we are pushing too hard or holding back too much. Fortunately, children help us figure this out; their behavior soon gives us the information we need. If we are holding on too tight, we are likely to get more rebellion and defiance either directly or in some more subtle form; sometimes passivity may be a reaction to great anger and frustration. When we push too hard we soon see evidence of anxiety, of reluctance to try new things. The child who is pushed into becoming a social butterfly, but isn't ready, refuses to go to dancing class; the child who is too heavily burdened with his parents' wishes for his intellectual success may begin to have learning problems; the child who is really not quite ready to start walking to school alone begins to "feel sick" every morning.

A respect for growth will help us look more rationally and logically at our children's problems. Struggle and challenge seem to be inevitable in the process of growth. A seed planted in the earth struggles, pushes, moves up toward the sun and air; the young, unsure bird is pushed from the nest and must fly or fall. In all of nature, growth is far from easy. It comes, as an innate force, from within the living thing—a dynamic relationship with the environment—pushing, struggling toward strength and maturity.

There is no way we can avoid the changes or ignore the signs of growth, and perhaps parents need time to reflect, to regain a sense of perspective, about how much they can do. A mother reports sadly, with a sense of defeat, that her happy, fearless infant is now, at four, afraid of the dark. She wonders where she failed. A father is disturbed because his three-year-old daughter is so selfish and possessive. Another mother wonders why her gay and friendly three-year-old has, at six, become shy and self-conscious with adults.

If we examine what we have learned about growth, about children's needs, we soon discover that every one of the "problems" mentioned above are logical, necessary stages in growing up; that we could add to the list of quite normal problems, almost indefinitely: thumb-sucking, nail-biting, daydreaming, sloppiness, rebelliousness, periods of fearfulness and unhappiness—on and on. In fact, the more we study children, the surer we become that within a certain framework of time and intensity, all kinds of behavior which distress and unsettle parents may be part of normal growth.

If expertness can't eliminate these problems, is there any point to our struggle to understand, to help? Of course there is—so long as it remains clear to us, as parents, that knowledge will not lead to the immediate un-doing of some kind of behavior that bothers us. Knowledge and understanding can help us ease the growth process, help our children meet its challenges with fewer hurts and succeed more frequently in moving on to newer levels of maturation.

If we know that four-year-olds have good reasons for being afraid of the dark, and that this is a sign of maturation, not regression, we can be more reassuring toward the child and more receptive to his need for a night light. Our confidence is reflected in how he feels about himself: if this need is met, he will know he has not failed. He is strengthened to move on when he is ready. If we understand that selfishness in a three-year-old is a logical step of development, a time for discovery about oneself, a time for needing reservoirs of self-concern and self-love before becoming able or ready to share with others, we can support the youngster's needs without fear that this is a permanent state of things, but rather a transitory behavior, part of the normal experimentation, soon to be modified by new learning experiences.

At each stage of growth, understanding of the meaning of behavior can help us to relax, to look ahead with perspective. Our own greater confidence and optimism is in turn absorbed by our children, who can then accept their limitations without feelings of failure and overwhelming guilt. In the long run, these attitudes will encourage growth. Children who are permitted to fulfill their needs at each stage of maturation develop the inner resources necessary for the next challenge, the next step.

Sensitivity to growth can help us watch for signs of real discomfort, unusual roadblocks that may call for more positive action than confidence and patience. True, we know that all children are going to rebel against adult authority, in different ways at different ages, in their continuing struggle to move toward independence and autonomy; but we should also know that if rebellion becomes continual, if it seems to dominate the parent-child relationship, it may be time for some self-examination; are we holding on too tight? Have we permitted new areas of freedom as the child feels ready for it? Have we been flexible enough to recognize a child's increasing ability to make decisions for himself, to be given some areas of independent action in which he can continue to test his increasing powers?

Knowing in general terms some of the logic of behavior at different stages of development, we are better equipped to observe with sensitivity and to recognize when a child's behavior seems out of keeping with his own development, when he seems overwhelmed by feelings that are not transitory but seem to persist and to be more intense than might be expected. Any symptom may appear for a short time at a reasonably appropriate age or under special circumstances; but there are times when we sense that children are under unusual tension and pressure, when symptoms seem to persist, to interfere with learning and social relationships—when we see a group of symptoms, a wide area of discomfort, when we may need special help in seeing what it is that is blocking growth and maturation.

Knowledge about child development can help us become more self-confident, flexible, resilient and resourceful, *but it cannot produce perfect children.* It will never mean that Mary won't stick out her tongue at a neighbor she doesn't like, that Johnny won't gleefully use his latest four-letter word in front of Grandma, that Debbie won't dawdle for hours over her breakfast, that Robbie won't fight with his older sister. Children will act like children, however wise their parents may become. But knowledge can help us enjoy the adventure, the challenge—and the never-ceasing wonders, delights and surprises that make up the experience of parenthood. We don't have to worry so much about our children's behavior.

Every normal, healthy child is upsetting, unlovable and difficult at times. We don't have to be so scared that everything a child does is going to be habit-forming. Behavior which is more typical of an age or a phase than of the child himself, will pass. A child who has been basically friendly and forthright isn't going to become a criminal because he goes through a stage of telling lies or stealing. A normally curious and courageous youngster isn't going to grow up a coward because he suddenly becomes afraid of the dark. A child who has seemed reasonably intelligent isn't going to grow up to be a moron because in fourth grade he's more interested in playing baseball than in learning division.

We don't have to worry so much about our own emotions and the way in which we express our feelings. A principal once told a group of teachers that on one of his inspection tours in his school he came upon a third-grade classroom in a state of bedlam. The teacher, on seeing him approach, said quietly and sweetly, "Now, children, wouldn't you like to quiet down?" Things went from bad to worse, so he hurried along down the hall so as not to embarrass the teacher further, and as he went out of sight, he heard the teacher shout, "Okay now, you kids, all of you SHUT UP for a minute, I can't hear anyone." All was calm! As a free and spontaneous person, she had communicated far more effectively in expressing her feelings, and the children undoubtedly respected her for it.

An ability to be flexible with children, and to bring some wit and humor into one's view of them, is an essential ingredient for survival and an indication of parental maturity. A pediatrician once told me how fatherhood had brought him down to earth. "When I started in practice, I had no kids," he said, "and I used to insist on absolute quiet in bed for three-year-olds with undiagnosed fevers. Now, with three youngsters of my own, even with serious illnesses I recommend 'modified bed rest'; by that I mean, 'NO swimming'!"

Being an adult parent involves some very thoughtful explorations of the question of discipline: what it is, what it means, what it should be. Extreme positions have been recommended in rapid succession, and parents have frequently been warned of dire consequences if they do not administer the "correct" discipline. For a long period of time we were scared to death to admit that we ever spanked our children; then it was all right if you did it calmly; then it was only all right if it was done in the heat of anger! Now, with the problems of society becoming more and more complex and our anxieties increasing about how to solve all our problems, we seem to return again to looking for the simplest solution, such as "back to the woodshed"—"let's beat the little b——." We long for a return to the simple life, and hope vainly to discover a panacea for problems which are part of change, industrialization, urbanization, a shrinking world and an exploding population.

Our problems cannot be solved by just being tough and getting our children to behave out of fear of our authority. It would be pleasant if we could all pretend to be Clarence Day, Senior, in *Life with Father*, and assume that our word is law and know that we will be respected and obeyed. How much easier it was to be a parent before we really noticed the children! Many of us have fantasies and dreams of the old-fashioned autocratic home, with a special and (very!) separate wing of a baronial mansion where a "Nanny" raised our very quiet, respectful, controlled, polite children, whom we saw for about one hour a day, and who never presented any problems! For most of us, the seen-and-never-heard child is as obsolete as the dinosaur.

Let's try to trace the events that have taken place in the exploration of the subject of discipline and then see if there might not be a general, basic viewpoint which leaves enough room for individual differences of opinion and feeling, and still provides us with a frame of reference that can guide us.

One of the first observations coming out of the earliest investigations in psychiatry was that people had many feelings they were terribly ashamed of, and their feelings of guilt were frequently a major factor in serious emotional disturbances: guilt could cause severe anxiety, depression, flight from reality, an inability to work or relate to other people. In considering the causes of neuroses and psychoses, as they appeared at the beginning of the century, this problem of guilt seemed to be of paramount importance. Mental health experts, anthropologists and others began to feel that antisocial and delinquent behavior could also be related to the problem of guilt. For instance, because a boy felt that it was evil and dangerous to hate his father, he repressed his anger, but since such feelings don't just go away, he might find an antisocial expression for his feelings, a kind of scapegoat—anger could become socially acceptable. We began to think that probably in countries with very strict, authoritarian and frightening moralistic controls there would be greater susceptibility to race hatred, group fighting against group, and the like. The feeling today would probably be that there is some truth in this connection between suppressed individual hostility and the outbreak of group hatred, but we know it is far more complicated than this simple formula.

I remember very vividly an experience I had about fifteen

years ago when I was the director of a nursery school in Chicago. A Viennese doctor and his wife, refugees from Nazism, had a little boy of four attending the nursery school. They were very cultured, sophisticated people, and as I got to know them, I found that they did seem to set awfully high standards for their children, and to be very strict and uncompromising in their discipline. When the mother came to school for a conference with me, she was full of complaints about Peter—he was naughty, disrespectful and defiant. I tried to explain how in America we were trying to understand young children, recognize their feelings and learn from their behavior. We talked about the fact that we had learned that all children, all people, have angry feelings, and that if we bottle them up completely we may create so much guilt that emotional difficulties of a serious nature may follow. She told me that her elderly mother, who was living with them, was very partial to Peter's younger brother, and while Peter controlled his feelings when he was with his grandmother, he expressed his unhappiness and jealousy toward his mother instead. She began to see that Peter's feelings made a lot of sense, but she was still afraid of permitting him to be "fresh and disrespectful." Everything in her own childhood spoke out against such behavior.

One Sunday afternoon my husband and I were invited to a Viennese *Kaffeeklatsch* at their home, where we met many of their friends, also refugees to this country. During the afternoon Peter, his younger brother and his grandmother came in from the park. Peter was scowling and looked ready to explode. His mother asked him to go upstairs and get washed up, and then come and meet the guests. Peter screamed at her, "Shut up! I don't want to—I hate you!" A deadly hush fell on the guests for a moment, followed by a heated discussion in which most of the guests warned the parents that if they permitted such behavior, Peter would become an "American delinquent, just like all those terrible children you read about in the newspapers." This bombardment went on for some time, and the mother seemed more and more embarrassed and uncomfortable, and finally, losing her temper, she said, "It seems to me you have all forgotten why you are in this country; better Peter should let me know *now* when he is angry than he should keep it all inside of him until it grows bigger and bigger and he gets so angry, he wants to put people in gas chambers!"

Although it is more complicated than that, we were learning, and still do believe, that hostility toward groups and antisocial acts toward the community stem in part from the repression of normal anger and aggression in children. This was another reason for our feeling that anger must not be completely repressed—lest it be taken out in social destructiveness.

A third major consideration in the development of a point of view opposed to repression was that people could become not only emotionally ill or socially destructive, but they could also turn anger toward themselves and become physically sick; the development of psychosomatic medicine did, and still does, suggest that physiological, biochemical changes can take place under the strain and tension of unacknowledged, repressed feelings. Changes in ideas about discipline do not seem so illogical if we recognize that repressive controls can lead to severe illnesses such as asthma, ulcers, migraine headaches and many other serious medical problems. This field of research is still very young, and we certainly don't know just how or when there is an interaction between psyche and soma. But we *can* say that while much of the complexity of mind-body is still a mystery to us, there is overwhelming evidence that the strain of repression and guilt plays a part in much physical illness.

Psychiatry came into being during the Victorian age; it had its greatest support in the United States, a country with a very strong Puritan, moralistic tradition. Certain kinds of feelings had never been acknowledged as being a natural part of all human experience. The early emphasis on sexual repression was natural, since this was a taboo subject. Sex and hostility were both cultural anathemas. Good people never had bad thoughts or wishes. In such a climate it was natural that normal, instinctual drives, needs and feelings would cause great guilt, which could then lead to some of the disturbances I have mentioned. Loving, altruistic feelings were good; if you had those only, you were all right. That is why socially acceptable feelings never had to be repressed and never caused emotional problems. We had no reason to be ashamed of love, compassion, self-sacrifice.

Part of the revolution in our thinking in the past fifty years has been the idea that there is just no such thing as a good person or a bad person; each of us are "God and Devil," angel and animal, with the capacity for being loving and good, and with an equal capacity for being primitive and animalistic. Furthermore, we *need* both sides. Much of our vitality, creativity, drive, ambition, healthy rebelliousness, is related to what is instinctual in us and may be expressed in curiosity, humor, the capacity to endure, the willingness to fight for principle. If we were all sweetness and light, half the vitality of being human would disappear!

Much of this kind of thinking went into the re-evaluation of discipline. We found that if we wanted children to grow creatively, without serious psychic handicaps, we should not continue to discipline in such a way as to bury all unlovely feelings. The price would be too high. Educational exploration was moving in a similar direction. John Dewey and the other early leaders of the progressive education movement said that if we wanted children to think for themselves, if we wanted them to be civilized human beings, we had to help them develop inner controls. We can't just make them behave out of fear; then they will always need strong police authority to control them. We would have to try to help children learn to live responsibly and constructively with each other, by example, through love and understanding. It was a highly idealistic and not at all foolish philosophy and does not deserve the criticism or blame now frequently heaped upon it. As in all new areas of exploration, its only crime was oversimplification. The goals were noble, but not enough was known about human limitations and the slow way in which children get ready for self-control.

Another important new observation was that behavior was highly significant: when a child did something that we felt was naughty or that seemed incomprehensible to us, he was really telling us something important about himself, and we could learn how to help him if we tried to understand instead of just punishing or stopping the behavior.

I remember an incident when I was a young practice-teacher; I was in the playground with a group of kindergarten children. It had rained the day before and there were some puddles in the playground, and some mud at the foot of the slide. Jackie came down the slide too fast and landed in the mud. At first he had an expression of shock and horror on his face, and then he became hysterical and unconsolable. I offered to take him inside and change his pants; I assured him I'd write a note to his mother and tell her that it wasn't his fault; but nothing seemed to have any effect on him. Because I began to feel so helpless and embarrassed I finally said angrily, "Now, stop it this minute, Jackie; there is no reason for you to carry on like that—if you keep it up you'll have to go inside and stay by yourself." At this point the head teacher, who had just come outdoors, hurried over and said, "Jackie, this is *mud*, nothing else," whisked him inside, changed his pants, washed the muddy shoes and sent Jackie out as quickly as possible, saying, "You are not a baby, Jackie." Later she told me, "Jackie is still young enough to remember his toilet-training, and how he had to learn to go to the bathroom. He probably had a terrible fright that his old, babyish wish to just have a BM in his pants had somehow returned, his secret was out, he was in danger of losing control again; that's why he got so hysterical." It was one of my first experiences in learning about the meaning of what appears to be irrational behavior.

A child expert wrote in a book in the nineteen-forties that if a young child became destructive of property after the birth of a brother or sister, we should understand that his natural jealousy was being expressed in this way. She recommended that we say, "That's all right Johnny, I know you smashed that lamp because you are really angry at us for bringing a new baby home." At the beginning of our new knowledge we were confused about the difference between understanding behavior, accepting the existence of undesirable feelings, and permitting expression of those feelings. It was again an understandable error that we are learning to correct. Feelings can be understood and accepted without our forgetting that there must also be controls on behavior.

But it *was* intriguing—this game of finding the hidden meanings! In discussing this once with a group of pediatric nurses, one of them told a story about herself: during the first world war, when she was about five years old, her older brother had gone to fight in Europe. When he came home there was a great family reunion; everyone was sitting around a big dining-room table while Bill told about the war—the "terrible Huns" who "stuck bayonets into children," the war orphans roaming the streets, etc. Marie was sitting at the end of the table, next to her brother and near the door to the hall. The door was open and the hall was very dark. Marie became absolutely convinced that a "Hun"—whatever that might be—was in the hall and was going to kidnap her and cut her into pieces. She was afraid no one would notice, because they were all listening to the returned hero. She suddenly leaned over and bit Bill's leg very hard! Naturally the family was outraged, and she was given a good spanking. "I was so relieved that they were paying attention to me, I didn't care what they did to me," she told us. "A least I was saved from that terrible danger in the hall." How hard it is to fathom the fantasies and confusions and fears of children!

Kenny was in a nursery group of mine many years ago. He was a very bright and active little boy, with lots of charm, a natural leader in the group. When his mother had a baby, he seemed to go to pieces in nursery school; he would come in looking sad and withdrawn, refuse to take his coat off, sit under a table sucking his thumb and refuse to play all morning. When we called his home, his mother was shocked; nothing like that was going on at home; he loved the baby, wanted to hold her and feed her, and help with the bath. He hadn't shown any signs of jealousy at all. The only thing she could think of was that Kenny never wanted to be left alone in a room with the baby, but she hadn't really thought about it until that moment.

I was getting nowhere with Kenny in school; the same behavior went on day after day. Finally I decided to take a chance—I seemed to have nothing to lose, and if I was wrong . . . well, Kenny would just think I was nuts! I got under the table with him and whispered, "I know lots of little boys who don't like it when they get a new baby. It makes them very sad. It's okay to be mad—you won't do anything bad." Kenny looked at me in horror, ran for the closet and sat in his cubby, more remote than ever, and I figured I had really made a worse mess of things, after all. Just before it was time to go home, however, Kenny came over to me and said he had a secret to tell me. He led me to the darkest corner of the closet and whispered in my ear, very softly, "I *do* hate her and she's going to die." We had a little chat about how angry feelings could *never* make a bad thing happen, and that everyone had angry feelings, but that this didn't mean they had to do angry things about it.

I was puzzled as to why Kenny had reacted more strongly than most other children, and I thought I ought to talk to his mother. I went to see her, and when I repeated Kenny's comment she began to cry. She then told me that when Kenny was two and a half she had had another baby girl, who had only lived for six weeks. She didn't think Kenny had been old enough to understand anything about it, and since he never asked what had happened to the baby, they never gave him any explanation. How terribly frightened Kenny must have been that his bad thoughts could *again* make a baby disappear!

This story has always epitomized for me why the experts spoke against the bottling up of feelings, the dangers of repression, the importance of finding the meaning of behavior. In many ways they were surely on the right track, and we did learn to respond more meaningfully and logically to such problems as Kenny's. I remember another day when a friend took me and his five-year-old son to visit a children's camp where he had been the director the summer before. When we got there, swarms of children climbed all over him in delight and with great affection. He told a group of children a story, and spent most of the afternoon surrounded by his devoted admirers. His son, David, followed in the rear, watching. Toward suppertime David seemed to go berserk; he knocked over a pitcher of milk, he hit an innocent bystander with a rubber-tire swing, he marched up and down the benches in the dining room and refused to sit down and eat. Suddenly his father looked very thoughtful, and stopping himself in the middle of shouting and threatening, he gathered David into his arms, rocked him like a baby and said, "David, you poor boy—did you think I forgot you? Do you think I love these boys and girls the way I love you? I'm just visiting some friends, but you're my *son*."

This seems to me to be one of the best ways in which understanding influenced discipline. This was a wise and conscientious and compassionate act, and the only thing wrong with it was that a lot of us assumed that this sort of thing would take care of *everything* and children would grow up without any problems if we could handle them this way. First of all, none of us could be that good all the time; many times we are tired, impatient, and can't understand at all. Sometimes we embarrass our children by understanding too much, and they lose a much-needed privacy to feel without being exposed. Understanding also doesn't change our basic personalities or our own problems, in work or marriage. Some parts of life are painful; we can't always get away from it, and it isn't always even so good to try. Some of these children who were "understood" and kept as frustration-free as we could manage, whom we treated with kid gloves so "God forbid, they shouldn't catch a trauma," are now young adults, and too many of them still can't take frustration or discomfort, and can't postpone an immediate need or wish, or practice any self-control; they want what they want when they want it.

Permissiveness often grew out of loving concern. It was not weak-minded or lazy in its origins. Disenchantment began to set in, however. Educators found that example and logic were not turning young savages into civilized human beings—all controls could not be internalized during the early years of childhood—and in fact all of us, adults and children, would always need external social controls in some areas.

Parents were finding that in the name of self-expression and freedom, children were sometimes being encouraged to be insensitive and cruel. I remember the genuine hurt and pain in one mother's eyes when she said, "All right, I know children get angry, but did he have to call me 'a fat pig' in front of all those people on the beach?" Another mother told me, "I got used to the idea of sibling rivalry and that it was normal for my kids to fight, so I didn't interfere if I could help it. Then, one day, while I was washing the dishes, I heard Jerry scream at Susan, 'And you're so stupid, you'll never get through sixth grade!' Jerry was eleven and a wonderful student; Susan was eight and having a very hard time, especially because she compared herself to Jerry, and I knew that what he had said was not just ordinary anger, but just plain cruel. I went in and told him I didn't care how mad he was, he must not hit below the belt; that I would not let him hurt anyone's feelings that way."

We began to see that accepting feelings and having a more realistic view of human beings did not necessarily mean permitting a child to say anything he wanted, any more than it meant letting him do whatever he felt like doing. We began to say instead, "I know you're angry, but you may not talk to me that way. It hurts my feelings and it is unkind. Go be mad alone, or tell me what's on your mind in a pleasanter way."

One Sunday many years ago my husband and I went to visit a young couple with a little boy of five and a baby girl of about fourteen months. As we sat talking in the living room that afternoon, the boy kept hitting the little girl on the head with a toy, and each time she'd howl. The parents would ask him to stop, but they made no move to make him stop. I was getting a headache watching this performance, and I noticed my husband wincing at every blow, too. The mother was terribly embarrassed and finally blurted out defiantly, "Well, what can I do—you psychologists are always telling us that jealousy is normal!" This was one of the worst kinds of misinterpretations of psychological theory. There is a vast difference between the pre-psychology-era technique, which would have been: "My son, you are a sinner. Good children love their little brothers and sisters, always. You are bad and we must beat that badness out of you," and what would seem more appropriate now: "You may NOT hit your sister on the head, and I will stop you since you can't stop yourself. I am a grownup, and I will keep you from doing things to hurt anyone else, just as I will not let anyone hurt you. Little boys often get angry at little sisters, and it is all right to feel that way, but you may not do anything to hurt her." Guilt can be just as severe from doing something you really know you shouldn't do, as from repressing a nasty thought altogether. In other words, when a young child who cannot yet control his impulses is permitted to act in a dangerous and aggressive way toward someone else, he will feel just as guilty as the child who would never do such a thing, but has been told it is evil. In between these two extremes it is possible to accept human frailty and acknowledge human imperfection and, by that very acceptance, know that external controls are absolutely essential.

In the heat of living, no parent can or should be expected to sit down and contemplate, "Now, how shall I respond to this?" every time a child misbehaves. It is just this self-consciousness which has made us anxious and unspontaneous and therefore un-human with our children. But we *can,* in some quiet and peaceful moment, over morning coffee after the children have gone to school, or over a bedtime snack after they've gone to sleep, decide what we believe discipline is in principle. The more we really think about it, and incorporate our thoughts and feelings, the more we will be able to respond sensibly, without thinking, when we need to.

In a certain sense, discipline is the way we handle our children in order to help them learn to live artistically with themselves and other people. Discipline is a tool that expresses our point of view about civilized living. But how do we pin that down to practical living? Well, for me it means that, being human, I will often make mistakes; I will be unfair or impatient; I may be more severe one day than another, depending on my own mood. What can I do about it? I can try to make amends; I can say, "I'm sorry." Part of being civilized is trying to have better relationships with people; trying to understand, to be sympathetic, showing I care. Since I can't possibly behave that way all the time, I can teach my child that all we can do is keep on trying. This means being flexible, changing my mind, admitting I've made a mistake.

At a morning discussion meeting, one mother arrived looking shaken and miserable. She said that for months she had been trying to find some way to make her ten-year-old daughter stop dawdling. She had been late to school three times, and the mother had tried threats, nagging, yelling, bribes, sweetness and patience—nothing made any difference. No matter what time she woke Laurie up, she managed to get behind schedule. On this particular morning, because she was trying to get out herself to attend the meeting, she was more impatient and annoyed than usual. She told us, "I just got so mad when I saw her sitting on her bed daydreaming—when I thought she was already dressed—that I gave her the worst bawling-out of her life, and before I knew what I was saying, I yelled, 'And I'm canceling your birthday party for Saturday —you can just tell your friends why, too! You are a selfish, inconsiderate brat and I'm not going to work to give you a party when you don't care how you treat me!' Laurie was so shocked that she just gasped, and then she began to cry as if her heart would break. I didn't know what to do. I wasn't thinking when I said it—I really don't want to punish her so severely—I was just having a temper tantrum of my own. How can I expect her to un-invite her guests? But what kind of discipline can I maintain if I give in and don't carry through?"

We all agreed she could have the very *best* kind of discipline, the kind that says, "I went too far, I made a mistake—I'm big enough to say so—forgive me." That didn't mean a whitewash of Laurie's responsibility for getting to school on time. That must still be worked at, of course. But the discipline that sets an example for maturity and civilized relationships is the best kind there is. And this doesn't mean just being sorry if we have punished too severely or been too unreasonable in our controls; it also means saying we were wrong when we have been too lenient! Since no one can ever be sure about what another human being needs or how something will work out, we have to practice the kind of self-examination and reviewing of experience that make it possible for us to change and try other ways. If we give a child permission to do something because we think he or she is ready, and then that child behaves in a way which indicates he wasn't ready for that much responsibility, we rescind the freedom temporarily, to be tried again later on. This is experimenting and learning for the good of civilized living.

Authority is essential. It provides a restrictive but secure outer world with clear-cut standards and necessary controls. Children of all ages feel relieved when rules are clear and when they can count on enforcement of these rules. As far as we can tell, children and adults alike will never be able to have all of life controlled from within; we all need a certain amount of social enforcement of necessary controls. We have all seen the relief and relaxation in our children's faces when they know we care enough to be policemen when we have to. To have the courage and energy to insist on certain basic standards is much more a sign of love than giving in—

which is easy. It's *not* giving in that is hard—and our children know that very well!

We were discussing this in a parents' meeting one day, and one mother told us of a memory from her childhood: her parents ran a candy store, and in order to support seven children they had to work from dawn to late at night. She remembered that as she would walk to school in the morning, she heard mothers shouting out to their children to come back for their rubbers, or yelling at them to put a sweater on. She saw that the children were furious, but she envied them terribly. Her mother had already gone to work, and was too pressed anyway to worry about such things. The girl felt hungry for the angry screaming of a mother: "I felt that those children were loved more than I was," she said.

One night we were visiting some friends, who began to reminisce about their honeymoon trip. Their nine-year-old daughter was enthralled with the story. Her mother said it was a shame: they had had wonderful pictures of their trip, but Kathy had torn them all up when she was about three years old. "Why did you let me do it?" wailed Kathy, and her mother replied in all honesty, "Because I didn't know any better."

At the same time that we recognize our obligations to act like grownups about important issues, we also have to give children permission to rebel; it is a necessary part of cultivating judgment and being able to function independently. I sometimes marvel at the wonderful force in children which seems to urge them on even in the face of great danger! They will suffer parental disapproval, anger, punishment, even the loss of love, in order to insist on growing up! Rebellion is really an act of integrity—it is a refusal to remain passive and dependent. There are many occasions when we want our children to be able to stand up against an idea or an act, and to use judgment and courage in making a decision. A child who is always obedient to every adult would be inclined to get into the car of a stranger—unless he has learned to think for himself and to discriminate about which adults he should listen to. A mother once told me that her twelve-year-old son had arrived home from school earlier than she usually expected him. Ordinarily he fooled around with the "gang" until suppertime. She asked him why he was home so early and he said, "Some of the guys decided to throw rocks at basement windows and I couldn't get them to stop, so I came home." Behind this simple statement was great courage and independent thinking. Gary had endangered his prestige, his acceptance by the group, and had not gone along with group pressure. That is the kind of resilience which comes with healthy rebellion and a sense of autonomy.

When you think about it, wouldn't it really be much easier for a child to let you make all his decisions, and do everything for him? It is really quite comfortable and pleasant, not having to worry about anything! What marvelous miracle of life and growth forces a child to try to stand up emotionally as well as physically? Compared to the comfortable safety of staying at home, why does any child want to go to nursery school—a jungle of other children who may hit him or not like him; why does he want to walk to school alone—he's got to watch for the light, and he may be ambushed by a big bully two grades higher up. Look at the havoc he creates when he starts to say No! People get madder than they've ever been before, all sorts of unpleasant things begin to happen. Rebellion is a kind of muscle-flexing. And at each stage of growth we have to figure out how much rebellion to tolerate—how much is possible, safe, endurable. There has to be room for a child to misbehave and to disobey us, and we don't have to be so frightened when this begins to happen. Children learn from defiance, as well as through imitation and guidance. By the time he is eight or nine, any child who is not a fool knows perfectly well what his parents' fundamental standards and values are, but he can't always measure up to them yet and he just has to get some things out of his system before he moves on.

Tolerance to rebellion also means being able to endure

some expression of open anger, and some rough and open warfare. After his mother had lost her temper and shouted at Peter, "Just stop using that tone with me," her son replied. "First of all, you're using 'that tone' too, and secondly, if I can't yell here, where CAN I yell?"

We are learning that it is not necessary to permit children (or ourselves!) to be completely uncontrolled in how we express our feelings, even verbally, but at the same time, life will be much easier if we don't take occasional flare-ups too seriously. We all say things we don't really mean when we're mad; if we nurse our wounds and overdramatize such familiar scenes, we just make for more problems. It is far easier on us and on our children to accept the fact that tempers will inevitably flare sometimes, and it clears the air, and that's that. The pressures and tensions of life add to the immediate family crises and by the time we are all at home together we are usually pretty worn out: Father had to keep his mouth shut when the boss bawled him out unfairly; Mother has had an argument with her own mother on the telephone about how to raise Junior; and Junior himself has had to sit still for long hours at a time in his life when he has more energy than he knows what to do with, and has had to memorize the nine-times table, when he is far more concerned with how to make friends with the boy in his class who has a new baseball. For all of us, the family serves as a safety valve, a place in which we don't have to try so hard to be controlled, polite and lovable all the time. Being grown-up really means accepting ourselves, accepting the reality of our human imperfections—and knowing that the struggle to become mature and civilized is hard and never-ending work. It is also the work that is more deeply fulfilling than any other.

A Constitutional Amendment

Children are as unlike each other in personality as in their fingerprints. I suspect that this single factor accounts for more of our troubles than anything else. Perhaps we shouldn't let it get around—we'd lose what little sympathy we may have garnered, and we have none to spare—but there are some babies who are angelic and who grow up so easy to raise we hardly know they're around, and who succeed without all the *Sturm und Drang* I have said is normal to growth. And then there are those others, at the other end of the scale, who, no matter what you do, are going to be screaming and fighting their way through life, manufacturing troubles if none are at hand.

Let us take the case of two sisters. Joan is nineteen and Sally is seventeen, and they have lived in the same house with the same parents in the same town, attending the same

schools, eating the same food, having the same relatives, doctors, dentists, recreational opportunities, and as far as anyone
can tell, they breathe the same air. That is where similarities
end. Life has been one long, constant, never-ending struggle
for Joan; nothing came easy, and if it did she made it hard.
She is mercurial, oversensitive, always assuming the worst is
about to happen. Although bright and attractive, her school
record is shaky and very uneven, and she has not been a great
social success. Her talents are extreme and so are her blind
spots. Her moods shift from hilarity to gloom, from shrieking
in fury at her parents to writing poetry by candlelight. She is a
nervous wreck before every new encounter, and despite the
fact that she is loved and admired by many people and has
had many triumphs in life, she is filled with self-doubts and
is constantly demeaning herself.

Joan is what I call a "wave fighter." Even in a relatively
calm sea, where it would be perfectly possible to lie back quietly and roll with the waves, she is in there splashing up a
storm and getting herself half drowned.

Sally had a much harder time as an infant than Joan did.
She was born with an intestinal obstruction, had several oper-
ations within the first six months of her life, and digestive disorders until the age of four. By the time she arrived, her parents were beginning to have financial worries, and when she
was two years old, her maternal grandmother died, a source of
intense grief for her mother. And you know what? Sally is one
of the steadiest, most successful young women you would
ever hope to meet! She has been a good student all the way
through school, doing well in everything. She is popular with
both sexes, self-confident, pleasant; she has a good sense of
humor, and the world is her oyster. One cannot explain her by
saying that she is dull or placid—she isn't. She is a sensitive,
responsive, vivacious person. But she moved from one stage of
growth to another with little or no pain; she has never been
hard to discipline; she is reasonable, lovable, charming, and
can and will do anything she wants to with her life, and she

knows it. Her view is pure optimism. Sally is a "wave rider."
Even in a stormy sea she would take each wave as it came
and ride it out.

Parents have always observed these kinds of differences in
children, but a great many of them have been brain-washed
into ignoring what they saw and felt. Most of the early child-
development research tended to look for generalizations about
children. The focus was on characteristic needs and behavior
at each age and stage of growth. Somewhat rigid and inflexible categories began to emerge as to what was normal or not
normal at each of these stages. Patterns of growth were emphasized rather than individual differences. One approach,
which used objective statistical observations of a small sam-
pling of children, led to the publication of "norms." A second
major approach to studying child development came from the
observation of patients receiving psychotherapy. Where certain experiences appeared to be crucial in their life histories,
theories were developed about the psychological forces at play
during these stages of growth. Any mother's son who failed to
roll over at the right month was a terrible disappointment
to some of the followers of Dr. Gesell, and any little girl who
didn't fall madly in love with her father at three and a half—
well, Dr. Freud's disciples would be crushed. Normality in children too frequently depended on whether you were raising a
little Gesell or a little Freud!

The early research on children was enormously important.
It was a necessary step, and it was carried on by able, imaginative and dedicated people. The research was as good as it
could be in relation to what was previously known and the
cultural, social and psychological orientation of the times.

But its effect on parents was very srong and has, in some
ways, led to our present feeling of dismay. When a theory
tends to bring all children together, it suggests very strongly
that what makes for differences is not internal forces within
the child, but the variations in the environment. Both Freud
and Gesell, by developing parallel theories of normal patterns

of growth, were frequently interpreted as emphasizing the constitutional similarities of children, rather than their differences. Much of the guilt, anxiety and uncertainty of many of today's parents lies in the fact that for twenty-five to fifty years they have been told that *handling* makes the crucial difference.

But what do you do with facts such as these: what about the schizophrenic five-year-old whose parents are intelligent, affable, no more or less neurotic than most people, and who did nothing at all bizarre or unusual in their handling of their child? Or what about a five-year-old girl who was born with an unusually narrow urethra; every few months she must be hospitalized for a painful dilation, involving the insertion of a catheter, and agonizing pain while urinating for several days afterwards. She has had severe illnesses involving sudden separations from her mother. Her mother is overprotective, terribly concerned and watchful. Her father is away from home on extended business trips, and an older sister is very jealous of her. And this child is gay, optimistic, sensible, untroubled. She has many friends, comforts her mother and delights her teachers.

The constitutional differences between children are so dramatic that sooner or later researchers were bound to turn more of their attention to this aspect of growth.

While so much emphasis had been placed on the environment before, new research is now looking at environment in relation to constitutional differences in children. By studying children very intensively from birth on up through grade school and adolescent years, today's researchers are finding that children have unique and entirely individual styles, ways of coping with the environment, and that differences in ways of mastering challenges are normal, healthy and need to be understood and respected.

This may sound like a calm and sensible statement, but for those of us who have lived through the "era of environment," it is quite a change. I was married and became a parent during a time when I believed, along with most of the other "enlightened modern parents" around me, that the environment I created would decide exactly what my child would be like. If I was patient and understanding, she would be loving and good; if I fed her on self-demand, she would be secure and happy. If I handled each stage well, a predictable picture was going to be very positive. I recently met a friend who was reminiscing about her college days, and the courses she took then in child psychology. We were taught that what happened to children was caused by parents. What a terrible burden this has been, and how illogical and untrue it now seems! This kind of thinking did a great deal of damage. It made parenthood a contest, a nightmare of fear, and it also caused us to guiltily overindulge our children because at times we really hated them for proving our imperfections and for taking up so much of our time doing it!

Wiser parents, who somehow maintained their sanity during all this madness, knew perfectly well that their children were very rarely alike, and that they could see these differences at birth; that while one baby nursed happily and quietly, and then slept like an old rag doll, another baby was colicky and tense, fighting and yelling and jerking. One child would have an optimistic view that life would be comfortable, with himself and others, while another started to fight for survival against the enemy at birth. Plenty of parents and pediatricians knew this and saw this in brand-new babies, and a few of the strong and courageous kept on remembering it. Dr. Margaret Friess, a pediatrician who later became a child psychiatrist, was one of the pioneers twenty or more years ago, who began to observe what she called "activity types" in newborn infants. However, it is only in the last few years that research workers began to follow up some of her work on a large scale. An observation parents and teachers have often made is that just as children seem to have a style or a unique quality, parents seem to react to these different types, to have strong likes and dislikes, and to know intuitively that one type or another is easy or hard for them to raise; we are constitutional types too, by golly!

A mother was observing in a nursery school. She had come looking for help with her son, who was two and a half. The teachers thought he was adorable; he had great big shining eyes with a devilish gleam. He was like quicksilver, wanting to try everything, be friends with the world. He was fearless and joyous—a real tough little devil, all boy, and enchanting. Mama was haggard and worn; this little "monster" was driving her mad. He was so wild and so hard to control that she just couldn't stand it another moment; the nursery *had* to take him even though he was six months too young. This mother was intrigued with one little boy who was standing alone, away from the group. For a while he had been picking leaves from a hedge, deeply absorbed in some inner fantasy of his own. He was pale and languid, and detached from the group. The teachers were terribly worried about him and planned to talk with the psychiatrist who had referred him; it seemed to them that this child might be psychotic. Bobby's mother looked over at Michael and said with a sigh, "Now, why couldn't I have had one like *that?*"

I remember seeing a great big muscular young man at a children's playland trying to persuade his four-year-old son to ride on a carousel. The little boy was obviously a quiet, pensive youngster, a little fearful and uncertain about his physical ability, a little unsure and clumsy. He might make a great chess player some day, but he wasn't ever likely to ride horseback, as far as I could see. The disappointment and hurt in this father was so acute and unbearable that he literally hurled the child on the horse and said, "You're my *son*, now *act* like it."

Sometimes parents and children react negatively to each other because they are so much alike. A father and his son seemed to ignite each other constantly into rages of anger. They would shout and scream at each other over the most minor events. His wife commented, "They're so exactly alike and adore each other, but one of these days they may kill each other!" "I see all my worst faults in him," the father explained, "and I can't stand it!"

A little girl, beautiful but lively and fresh, was driving her mother, a very sweet and passive woman, crazy. What we saw as a healthy struggle for independence, a joyous and vivacious individual, this mother saw as a constant threat to her peace and her authority. A rough little boy with lots of open and direct feelings of anger was causing a very compliant and obsequious mother to try desperately to pretend his feelings didn't exist. A sensitive and introverted father felt embarrassed and uneasy with his flamboyant little girl. These examples seem to suggest that while environment certainly does color what may eventually happen to children, parental responses to children also reflect reactions to basic differences. In other words, when parents and children are well matched constitutionally, life is probably a lot simpler all around, but that doesn't happen very often, and so, a great many of the difficulties we encounter probably are rooted in these differences.

I was discussing this question of constitutional differences with a mother of two girls, just twenty months apart, so that their life experiences can be assumed to have been quite similar. Both were nursed, both were wanted, and the family was well off financially, and happy. The mother told me, "It is incredible how different these two children are. One is affectionate, outgoing, secure, happy—I can yell at her and she doesn't even hear me. The other is very independent, undemonstrative, insecure—if I yell at her even slightly, she is deeply hurt and crushed. She was a thumb-sucker even during the months when she was nursed! Here is a typical example of their differences: when one was three and the other four and a half, they were invited to a birthday party, where they were each given a box of crayons. Both of the boxes of crayons had a few broken ones. One child cried and wanted a new box; the other said, 'Now I have *two* green ones instead of one.' "

At the present time there must be literally hundreds of

studies going on all over the country which will provide us with a new appreciation of the constitutional differences in children. I will mention here only three that I have followed with interest myself and which I think give us the new perspective we need.

The first is reported in a book called *The Widening World of Childhood*, by Lois Murphy. It describes a project undertaken at the Menninger Foundation in Topeka, Kansas. Dr. Murphy and her associates had felt for a long time that there were serious flaws in earlier studies of children, and that the psychoanalytic interpretation of the differences in child behavior was not adequate or sufficiently convincing; something was missing. They began an intensive study of a group of children almost from birth. They collected a great deal of information about family background, and they developed various methods for careful and intensive observations of the children in many different kinds of situations. This was to be a long-term study of a group of children with some variety in family background, but in general representing an average middle-class, Midwestern community.

With a similar point of view, another study was being made in New York. A preliminary report has been published, entitled *Behavioral Individuality in Early Childhood*. The chief investigators are Alexander Thomas, M.D., Stella Chess, M.D., and Herbert Birch, M.D. It is also a longitudinal study of one hundred and thirty-six children from early infancy, and will eventually follow them through adolescence. The families in this study represent a somewhat more varied group in terms of social class, cultural and ethnic background.

A third study, which was recently concluded, was reported on in the *New York Post* by Susan Szekely:

Many mothers may have breathed a thankful sigh to learn that they're not totally responsible for what their children become. The recently concluded research at Albert Einstein College of Medicine, which showed that each baby is a unique individual from the day of his birth, relieved the minds of many women. . . . Dr. Beverly Birns decided to investigate her suspicions about the individuality of each child on a scientific level for her Ph.D. thesis. Previous child behavior studies usually began when babies were three months of age or older and their mothers had already had time to influence them. Dr. Birns' research was carried out on newborns between the first and fifth days of their lives.

She found that even at this age, babies had their own individual ways of behaving. Some were innately passive, quiet and undemanding; others were active and responsive from the very beginning . . . The implication of Dr. Birns' work is that no set theory of child care is the right one. Different kinds of children should probably be treated differently . . .

The first two studies reveal that those differences in the first days of life have a remarkable degree of consistency later on. In her book, Dr. Murphy suggests that we need to look at child behavior in a new way. Much of what we have known has been problem-oriented. We need now to study the child's adequacy, we need an emphasis on the positive aspects of growth. Her point of view is that children use their own strengths and resources to cope with life in relation to their own basic constitutional style. We need to respect the child's efforts to achieve mastery in his own way. She says:

It is something of a paradox that a nation which has exulted in its rapid expansion and its scientific-technological achievements should have developed in its studies of childhood so vast a 'problem literature' . . . concerned with adjustment difficulties, social failures, blocked potentialities and defeat. Studies have been burdened by rigid biases, statistically conceived genetic factors, standardized criteria of developmental norms.

Wanting to see if I could look at children from this fresh viewpoint, I spent several weeks watching three children enter a nursery group for the first time. Jonathan came in on the first day like a whirlwind. He could hardly wait until his mother had taken his coat off before he tore around the room, touching everything, playing briefly with each toy, then pushing it aside and going on to something else. Jimmy, having been offered a cup of juice, sat himself down at a table and seemed to be concentrating on sipping it slowly, but he was also looking at what was going on around him with intense interest. After sitting guardedly for about a half-hour he got up and asked a teacher if he might paint. He continued his observations from his position at the easel. Elsie was glued to her mother's side—she would have none of this new place. Despite all kinds of suggestions and overtures from the teachers she kept crawling back into her mother's lap.

By the end of the first week Jonathan and Jimmy acted as though they had been coming to nursery school for years. Jonathan was calm and steady; he has since become an imaginative and sensitive leader in the group—with no sign of the frenzy he showed at first. Jimmy is actually an aggressive little boy—he fights for what he wants; he demands attention when he needs it; there is no sign of that watchful and tentative beginning. Elsie could not make the next step herself; after a week of clinging, mother was asked to leave for a short time. It took another three days for Elsie to accept the separation. Thereafter she seemed happy and animated in her play.

When I was a young beginning nursery teacher, my first impressions of these three children might well have had a pathological slant; I'd been trained to look for disturbances. I might have decided that Jonathan was unstable, emotionally immature, tense and uneasy; Jimmy, overcautious and lacking self-confidence; Elsie, overdependent and anxious. Now, having tried to look anew, in terms of some of the new research, I could see something quite different: I could see the healthy strivings of three children, coping in their own unique and special styles with a new experience. Before jumping to conclusions about pathology, one must know children very well, know how they have reacted in the past, their individual ways of mastering life experiences.

The research projects I mentioned all emphasized this in their findings. By very careful and astute observations of children from earliest infancy, they all found that there were qualities that one could observe with great consistency in a child's development. One of these consistent patterns had to do with motor activity. Some babies move a great deal, others seem to be more passive. The very active babies tended to become very active children; the more passive babies, quieter as older children. Responses to external stimuli was another consistent quality. One baby would react with a great startle at a sudden noise, while another might hardly notice. Some babies reacted to a very small noise, while others would not show any awareness until the noise was very loud. Rhythmicity was another category in which one could observe consistent patterns. Some babies seemed to be born with a certain inner rhythm: they were hungry at regular intervals, their sleeping patterns were regular, elimination occurred at regular and predictable times. Other children seemed completely erratic; whatever routine or regularity there might be in their lives had to be imposed by the external environment. Other consistent constitutional differences had to do with such things as attention span, approach and withdrawal responses, and general mood. Some children showed consistently in all the observed situations that they could be very easily distracted from what they were doing. Others would stick to a focus of interest no matter what was going on around them. Some children, coming into a new situation, would always approach it the way Jonathan did—taking it head-on. Others consistently showed they had to have time to "case the joint" before they could feel comfortable about it, like Jimmy. Some children appear to have a consistently more sunny, optimistic, hopeful view of life, while others seem to expect the worst.

The important element in this view of children is that it suggests very strongly that while the environment influences a child's life experience, it can only work with the constitutional qualities the child presents. For example, it is easy to see why encouraging all parents to use demand-feeding with newborn babies couldn't work successfully for all babies. Those with a steady inner rhythm would react beautifully; those with no such inner rhythm would not be able to establish their own pattern. For example, an arhythmic baby, without a definite sleep pattern, might get overtired and begin to cry. Mother might think he was hungry and because he was not, he might get colicky. The baby would be as confused as everyone around him. This kind of a baby might have been much happier in the era of strict schedules, because he needs to be provided with some external structure to his life.

We cannot change the basic nature or constitutional differences in children; but if we watch for the emerging patterns, if we get some sense of the natural tendencies and consistencies in a child's responses, we can help him to live happily within that framework. For example, if Jimmy is the type of child who must have a chance to look things over before getting involved, it makes a great deal of difference if his parents accept or reject this need. If Jimmy is made to feel ashamed because he hesitates and holds back, this sense of failure will affect other aspects of his growth. If Jimmy is accepted as a perfectly nice little boy who needs to take his time, and who does just fine if you let him meet new situations in his own way, his self-confidence is bolstered. An active child who reacts with great sensitivity to everything that is going on around him will react differently to stressful situations than a more placid and less reactive child. If a third-grade class is in turmoil because it has had to adjust to three substitute teachers, the differences in disturbance in the children is a difference in their natures, and the child who is more distressed is no better or worse in terms of emotional adjustment—just different. This concept of the constant flow between inherent differences and environment makes it possible to be far less frightened as parents and more helpful to our children. A sensitive, highly reactive child may need more reassurance, but he isn't necessarily a more disturbed child than the one who can take things more easily in stride. However, we must be careful not to go to a new extreme. This awareness of inherent differences does not mean that we can become indifferent or unconcerned about signs of genuine unhappiness and emotional disturbance.

.   .   .

There are times when we and our children simply cannot solve our problems without help, and we are fortunate to live at a time when this help is becoming more and more available. I do not mean at all that we should run to the nearest child guidance clinic at the first sign of difficulty. First we give ourselves time to observe: Is this the way my child has to meet this life crisis? Can he master it? Is this a part of his normal growth or is his growth blocked in some way? We wait until we see a consistent and general pattern of failure, immobilization and unhappiness. Why do we wait? First of all, because pain and conflict are so often normal and necessary. And secondly, because psychotherapy or counseling are neither perfected tools nor always helpful. Professional guidance is no panacea, and especially in the case of young children should be approached with great care and caution.

The *kind* of help is just as important as the decision to seek it. The first step might be a consultation to try to get a better perspective on the problem oneself. Maybe there are some relatively simple things we just haven't noticed because we are too close to them. Maybe there are things we can do, once we have a better understanding of what may be going on. Many parents find that they can get help for themselves that in turn helps them with their children, and that the child need not be brought directly into treatment. Sometimes psychological testing of the child, followed by a brief series of counseling sessions with parents, will help.

We have every right to insist on getting the kind of help we want. If we think we need some direct advice and information, we must not let anyone tell us that this is impossible, and that first we must go through a long exploration of our past. Maybe we will want that too, someday, but we have a right to choose. A mother told me this story, "Kenneth was about four and a half, and it was during the period when Dena had just arrived and was exhausting us as a colicky, miserable baby—vomiting a lot, and the like. Kenneth was holding in his bowel movements—a combination of pleasure and pain, I guess: 'this is mine'—and the situation was becoming dangerous, as the stools were huge and hard and frightening by then. Herb thought we should give him an enema for medical reasons; I refused, and we went to see a child psychologist. She was very cozy and a little condescending as she leaned over to Herb and said, 'Since most doctors are interested in the theory behind these symptoms and the dynamics involved in treatment, would you like me to explain?' 'No,' he said, 'no theory, please! We came to get some little gimmick you can give us to ease the situation.' She recommended some cellulose product to soften the stool—it was not a cathartic—and some perfectly sound procedures to follow to reassure the kid—such as respect for his privacy and autonomy. I seem to remember going with him to the store to buy very fancy soft toilet paper too. P.S. It worked."

Sometimes the question of psychological help will be raised by someone outside the family. Most frequently the suggestion will come from a pediatrician or from the school. This may be very helpful, if, co-operatively you and they have been talking and working together around a mutually felt concern. But parents can be bowled over if they have not been aware of any serious problems and have been told their child needs professional help. Here we will have to really use our judgment very carefully. Is the person recommending such help really qualified to do so? How well do they know our child? Are they sensible, down-to-earth people, or would they be inclined to make such a recommendation too readily? Some experts are "therapy-happy" and make this suggestion too blithely.

This pattern has developed quite often in schools. As more and more schools sought out the services of mental health workers, a pattern frequently emerged that made teachers tend to see the hopeful signs of health in children, while psychologists and social workers tended to be preoccupied with pathology. Many parents, caught in the middle, simply could not tell who their children were any more. One mother told me that when she went to see her child's teacher—a woman in her sixties who had been a pioneer in progressive education—she was told, "Susie's a rebel—she wants to know why and how and what, and if you want her on your side, you have to give her straight answers. She has energy and restlessness, but when she's older and this can be harnessed, she will do great things. Right now, she just isn't very concerned with doing well in academic subjects, but most eleven-year-olds aren't, and we discourage them by making them sit still instead of letting them follow their own curiosity. She's sensitive and feels things deeply, and while she may suffer from this, these are also qualities that will bear rich rewards later, so long as she doesn't become discouraged with herself." Because the school was primarily concerned about Susie's grades, she was tested by the school psychologist, who then reported to the mother, "Susie has a basic sense of insecurity. That's why she's so defiant and restless, and can't take criticism. Her sense of inadequacy and her uncertainty about parental love causes her to test the limits, to refuse to work for results in her school work. We feel she needs psychiatric attention."

Unfortunately, teachers were sometimes too easily impressed by the mental health experts and gave up more easily on children who could make it all right if the adults around them had a little more faith in the processes of maturation. Many of us have become so clinical and psychologically self-conscious that unusual behavior, which has always been part of childhood and which frequently is accentuated in children who are going to be particularly talented and intelligent as adults, upsets us disproportionately.

A mother told me that she had been seeing a school psychologist several times because her son was having learning difficulties. At one point she disagreed with an interpretation the psychologist made, and the psychologist said, "But how do you know what's best for your child?" The mother replied, "How do I know? Because I'm his *mother*—and that is just as good a reason as your tests!"

However, it is not at all uncommon to find that some children who do not show their emotional difficulties at home will do so away from home, and in such cases it would be foolish to ignore the observations and genuine interest of qualified people who see your child in a different light. The best safeguard is to move slowly, get several opinions, have some testing done perhaps, and try to evaluate the problem from many different angles.

Because children cannot bring a conscious sophistication, a sense of judgment, to therapy, we must be very careful about bringing a child to it, and if we do, in choosing the therapist. Many parents have been so thoroughly frightened by the experts that they often fail to use their own good judgment and instincts at a time when they need them most. If we consult a child guidance clinic and don't like the person we talk to, we needn't assume that we are not trying hard enough to get help for our child. There are wonderful, there are mediocre, and there are terrible therapists. We *must* use our own judgment; get all the information we possibly can, use all the referral services available, look for accredited clinics, and licensed and highly trained personnel—and after we've done all that, we *still* have every right to make our own decisions. If our child strongly resists going to the therapist he is seeing, if we can't get answers to our questions, if we are made to feel uncomfortable and uneasy, then it is time to look elsewhere for help. Many parents say that when they bring their children and themselves into a therapeutic situation, they feel that they have lost the ball. Suddenly, after knowing a child for five or ten or more years, they are made to feel that what they know has no validity at all, and only the searching eye of science and the objectivity of a stranger, who neither lives with nor loves the child, and has seen him for perhaps as little as twenty-five hours, provide all the right answers.

I am saying these things only because they are not said often enough. But this is not the usual experience for most people. The large majority of people who work with the emotional problems of children are dedicated and honorable. Most of them behave as warm, interested, honest people, ready to share with us candidly, eager to be of real service. We have every right to seek out those kind of people and never to settle for less, especially where a young child is concerned.

There are situations in which we cannot wait patiently; there are children who suffer from serious emotional disturbances. Many parents have delayed getting help because they are so afraid of being blamed. Up to this point in time, they have probably been right to have such fears, but the situation is changing. There is a new humility abroad in the land which accepts the fact that some children who are treated terribly get along just fine, while other children treated in the opposite way may become psychotic. There are ways in which environmental pressures can kick off some special sensitivity in the child, but (and this has been painful for therapists to face!) some children who are rejected by their mothers don't get asthma, some children who get yelled at a lot don't have nightmares, and some children who are told it is perfectly all right to be angry sometimes, still do stutter and wet their beds at night! Any parent who seeks help today should feel assured that he can find counselors and therapists who will be as eager as he is to help the child, without having to blame anyone.

When therapy is undertaken for very good reasons, a child can often be helped enormously. Children are more flexible, they bounce back more quickly and dramatically, and one can see the relaxation, the opening up, the self-confidence that come with breaking through the barriers of fear and anger. As one little boy said, toward the end of his therapy, "When I came to you my heart wasn't in very good condition, and you mended it."

One of the best examples of a new and more flexible approach which has been developing occurred when I was attending a staff conference in a child guidance clinic. A very well-known and highly respected psychiatrist, who has kept on learning and growing all her life, was asked, "What school of psychiatry do you belong to now?" She answered with a smile, "How can I tell until I see the child?" Our accumulating wisdom can be of value only when it is used in this humanly sensitive and perceptive way.

The new research on child development, and the more balanced and realistic approach to psychotherapy both offer a constitutional amendment to parents as liberating as the Emancipation Proclamation. Our children, it seems, are not putty in our hands! Perhaps now, freed of the heavy weight of culpability and guilt, we will be able to use our good sense and good will, to accept our children as they are, and provide an environment that measures itself in terms of differences. Being less fraught with anxiety, we may be able to accept what can't be changed, and change what can be changed. D. K. Winebrenner, quoted in *Today's Child*, says:

> Some children—like trees—are best planted in groups, while others are best standing alone. Some grow strong and sturdy against the forces of nature. Others need protection from the winds and storms. Some resist rot and stand up well against the elements which rapidly deteriorate others. Some children are like sturdy oaks, or lonely maples, or beautiful pines. Others, like quaking aspen, shimmer and tremble with the slightest breeze . . .

Surviving parenthood would seem to mean accepting and honoring nature, and providing the elements that will aid nature in its work.

CHAPTER

❦ *5* ❦

"Tommy Did It!"
The Preschool Years

During the preschool years, the crucial aspects of growth are not as easily influenced by external forces as is true later on—children are then more products of their homes than of society. Usually parental concerns center on the following areas:

1. Parents feel helpless in the face of the young child's fears. How could such a happy baby become so filled with apprehension? There doesn't seem to be any way in which to give reassurance—and adults begin to feel angry because of a sense of impotence. "You stand there, it's three o'clock in the morning and there is Maria, screaming in terror because the lamp post outside the window makes a shadow on her wall that looks like a tiger. You turn on the lights, you feel the wall, you offer to leave the lights on, you explain that tigers are all securely locked up—but she goes on yelling, and be-

cause you are so helpless you feel as though you could strangle her!"

2. Parents become panic-stricken that behavior won't change. They expect to be awakened every night, forever, they are afraid that their child will always wet his bed, cling to them when other people are around, eat like a hummingbird. (These are the easiest things to offer reassurance about. When my daughter went on preferring strained foods, after what seemed to me a suitable time for moving on to chopped foods, I consulted the pediatrician, who assured me that by the time she got married she would be eating solids! That time scale covers anything that's bothering you!)

3. Parents find themselves becoming perplexed and uncertain when their children begin to really rebel. We feel we are losing control, that we aren't respected. We find ourselves overreacting, and we don't know why. It is hard to let go, our children are still so helpless that accepting the evidence at hand that they are becoming ready for some opportunities for independence makes us confused and uncertain. Our children's rebellion and defiance reawaken old and forgotten conflicts in our own childhood, when we too behaved in unacceptable ways, were punished and had to learn to control our impulses. Selma Fraiberg, in an article in *Parents' Magazine*, "Life and Times with a Two-Year-Old," wrote:

> This period of our own childhood is forgotten . . . we don't remember that, at two, we were stubborn and defiant, that we lied, had aggressive feelings toward our parents, committed a host of misdeeds, enjoyed dirtiness and naughtiness and were without shame . . . When we are confronted with a small child who is like that, he represents tendencies, impulses and wishes in ourselves which we had long ago banished from memory . . .

There are definite tendencies during the period of growth from about two to five years that seem to me to form the basis for our concerns. Language—its meaning, its use as a tool of communication—is one of the crucial growth areas; the other is an emerging sense of self, and an awareness of what it means to be a human being. A central theme that runs through these years of growth is, "How do I learn to live with my imperfections, especially after I know what they are, expressed in words?"

When our daughter was about three years old, she became a paragon of virtue, she never did anything wrong. Whenever it appeared to our confused minds that she *had* done something naughty, she set us straight immediately; she was always the innocent bystander, the victim or horrified spectator; the explanation was really quite simple: "Tommy did it!"

There really was a boy named Tommy on our block and he really did manage to get into considerable difficulty with grownups and children alike, but we began to have the feeling that he just wasn't capable of getting into as much trouble as our family reporter would have us believe. He would have to take some time off for eating and sleeping—and anyway, some of his crimes sounded too interesting and original, and we just didn't think he was that talented. During this period, however, when all the crimes were being heaped on his head, his accuser was having nightmares quite often and was afraid of the dark, of thunder and of wild (imaginary) animals. Eventually Tommy was accused less frequently, and as he became less a member of the household, the fears diminished too. The time came when it was possible for our child to endure being human—both good and bad—and to incorporate all this into her one self.

"Tommy did it" became a standing family joke and now we all use this to cover a multitude of sins and catastrophes. Sometimes it is a room that is left in an awful mess, sometimes it's a sloppy job on a homework assignment, sometimes my husband and I have called on Tommy to be blamed for a leaking roof or a broken dish. When I meet and talk with the parents and teachers of nursery-age children, I am frequently reminded of the "Tommy did it" stage in our home. It seems to me that it epitomizes one of the most important and basic aspects of growth in the preschool period; an aspect of growth which, if understood, can make the job of parenthood a little easier.

Not all children find a scapegoat to blame all their sins on, but in one way or another, a central struggle at this time of life, for all children, is what to do when they discover anger, jealousy, rage—the unlovely or socially unacceptable parts of being human. Let's look back for a minute at the time before language, or thinking-in-words, began. When a baby or a toddler feels uncomfortable or frustrated, it is just a generalized feeling all over his body. His face may turn red, he may howl, his body gets rigid, he may wave his arms and legs. If he is uncomfortable, if something hurts, or if he is angry because he has been left alone, all we can observe is a kind of generalized physiological reaction all over him—something for which he hasn't any words and no conscious thought. As he gets older he learns words—and one part of his developing vocabulary has to do with feelings. Now such things as love and kindness and sharing and friendliness take on form and shape. He can think in words: "I love Mommy—she gave me chocolate pudding," or, "I was a friendly boy—I shared my truck with my little brother." Children learn attitudes along with language, and they figure out that certain kinds of thoughts, and the actions associated with them, are acceptable, appreciated and desired by adults, and others are not. I suppose that if there is a culture somewhere in the world where it is considered evil to love, children at the language-learning stage of development would develop guilt feelings about being affectionate and nice! In our society, it is anger and hate, aggression and hostility, that are considered naughty or bad and have to be overcome. But they are *felt*, and now they are thoughts-in-language. If we watch nursery-age children, we begin to see that some of their growth problems are related to the fact that really for the first time conscious thoughts can be troubling, not only unconscious feelings.

When language first develops, it is quite primitive. Young children think magically. We never completely lose this quality even as adults—there is still a kind of instinctual, primitive feeling that words or thoughts can make things happen. If we talk about some good fortune, we knock on wood lest some evil destroy our luck because we have put it into words. The other day I was talking to a friend on the phone and she said that her husband might be getting a much better job. When I asked for more details, she said, "I don't dare talk about it—wait until it's more definite." This is a holdover from childhood, when all language was so new that it seemed to have infinite and magical powers.

We think, very often, that because a young child's language is limited, we can say a great many things in front of him because "he's too young to understand." The truth of the matter is that he is too young to look at our words with the sophistication we bring to language, but he understands something. Frequently we underestimate the two- to three-year-old's reactions to a death in the family, the arrival of a new baby or any major family crisis. He doesn't *seem* to notice or react. Several years later, we may discover confusions and misconceptions that have completely distorted his view about what took place; his language was too primitive and his perceptions often strange and magical.

The language-learning child faces one of the greatest tests he will ever have to encounter—a crisis that has been written about by poets and philosophers, and which figures as a central theme in all religions: once you discover that, being human, you are imperfect and that you have angry thoughts and feelings—you really don't love everybody all the time; in fact, there are moments when you could gladly kill—what in the world can you do with this shocking information? Well, for one thing, guilt becomes part of the human experience. Whether this will be the beginning of constructive self-control or of destructive self-hatred depends on what we do to help a child through this deep personal crisis. He'll go through it, no matter what—and he will hurt and he will suffer—but if we know what's going on, we can help him solve his problems to some extent, so that he will be able to move on to new challenges without the deep paralysis or distortion that can stunt his emotional growth.

Some children, in becoming aware that they are partly "devil" as well as partly "angel," find a Tommy; *they* are good —it is someone else who is bad. This is the age for the emergence of an imaginary playmate who can serve as the "shadow side" of oneself. Some children will say, "Yesterday I was the bad Billy, today I'm the good Billy." Each part is still distinct and separate even within oneself. A child comes to nursery school—a pretty, dainty little lady. She kisses the teacher and then, sliding off her lap, makes an absolutely terrifying, catlike face and says, "Now I am a terrible lion. I will scratch your eyes out, and I will take my claws and then I will kill you!" Some awfully sweet and docile children are almost never themselves—they are constantly playing at being a galloping horse, a mean, biting cat, a naughty little dog, a jumping rabbit who bumps into everything and knocks things over. Goodness is expressed as oneself, badness has to be externalized and dissociated from oneself, because it is just too painful. Why is it painful? Because if you think bad thoughts, terrible, terrible things can happen, things you really don't want to come about, but your thoughts can make them happen. Think only good thoughts, and you'll be safe—the bad thoughts belong to that tiger or horse, not to you.

During the "Tommy era" in our house, my daughter also went through a period of wanting me to stay very near her bedroom when she went to sleep. She had a light on in her room, a light in the hall and I was NOT to dare go downstairs—she wanted to hear me moving around. After several weeks of this, during which I was confused and frightened— just like any other parent who thinks to himself, "Suppose she's still this afraid when it's time to go away to college or get married?"—but finally, in a moment of quiet reflection I tried to remember some of my own theories, and I said at bedtime one night, "You know, no matter how angry you would be at me, no matter how much you might wish inside your head that I would go away and never come back, that would

NEVER happen. Thoughts can't make things happen and every person gets mad at other people sometimes." Within a week or so I was allowed to go downstairs. But I don't want to imply that this is a simple matter. Children who are helped to limit the magic power of thoughts may still need a night light in the room until about six years of age, a hall light until ten and a light in the bathroom until twelve. Magical thinking, guilt about naughty thoughts: these are deeply, instinctually, primitively human, and it takes years and years and years to come to terms with them—and none of us ever does, completely.

This tendency to try to disconnect, to separate the good and the bad in oneself, is human and natural and apparently inevitable. The fears that are so characteristic of this age are also part of this tendency to push away not only anger in oneself but awareness of anger in others, and the fear which that generates. When I have asked young children to explain the things they are afraid of, here are some of the answers I have received: "Thunder is something very big and powerful. It rumbles and roars and it makes you scared because it's so big. It is an angry sound and it could maybe kill somebody." Fear of horses: "Well, a horse might do almost anything, he could run away and trample on people, he could bite someone's head off because he has such a big mouth, he could tramp, tramp, tramp, on some little animal—he could suddenly run away so fast that no one would ever know where he was." Fear of cats and dogs: "Well, you can't tell what they might do—a little kitty could be all curled up and very friendly, and then suddenly, without any warning, it could jump and hiss and scratch, and a nice little dog who is just standing there wagging his tail could suddenly race all around the room and knock everything over, and he could suddenly snarl and bite, even though one minute before he was a friend"—all descriptions of the less lovely aspects of human feeling and behavior.

Here, for all of us adults to see, is the terrible dilemma of the two- to five-year-old: "Now I know, now I feel, now I see.

People are a mixture of nice things and terrible things. What shall I do? Am I all bad, or could I be all good if I push the bad part out? Grownups aren't good either—they can yell and scream and be very scary too. I am afraid. I am evil. I am guilty."

One night when we were trying to comfort our daughter after a nightmare, and talk about the dark in realistic terms, she finally said, "But I'm afraid of *my* dark," and of course this is the crux of the matter. It is at this stage of life that each of us had to face our "own dark"—the dark side of man's nature—the primitive fantasies and wishes, the uncivilized part, the part that remains the animal aspect of us. It is pretty perceptive of our children to choose so often at this age to be afraid of animals, since in reality it is the animal in them that is so frightening.

There are many ways in which understanding this struggle can make life easier for parents. First of all, we can be quite sensible about it by not being afraid, as I was, that because a child is going through a period of fears and nightmares, this will go on forever. It is the logical growth work for his age, and it will NOT go on forever. Secondly, we can ease the symptoms somewhat by speaking about the problem, not around it. Instead of saying, "There's nothing to be scared of," we can say, "Tell me what the thunder makes you think of," or, "What makes that kitty so scary?" and we can help our children say out loud what the qualities are that they are having such difficulty internalizing and accepting as part of themselves. I don't believe that we should ever walk around with couches on our backs, and become our children's psychiatrists, nor should we ever, at any stage of growth, make our children feel that they have no privacy and that we should examine all their thoughts. Everybody needs the right to be free in his innermost thoughts, the right to the dignity of privacy, but we can speak generally.

A friend of mine told me that her four-year-old son kept having a recurrent dream that a lion was roaming the streets at night and that he was putting his paws up on the glass part of their front door and would break the glass, get in, and eat the whole family. This mother was getting more and more exhausted from lack of uninterrupted sleep, and asked if I could think of any way to help her child get over this nightmare. I suggested that next time he had this dream, she sit on his bed and ask him to tell her all about the lion—what sort of lion he was. Her son was delighted to give a full report. Sometimes the lion seemed like a friendly lion daddy. But then, when you least expected it, he could bellow and roar so loud that you would shiver and shake. Then, sometimes he would like to play with the other lions when he was in the cage at the zoo, but when he got out and was roaming the street, he got angrier and angrier and he wanted to kill anybody he met. Suddenly Chris seemed to change the subject, and asked, "Mommy, if a four-year-old boy killed somebody, would he be put in jail?"

What can a parent do with such material? Let us hope—not spend hours in psychoanalyzing the deep symbolic meaning. There is quite enough to work with on a nice, conscious level of sensitive parent and scared child. First of all, that lion sounds very much like a father—or a mother—who seems so terribly big and powerful to a very small boy; little children do shiver and shake inside when parents get very angry or impatient. Nothing too deep or complicated about that. A parent might say, after such a midnight talk, "You know, Chris, sometimes Daddy and I forget that you are little and we are big. I guess most boys and girls your age get scared sometimes when big people get angry at them. People shout loud when they get mad, but they don't really mean it, and they get over it quick!" Such a comment isn't going to change the world or cure all childhood neuroses and problems—but it may offer some relief and comfort, and it can set the stage for a child's becoming ready to accept, inside himself, his natural fear of grownup anger.

What about the lion's being good when caged, and bad when left roaming? That's not very subtle either. Most of us feel more comfortable with our uncivilized parts when we know there are external controls. Laws make us feel more comfortable. We know the danger of a mob, the uncontrolled passions that can be released when law breaks down. Children are learning about this at three and four and five: "Don't leave me alone with my bad thoughts—I might do something awful—would you stop me?" In the first place, we can tell children over and over again, in a general and nonspecific way, "Bad thoughts cannot make a thing happen. Lots of children and even some grownups get mixed up about this, but it just isn't possible. The things you think are the same as what other children think. But you will not need to do any of those things you think. No child who thinks about killing has to do it—thinking is enough!" Questions about jail beg for answers that say, "Thinking won't make you do it, angry feelings are normal, everybody has them, and yes, we will never let you do anything to hurt others, we will keep anything bad from happening. Grownups are here to stop you, and you will never be sent away from us. Parents help little children control their actions—not jails."

The magic power of words—and the thoughts they bring—this is the central issue. It can lead to paralyzing fears if unrelieved. When an especially imaginative and intensely alive child goes through this growth experience, it can block growth and learning if we don't do anything about it. One little girl went through two and a half years of never being herself when she was naughty—she would become a cat or a crocodile—and so realistically that she scared her nursery teachers! She was exceptionally bright, but this absorption cut down on the amount of energy she could use for play and growth; although she could paint and do marvelous improvisations, her energies were sapped by her central concern, and although she did get over it, and did resolve her conflict eventually, so that at least she stopped being an animal, some of her talent and vitality had been wasted and even her resolution was not as good as some other children's. The reason for this was in part the fact that try as she did, her mother simply could not accept the imperfect, the shadow part of herself, so neither could her child. The mother was a sweet, soft-spoken, sensitive person, raised by her parents to repress and push away any aggressive or angry feelings, and she could not forgive herself if she lost her temper, nor could she tolerate jealousy between her children, or anger expressed toward herself.

We help children most through this phase of growth when we ourselves can be tolerant of the human condition, when we have made peace with the idea that we are each many things. We strive to be civilized and social, but we also accept and try to love that part of ourselves which refuses to be tamed or intimidated by civilization; that part which can take the form of drive, vitality, creativity, imagination, and which comes with the package deal, including the primitive instinct to fight for one's individuality, to resist interference, to refuse accepting compromises. When we learn to balance and accept the social and the instinctual, our children also learn to live with both sides—and the best thing about this is that then our resources can be freed: we aren't using up a lot of psychic energy in keeping the deep dark secret that we are not perfect or always lovable and sweet. Knowledge of our deepest and darkest parts makes it possible for us to bring them under control and to help us become the masters of our fate.

One of the things that often bothers parents when children begin to show their less admirable feelings is the terrible fear: "If my child feels like killing, doesn't that mean he might do something terrible? How about the children who *do* do awful things?" The children as well as the adults who "do awful things" are almost always the ones who do not integrate the dark and light sides of themselves—they really do not even know both sides at all. Haven't you been puzzled when you hear about a criminal who has committed a ghastly crime and who is described as a docile person? I am always interested when I read reports of teachers and neighbors about young people, especially, who suddenly go berserk. The typical newspaper quotation usually goes something like this: "We interviewed Burt Smith, the next-door neighbor who runs the local gas station. He was shocked and stunned by the crime. Dazed, he told us, 'Why, I just can't believe it. That boy was a good boy. He was quiet and well mannered and he helped his mother more than any other boy I know. You couldn't ask for a better boy—went to church, never was wild or sassy, I often said to the missus, why can't our boys be like him?' "

These are frequently children who are never able to accept, deep inside themselves, that they are all things human; they are children who remained, far beyond the normal age for this, three to five—unable to make an association between goodness and badness, good and evil, as all part of man's nature. The bad side was still externalized and never really brought under any kind of synthesized control. No one helped them to understand: "We all think bad thoughts sometimes. It is normal and natural. Thoughts can't make bad things happen. We will help you learn the difference between thinking and doing." It is the process of consciously coming to this realistic understanding of oneself that provides the ability to control one's acts and not be at the mercy of uncontrollable impulses.

These are the years for a beginning sense of "me"—what is this person, this body, this thing I see in the mirror—what is it to be "I"? Because this is a period of this kind of growth—self-discovery, self-awareness—and it becomes important to do what we can to help a child get a good image of himself, an image that will help him feel he is lovable, and capable of mastering life's challenges and problems.

When he is afraid, for example, a reason for not saying, "There's nothing to be afraid of," goes beyond the question just discussed that there *are* things to be afraid of, inside oneself. There is another reason for respecting a child's fears lest he get the idea that he is already a failure at the age of three, because, obviously, if it is silly to be afraid, then something is wrong with him if he can't *not* be afraid. "You're too old for a light," "You're too big to be biting Jenny," "You are a big boy now, you don't have to cry at the doctor's"—all these comments (and all of us have said them, and can't help it sometimes) suggest failure.

We know that the reason for immature behavior is because the child *is* immature, and really, we do know he'll outgrow it. But the young child doesn't know anything of the kind—his time sense is too limited, he can't imagine a time beyond tomorrow—so how can he be optimistic about getting over being immature? A cartoon showed a little boy trying to fight off being put into the dentist's chair, and saying, "You're always telling me I'm too young for this and too young for that —now all of a sudden I'm a big boy!"

Most of the things that our children do which we wish they wouldn't, and which we admonish them to stop doing, are normal for their age and perfectly appropriate ways of coping with life. Crying when you're scared, for instance. This is nature's own way to help a child express fear and release the accompanying tension. When we let a child know we respect this natural reaction, we release his energies to try and control it to some extent. When we make him feel ashamed and inadequate, we increase the tension and force him to struggle so hard for self-control, on such a high level, that fatigue makes it twice as hard for him to cope successfully.

Many years ago, when my husband was stationed at an Army hospital, we met a dentist and his wife who were desperate about their little girl. Paula had something wrong with her—I can't even remember what it was any more, but she had to have two injections a week for this condition. She was being treated on the Army post, and she carried on so terribly every time that she was disturbing ward after ward of patients as she was brought screaming down the halls. Sometimes she managed to squirm away and would race down the halls with two or more adults running after her. The parents were beside themselves with embarrassment and were offering all kinds of bribes if Paula would behave: if she acted like a big girl, they would buy her a doll; if she didn't cry today, she'd get an ice-cream cone.

Everything depended on her being a big girl. There was just one problem, she *wasn't* a big girl—she was a little girl, just four years old. When the parents asked our advice, I suggested they tell Paula the truth. What she had to go through every week was just awful for such a little girl. She was so scared and it did hurt, and she needed to cry very, very hard. That was all true. It was also true that her mommy and daddy had to take her to the doctor—they wanted her to be strong and well because they loved her; it was their job to make her go to the doctor because, of course, such a little girl couldn't make herself go—it was just too hard to be good or to be brave, she wasn't old enough. So, what could be done? They would have to make her go, and she would have to be scared and cry. Maybe, since there were lots of sick people around who were resting, they could help her by carrying her *very quickly* and hugging her tight *while she was crying.* Daddy would pick her up and run just as fast as he could from the car to the doctor. Paula could put her head very hard on Daddy's shoulder and cry with her head buried in his lapel, and that would cut down on the noise. When they got into the doctor's office she would sit on her mother's lap, and because no one could expect her to go through it all by herself, they would hold her very tight while the injection was given. It was perfectly logical for her to want to run away at such a time, so they would do the holding, she didn't have to try herself, or worry about getting away—that was the grownups' job. She certainly would need to cry a little, but after the injection was over, she would be able to stop because it was finished, and she and everyone else would be feeling happy then. Each time they would do the same thing; Paula could just be a scared little girl, and her parents would do what had to be done. If she still felt scared later, and if she had tried not to cry too loud, maybe she could save some of the being scared and hurt until they got back in the car, and then she could *really* yell until she felt better.

Paula was in a state of shock for a while after this plan was suggested! All along she had thought she was an awful little girl, a terrible failure. Now they were telling her she wasn't. The parents explained that they hadn't realized how frightening all this was for a four-year-old girl, but someone who knew lots of children had told them that Paula was acting just like any other four-year-old would act. Within two weeks Paula herself, with all the energy and strength released, now that she felt like a good girl, a nice girl, a successful four-year-old girl, was able to begin controlling herself. She whimpered quietly in the hall; she told her mother, "Don't forget to hold me tight"; she squeezed her eyes shut and shook a little—but she could now work at controls, since she knew she was no longer alone but could count on support and genuine approval.

If children can be relatively comfortable with their own ways of growing during these early years, it may help them feel more competent and comfortable with later ups and downs of growth. One example of this seems to be what happens when young children who have already learned to keep dry at night begin to wet their beds again. For many children almost any change or transitory tension or fatigue may cause this "fall from grace," and certainly the more obvious events such as the arrival of a new baby, moving to a new house, some strain or unusual tension between parents, too much partying over the Christmas holidays, tend to be related to a return to bed-wetting.

At this point, many well-intentioned and well-informed parents will smile fixedly, grit their teeth and say, "That's all right, darling." When it happens the next night, and the next, they pick Junior up at eleven, and tell him he can't have his usual glass of milk before going to bed. They are now getting a little annoyed, and even if they continue to refrain from punishing the child, there is an atmoshpere that is more and more loaded with reproof and parental despair. Junior, who may now really be over the initial fatigue or tension which caused the bed-wetting in the first place, is now more anxious than ever: why is he doing this babyish thing? It seems perfectly clear from the behavior of the adults that he could stop it if he really wanted to. Feelings of shame and failure become more pronounced, and the snow-ball effect is in operation; the more upset the child becomes about his inadequacies, the less likely it is that the bed-wetting will cease.

For the past two years I have suggested a course of action to nursery school parents that seems to be reasonably effective. First of all, preschool-age children simply *don't* have any conscious control over bed-wetting, and secondly, thinking they do makes the situation worse. I have tried to help mothers really believe that the child is not able to do anything about it. There is no reason why they can't react like normal, harried, annoyed mothers, and grumble about washing the sheets —it *is* a nuisance, so why pretend that it isn't? At the same time, however, it is very important to make it clear that the nuisance is just one of those natural things, and someday it will go away. One mother told me that when she caught herself muttering over the extra wash, she explained to Danny, "Listen, this has nothing to do with you. It's a nuisance to clean things up when you're very sick and you vomit, and sure, I don't enjoy it, but you know perfectly well it's not your fault. And this isn't either, you can't do a darn thing about it. Lots of children your age have accidents and then someday it just stops by itself, so don't worry about it."

Another mother said that at first she found it difficult to explain to her daughter how bed-wetting could be an automatic action. Finally she thought of an example. She said, "Ginger, suppose when you went to bed at night I told you, 'Now I want your stomach to digest your supper and I want your lungs to breathe in the fresh air.' That would be silly; your body takes care of those things—you don't have to think about it and you can't make it happen, it just does. Well, wetting the bed is the same kind of thing."

Whatever theories there may be—and there are many more than I have mentioned—the point of this method of handling is that it removes a major obstacle to growth of any kind; it takes away that sense of personal responsibility for failure, and removes something that often paralyzes a child in his efforts at surmounting difficulties: his sense of incompetence, his feeling that somehow he is different and is not living up to his or our standards.

A father told about getting a report card from a nursery school which stated that his four-year-old daughter "is quite immature." Furiously, he wrote on the back of the note, "If you can't be immature at four, when CAN you be?" and returned it to the school. Sometimes we need to make it clear to our children that it is appropriate to behave immaturely if one is a child!

For many children of this age, it is very difficult to know how to behave in new situations. Where an adult assumes that birthday parties are cute and fun, they may be an ordeal for a child. If we absolutely insist, "You're three years old now; don't be such a mama's baby—go and play the games and stop hanging onto me," then we are saying, "You are failing. Why can't you act like a six-year-old?" If we say instead, "I think Patty is a little tired so we are going home. Maybe next year she will like parties better," then we are saying, "You're okay, honey, you don't have to be ready for that yet, there's no rush—take your time." One approach brings a sense of failure and inadequacy, the other makes you feel comfortable and at ease with yourself and growing. For many children at this age it is extremely difficult to find suitable ways of defending your own rights. It feels natural and right to just bite somebody if they bother you—but grownups are horrified, and act as though you have no right to claim membership in the human race, so after a while, if you're lucky, you can remember not to do that. Then some grownups want you to fight back, but not by biting; you're supposed to fight back by hitting, which is a little confusing since hitting is also, under other circumstances, not allowed. One little boy was constantly being pushed by an adversary in school. His mother was very ambitious and had high expectations for her son. There were very few areas in which he felt he was doing all right. One day, when a boy hit him, and he didn't do anything about it, he noticed a teacher had been watching. He went over to her and said, "I'll give it to him—when I'm six years old." That little boy had more sense than a lot of grown-ups—he had a perspective on growth!

One of the sources of our confusion in living with young children is that frequently behavior that looks like regression is really an advance in maturation. The infant often seems to be much more self-confident and optimistic than the three- to five-year-old. Well, just think about the differences in what they know and understand. The preschooler may have discovered death—his and everyone else's mortality. He is aware of real and present dangers in life. He perceives other people and events more sensitively and acutely. Of *course* he worries more—he'd be a fool if he didn't! Growing up means taking on the burden of knowledge—and much of what we discover is painful, frightening, frustrating. The young child feels over-powered by our size, our strength and our abilities. The miracle of life is that he struggles for his own autonomy even in the face of our power and apparent omnipotence.

There is the apocryphal story told about H. G. Wells and his four-year-old son. They were sitting on the cliffs of Dover looking out over the water, just at twilight as the sun was setting on the horizon. H. G. Wells was smoking his pipe and musing to himself, "Going, going, gone." At that moment the sun disappeared and his son turned to him in adoration and said, "Do it again, Daddy!"

No four-year-old is ready to go out and earn a living. He can't even be permitted to cross the street alone, or decide on his own whether or not he'll have a polio shot. He can't even be allowed to decide to hit people just because he feels like it. There are many times when, if a child wins, he really loses, when we permit him to do something that he himself knows is unrealistic and about which he may become guilty and anxious. But he is growing, and he is moving in the direction of self-control and self-determination and he has to begin somewhere. We have to be careful that we don't initiate the armed-camp approach. If we set ourselves up as opposed to independence, then we are in for a long war. If, on the other hand, we control what still must be controlled, but are flexible enough to allow some dignity and self-respect, we can be our children's allies in growing, at least part of the time. Not always; growth often involves some downright hatred and some clear and open warfare between adults and children—that's part of becoming free, too, but not all the time. If we look at the children we live with, we can see that there really are many ways in which we can begin to encourage choice and opportunity for experimentation. Many young children don't naturally take to three big meals a day, for example. It's too much food at one time, and table conversation is an art that is at least five years ahead of them. Under these circumstances, can we be flexible enough to avoid unnecessary battles, saving our ammunition for the truly vital issues? For instance, I don't understand why so many mothers are terrified at the thought of ever letting young children watch TV while eating. This age group isn't ready for the social skills related to eating, and anyway, they are rarely very hungry. Eating is all too often a boring chore, since appetites are almost invariably smaller for a couple of years. And how civilized do you have to be at such an early age—why are three big meals better than five small ones when you're three years old?

Audrey's parents were so afraid she was starving to death that they both came to nursery school for a conference. Audrey certainly wasn't a fat four-year-old; she was more like a string bean. But she had grown three inches in six months and she'd only had one cold all winter. Despite the pediatrician's reassurances, her parents were sure she would starve to death. She could never finish what was put on her plate, no matter how small the portions. She ate so slowly that it took hours to get anything into her, and every mealtime was a nightmare. Apparently Audrey had found one way to show she was growing up; she sure could get people worked up and mad, and still she would win every time. If she had to prove her right to some decisions, she was going to do it, even if she got a little hungry once in a while! If we have some one area in which we have very strong feelings, we can be sure our children will discover it! Some nursery-age children whose parents are very relaxed about their food but are terribly nervous about rubbers and sweaters, eat just fine, but run out without the proper clothing in really cold weather. Other children who are real lambs about co-operating in dressing decisions, since no one seems too concerned, will refuse on principle to clean up their rooms after playing, because nothing in the whole world could make Mama madder, and there is, in the midst of the ensuing battle, a sense of personal triumph.

With Audrey, we suggested that she be told that her parents had found out she was really much too young to eat so much food at one time, and it was silly to force her when she really wasn't ready to sit at the table for a long time. When she came home from nursery school, she could have a half of a peanut-butter sandwich and a little box of raisins and some nuts, all of which she loved, while she walked around the kitchen watching mother do her various chores. Later in the afternoon, if she wanted an apple or if she wanted to have a little picnic in the yard, a snack could be prepared. For supper she might help in the preparation and see how she liked the taste of raw vegetables while her mother was washing the string beans or shelling the peas. Maybe just a small lamb chop would be pleasant to have while watching her favorite cartoon—and then at bedtime, while Daddy read a story, she might enjoy a glass of milk and some bread and butter. If her parents could leave the battleground for a while, Audrey might find that there were other and maybe better ways of asserting herself: she could choose which overalls she would wear to school; she could decide what she wanted to do in the afternoon, play in the yard or go visit a friend; she could choose which toys to take to bed with her, she could pick out her own new book at the library—all signs of growth, all new ways of feeling increasingly self-determined. When Audrey stayed in school for lunch, she ate almost everything she was offered—a fairly clear sign that when no one made this a test of power, she did what came naturally.

How fearful most of us are of some of the most healthy behavior! I am far more comfortable when my teen-age daughter is reasonable, thoughtful, loving. When, on the other hand, she flexes her emancipation muscles and rages against me, I am soon shaking with anger myself, and am filled with misgivings. And yet an obsequious and overdutiful child is likely to be more reluctant to give up dependence, and may mature more slowly than the one who fights and screams for being a person in his or her own right.

I recently had a conference with a mother at the nursery school that brought with it this sense of surprise. Last year her son had attended the nursery school. Roger was a slow-moving, passive, intellectually limited child who would probably need special schooling and would not be able to achieve with his peers. His mother adored him, never had the slightest difficulty with him at home, and in most of our talks her only complaint had been against other parents who refused to make dates for their children after school with Roger, and neighborhood children who were reluctant to play with him. Roger was very big and he loved to hug and pat people; unaware of his own size and strength, he was often hard for other children to cope with; but even after accepting Roger's difference from the other children, his mother seemed unable to see that Roger might not seem attractive and lovable to others. From our point of view it was a sad situation.

This year her younger child had arrived in our three-year-old group. Patsy was one of the most enchanting children we had ever seen—shining black eyes, a quick wit, a natural leader in the group. The teacher's joy in her was never-ending. Patsy was imaginative, she was compassionate toward other children, she was always ready to try something new and threw herself into every activity with great zest and genuine delight. We all adored her, and whenever I observed in her classroom, the teacher and I would marvel on nature's balance; if the parents had to face the problem of Roger, at least they also had the joy of this wonderful, delightful, miraculous little girl.

When the mother came in for her conference, she had a long list of things she wanted to discuss with us. Patsy was "an impossible child," she was at her wits' end with her. Patsy was constantly defying her, she fought over every mouthful of food, she couldn't be reasoned with at all. She added, "I suppose I've been spoiled—Roger has been such a pleasure to live with." It took several seconds for the teacher and me to recover. What strange twists and surprises life presents! She liked docility, and that was something she got from Roger. Patsy, a robust, healthy youngster, was being held back from growing at her own marvelous rate so that she would not outshine her elder brother. Her mother said, "Look, she's only three, it won't hurt her not to ride a bicycle for another year. If I let her now, she will be doing better than Roger." She was distressed by the fact that Patsy was curious, that she had already asked her mother to teach her to write her name, that she wanted to skate, that she could paint "real people." Patsy's self-assertion, her drive to grow and to become a person in her own right, were more threatening to her mother than Roger's mental deficiency.

A major task for the preschooler is communication—with himself and his own inner being, as well as with others. What do you have to do to be loved? When do other people get angry or dislike you? How do you figure out what and who you are, and then keep other people from taking this slowly emerging image away from you? How do you keep yourself intact and still give to others? One of the most interesting ways in which we see some of this struggle going on is in the possessiveness of young children—what we too quickly think of as selfishness.

A friend of mine told me that when she was explaining where babies came from to her four-year-old, she told him that he had been in a wonderful, safe warm place in her body called the uterus. Steve sighed contentedly and said, "Did I have my special blanket when I was in there?" It is very hard to figure out where you begin and end, what it is to be a person. If you love and need something desperately, is it part of you? Almost as much so as an arm or a leg? Suppose when you go to bed at night you feel sort of tired and mixed up, and you are thinking about so much that you can't go to sleep. You suck on a blanket, and every single night that blanket makes you feel good. If anything is that important to you, is it part of your own body, your own self? Suppose someone gives you a beautiful shining new truck and you love it a lot more than you do your baby sister, or even your mother, at least for a while. Isn't that truck part of you? How can anyone ask you to let someone else touch it? How can they say you're being selfish—they never ask you to give your sister to someone else; they never say, "Now, Johnny, you have to take turns, you have to share your leg with Peter." No one ever says things like that.

Precious things are a kind of extension of oneself when one is very little and uncertain of what "self" means. If we say, "You're being selfish," we are again suggesting a failure, and the more we think we are failing, the more likely we are to dislike this failing self we must live with all our lives. Suppose someone says instead, "I know how you love Teddy. You need him all for yourself. Maybe when you are bigger, you won't need him so much. Right now it is too hard to let anyone else play with him. When Ronny and Jerry come over today, let's put Teddy up on the shelf in the closet, safe just for you. Then you can look for some other toys that you don't care about quite so much and you can all play with them."

Such a response respects what a child is working at; his discovery of what is intrinsically himself, and what is outside himself. It isn't an easy thing to learn. If he feels protected and supported, he will probably be relaxed and free enough to begin to experiment with lending, sharing, taking turns; if he feels threatened and uncertain, if he thinks he's been a mean, bad boy, he has to spend a lot of time and energy protecting himself and hating himself, and so has less time and energy to go on experimenting and trying other ways.

Communication also means learning that you can feel something and communicate with yourself, but you can't always let yourself impart your ideas or feelings to others, through action. We can communicate with words, and this may cover a broader range of possibilities than communication through action. You can get mad at Danny and you can say, "*Boom, boom,* I can kill you and I'm going to get you," but you are not going to even hit Danny—this time, anyway. Communication, both in language and action, is the way in which we learn what it is to be human, to be civilized, to be an individual, to be a friend, to be an enemy. We can sometimes begin to help this process along when we take the initiative in using language to help a child come to terms with his feelings. When one little girl howled as I took her from her mother, after the first week of nursery school, I was convinced that she was angry at being thwarted, but that she was more than ready for someone to place some limits on her separation from her mother. I said, "Boy, Linda, are *you* mad at me!" Linda looked very surprised, yelled louder, and then asked to be allowed to play the phonograph. Another little girl, on the other hand, was really suffering at letting her mother go, and wept quietly for some time. I commented, "You are certainly very, very sad." The teacher looked at me askance; wasn't I encouraging more tears? Apparently not. The next day it was over—the verbal recognition of a fact seemed to have cleared the air.

We can easily make a mistake in an interpretation, and if we're wrong it won't make any sense or any difference, for children know when we are trying to understand. If you're right, you are helping a child use a potential technique of communication with himself.

When we can understand the life work of the preschooler, and when we can respect his way of growing and of gaining mastery over himself and his environment, we help him to learn his most crucial lesson, which begins at this age and goes on for the rest of his life: how to live artistically with oneself and others, how to listen to one's own inner voice and be oneself, and still live with compassion and sensitivity with others. Approval and acceptance of one's own way of growing is one way. A feeling of safety to be oneself and to learn in one's own way is another.

I read an article a number of years ago where the writer described a nursery group in which the teacher was trying to help children increase their awareness of their own senses. She held up a flower and asked the children what senses they could use in appreciating the flower. Dutifully, the children said, "We can see the flower with our eyes, we can smell the flower with our noses, we can touch the flower with our hands." But then one little boy said, "And I can hear the flower." The teacher responded, "Oh no, Johnny, we can't hear the flower." And the observer wrote: "What kind of world would it be without those who can hear flowers—what of our poets and dreamers, who help the rest of us to hear flowers?" In our contacts with young children, we can help them communicate and feel good about themselves if we leave plenty of room for flower-hearers.

Many years ago, I heard a story that still moves me deeply. When the United Nations met at Lake Success on New York's Long Island, a nursery school was set up for the children of the delegates. Teachers had to be sensitive to many differences, they had to speak several languages, and they were a devoted and dedicated group. The children came from all parts of the world. At one time, a Chinese delegate arrived in New York. During the flight to America, his wife had become very ill, and when the plane landed an ambulance was waiting to rush her to the hospital. The delegate was needed at some important meetings, and so he had to bring his four-year-old son to the nursery school. The child knew no English, he had just flown from his home to a totally strange and unfamiliar land, and as if that wasn't enough, he had even lost the comfort of his mother's presence, in transit.

When his father brought him to school, he accepted the situation without protest, and simply stood quietly, weeping. He was inconsolable, he would not let anyone touch him, he would not play or eat or take a nap. He stood all day long, quietly brushing away his tears. None of the teachers could speak Chinese, and they were greatly distressed about this little boy's misery. That first night, one of the teachers went to Chinatown and bought some Chinese toys. Another teacher was able to find a Chinese picture book. But the same pattern occurred the next day and the next. At the point when the teachers really felt desperate about helping this little boy, a strange event took place. An American girl went over to the little boy and said something to him that sounded like gibberish or nonsense-words. The boy looked up very seriously, took her hand and went with her to the table. Still holding hands, with the little girl still making sounds that no one could understand, he ate some lunch. Later the two children, still holding hands, lay down on cots pulled next to each other. Still later they sat holding hands in the sandbox. The teachers were terribly curious about what was going on and delighted at the turn of events. When it was time to go home, and the Chinese boy had been called for by his father, a teacher asked Anne what she had done to help Lee so much. Anne said, "Well, I thought about it a lot, and I couldn't talk Chinese and he couldn't talk American, so I decided to talk to him in make-believe Chinese."

That is the artistry of living, and it can begin to happen so very, very early in a child's life.

The
MIDDLE
YEARS

measured and found wanting, and where personal feelings of failure may already have occurred, one now feels that one's failures are on public display.

What are our children like? When she was ten, our daughter was a lady roughneck; part bluejeans and which-boy-can-I-beat-up-today, and part mooning and moaning for the love of the handsomest boy in class. When her class gave a play having to do with Greek mythology, her part called for a grotesque headdress and very large wings on her back. During the performance the children who were not on the stage sat on a bench at the back of the room. At one point I noticed her sitting next to the music teacher, who seemed to be having convulsions—or else to be doubled over in pain. When the play was over and my half monster–half fairy had disappeared down the hall with her friends, he came over to me and said, "Your daughter had me in hysterics there for a minute. I went over to sit down on the bench next to her, and she shouted at me indignantly, *Don't sit on my wings—I'm an angel!'* Boy, if that isn't the story of these kids' lives! It's so hard to remember they're angels, and not to sit on their wings!"

School-age children aren't so cute any more; they are not always lovable, if we want to be honest about it. They squirm, they jiggle, they twitch, they run in packs, they are noisy and sloppy, and they never remember to do anything we ask. Worst of all, they don't think much of us any more—we have lost our halos forever; practically *anybody* is smarter than a parent. And then, just when we think we can't stand the feet kicking under the table one more minute, or the droopy socks, or the silly giggling that is so loud the house shakes—just then something marvelous happens. We look out a window and see a son courageously resisting group pressures to exclude the new child on the block from a game; Helen tells us that she's decided to be a veterinarian and has arranged to meet her science teacher after school to dissect a frog; Bob offers to dry the dishes on a day when you were too weary even to ask. One of the loveliest stories about a grade school child I ever heard was about the mother who said that for her birthday her eleven-year-old son had given her a beautiful nightgown. The only trouble was that it was a size 16. When she took it back to the store, the saleslady remembered her son, and said, "Oh yes, he wasn't sure of it, but he said you were about my size, so I gave him a sixteen!" Both ladies laughed as the nightgown was exchanged for a size 42!

For all the external appearance of things, school-age children are sensitive, idealistic, proud, eagerly curious creatures. Given a lot of room for real adventure and exploration—their own kind, not what we decide is good and then supervise for them—they can take off and fly. It is so hard for most adults to tolerate the outward behavior of school-age children that a good many wings do get clipped. There is a very real difference in today's attitudes toward mischief—no longer any room for "boys will be boys." Society will not tolerate what was once accepted and taken for granted—that childhood is a time for explosive energy and vitality, secret and impulsive and anti-adult activities.

School-age children are restless and require genuine release for their high spirits. Adults tend to emphasize the need for docility—"keep the kids in their place." Many social and economic factors contribute to an increasing adult intolerance of childhood, but the fact remains that much of what we fear the most in our children are qualities we once accepted as part of nature's plan.

The first rule for enjoying the fives-to-twelves is to tolerate what this age group is like, naturally and inevitably, and NOT spend hours every day in desperation and worry because these savages will never be tamed. Time and living change a great many things without our having to be in there doing battle every minute. One mother told me how she learned to wait. When Fred, her first child, was three years old, she congratulated herself because she was doing a good job of giving him the habit of cleanliness; why, he could sit in the bathtub playing with his boats for hours, and you just had to drag him out. He wasn't just clean, he was "blue-white"! But when he got to be about nine his mother really was worried—where had she failed, what had happened to all her earlier training? Fred was now allergic to water. It took days of imploring, hours of dire threats, to get him into the bathtub once a week, and at that, he made it quite clear she was torturing him more diabolically than if she had used the rack. What could she do to make him change? Suddenly, when he was twelve, she noticed that it was very hard for any other member of the family to get into the bathroom—Fred was doing his hair. This involved a long shower, followed by an hour or so in front of the mirror with a comb and some kind of hair goo. Fred testily asked where his clean shirt was and sometimes took two showers in one day. She started to congratulate herself—after all, her nagging had paid off, she had done a good job—and then, suddenly, she stopped kidding herself: it was that beautiful little girl who sat in front of Fred at school. "With my younger children, I just relaxed, and exactly the same sort of sequence of events took place. I didn't have to do a thing!"

If we spend all of our time trying to make our children outgrow their age instead of letting time do much of the work, we can really lose touch with them and spend a good deal of time alone and angry. Another mother told me that she had been nagging her son Jeff to hang up his pajamas before he went to school and she was getting nowhere. One morning when she had a lot to do and was feeling put upon, she walked into his room and found his pajamas rolled up in a ball on the floor, all his dresser drawers open, absolute chaos inside, the bed unmade—and she decided in seething wrath that she had *had* it and that he was going to get it. All day while he was at school she muttered and growled and planned her attack when he returned. A little after three, when he galloped up the front walk, she had the door open and was waiting with ammunition ready. The eager, excited look on Fred's face disappeared as Mama yelled. He became grim and quiet; without another word he went upstairs, slammed his door, didn't emerge until dinner, seemed more angry and hurt than his mother had dreamed would be the result—she had succeeded too well. Jeff said almost nothing while eating, then slunk off to do his homework. A friend arrived, dashed into the house to see Jeff and shouted on the way upstairs, "Isn't it *marvelous* about Jeff being chosen from the whole school to be on that radio program?" This was the news event Jeff never got a chance to report. His mother said, "I learned something that day. I learned that if you want to be friends with a child, and if you want to have the good times you need with him, you just can't waste so much time in yelling and nagging. You have to make a choice: take them as they are and get some fun out of it, or turn into a shrew and hate yourself and your child almost all the time. I could just as well have said quietly, 'Before you do anything else, Jeff, you have to clean up your room.' I didn't have to harbor all that rage and self-pity all day."

Humor helps a great deal. The very things that are most annoying can be the funniest. I was going out of my mind because my daughter could never find anything; she could be looking for a red sock to wear to school for ten frantic minutes, screaming that I had stolen it, and then, when I walked into her room, it would be lying on her pillow—bright red against all that white! It is an exasperation that doesn't have to be explained to any mother! Then one day I went to a PTA parents' meeting, where one mother told us that her husband had made up a name for this disease—he called it "Thing Blindness." We all loved that, and when I came home and told my husband and daughter about it, they did too. For some reason, I never was as bothered by it again—now it seemed funny—and it had such a cute name!

A friend told me a similar story about mealtimes. She said, "I defy any parent to suggest that we did not have title to the worst table manners of an eight- to ten-year-old in captivity. One day when my husband had really reached the end of his endurance, and figured he had suffered his last belch from across the table, he yelled, 'Now CIVILIZE UP!' This was so clever, we were charmed by it, Cindy included. It was a sort of grudging acknowledgment that out of pain and desperation Daddy had come up with a good one. The phrase made life much easier—for future reprimands it lent a light touch."

Being tolerant of what is natural doesn't mean becoming a mat that children can walk on. If you live with children, you just have to expect that there will be noise and mess and excitement and a general atmosphere of disorganized living, but while we can try to tolerate some of this, it is a two-way tolerance program; children have to tolerate us, too. We have rights that must also be respected; maybe their own rooms are chaotic, but we have a right to an orderly living room; it may be noisy with lots of friendly children around, devouring every scrap in the refrigerator, on a couple of afternoons or on a Saturday or Sunday, but there are other times when the house is to be quiet and parents are to be allowed to take a nap or read a book or the newspaper in peace. We will do what we can to help our children have time for running, jumping, shouting and "messing around," but at the same time we will make it quite clear that there are some rules and laws which are to be respected. A father once told me that when the chips were down and he had decided that his children had to do what he said, he used the old Army method; when they questioned the rule or his authority to make it, he would stand stiffly at attention and in a deep voice announce, "It's Policy." He was amazed at how well that worked!

Most of us have trouble tolerating the tremendous variability of behavior and interests at this age. Adults like to have their own sense of order imposed on the universe, and school-age children are usually churning masses of changes, of inconsistencies, illogical and unpredictable. Behavior, interests, level of maturity, all vary so excessively from day to day that we have a vague, constant, free-floating anxiety that we are losing our minds! A big strong nine-year-old boy, who would rather die than let you kiss him, gets the measles and lies there wanting you to feed him his soup and sing him to sleep; your shy, diffident eight-year-old daughter, who can barely speak above a whisper in school, gets so mad at her younger brother that she hits him over the head with an electric train; or you get the kind of camp letter quoted in *The New Yorker*: "Dear Mother and Daddy, Your worries are over. I am really growing up. I am in a tent with older girls and all we talk about is boys and sex. Please send me a water pistol. Love, Linda." It is very hard to get your bearings! You are ready to murder your little monster because he is so irresponsible, unfeeling, self-centered—and then he marches home from school on the Friday before Mother's Day with a beautiful spice shelf he's been working on all year, and which has some of your best recipes etched beautifully and carefully into its high polish. You are fit to be tied when ten-year-old Jan refuses to help you by setting the table for supper; you have been downtown shopping for her all day and you're tired. When she says *she's* too tired, you decide that you have spoiled her rotten and she's just a brat, and if you could you'd disown her. Then you go to a meeting at school and the gym teacher tells you that there is a new girl in school who is trying to buy Jan's friends with after-school candy and sodas. She was quick to recognize Jan's leadership and knew she couldn't take over unless she got rid of her. Jan has been going through her own private hell in trying to handle this on the playground after school, and the teachers are watching and say proudly, "She's not giving up and she will win them back fairly." You remember that when the table-setting episode was in full swing a few hours earlier, you shouted, "Here I've been slaving for you all afternoon and all you did was play!" One minute you are filled with righteous indignation—the next with guilt and shame because you have misjudged your child so cruelly! The only way to survive is to accept the situation as it is; we just can't predict and we do the best we can from day to day. We acknowledge the ups and downs, the backing down and moving forward, the lovely and the unlovely, and we keep telling ourselves that children do grow up—and no faster or better if we worry all the time.

· · ·

So far, I have talked about the things in children themselves that bother us. About those things, we need patience and endurance and a sense of humor. We also need a few good, logical rules, and we can protect ourselves by demanding some rights and privacy. (By now, most of us know that the "open floor plan" was invented by architects who were not parents, and we have been busily putting back the doors and walls they took down to make our rooms look larger! Most of us are happy to sit quietly in a closet with the door closed, in preference to a forty-foot living room with no barriers between us and the enemy fire!)

But many of our difficult problems with children have been created by adults. And these things we better change if we want to survive and enjoy ourselves and our children more. I have been meeting and talking with parents of school-age youngsters for about fifteen years and I know that children are really very co-operative and pliable. Once we make it quite clear to them what we want, they go out of their way to give it to us, and only then do we discover that the worst thing that can ever happen to anyone is to get what he wants!

Fifteen years ago we were anxious to have well-adjusted children. That meant children who were not different, and who got along very well in groups. Many of us didn't want little geniuses, because we had the feeling that such children didn't do very well socially. I remember a mother who told me that her twelve-year-old daughter had won a statewide scholarship to study the violin with a great and renowned violinist, but had turned it down because the other children were calling her a "square." Despite a genuine talent, and a joy in that talent, this mother permitted her daughter to renounce her gift and her award. "It's more important for her to be popular," she said. I remember a mother saying, "Look, I don't want Mark to be a genius. I just want him to be happy. People who are too smart aren't happy." Because we tended to want our children to be well adjusted, and since we equated that with being popular, we got exactly what we deserved: a conformist but devastatingly sophisticated group of children. We looked on in horror at nine-year-olds going to parties and ten-year-olds wearing stockings and twelve-year-olds going steady—but everybody was doing it, the children wanted to be members of the group, and popularity reigned supreme. I remember one mother who said she was shocked and horrified at her daughter's behavior, but oh my, how she loved telling us all about it at the parents' meeting. "It's just terrible," she said, "but I can't do anything about it. Imagine, a thirteen-year-old girl insisting that her shoes had to be dyed to match her dress, and wearing high heels and eye make-up—it's just ridiculous, I know, but she is invited all over and the boys are crazy about her, and after all, I can't put her in a nunnery, can I?"

Nobody went to a party or dressed inappropriately without the tacit approval of some adult. If we think we are having trouble surviving—well, we made our own little nonsurvival disasters. We also got so terribly eager and overconcerned that we watched and supervised and organized every moment of our children's lives. We encouraged a frenetic, meaningless *doing*—which had the effect of making our children incapable of being alone to dream. (One girl, a victim of the overorganized life, reported that what she liked best about her camp was that they didn't make her do anything. "I just meditated," she said happily!) We wanted to be our children's pals and then we were stuck with not merely tolerating childhood but joining it. Baseball, dancing class, musical instruments, religious instruction, dramatics and creative arts are now family events, apparently on the assumption that there's nothing wrong with going through childhood twice! We have been discouraging resourcefulness and imagination, and there is very little real adventure or challenge in the lives of many children. Everything is planned, nothing is mysterious, uncertain, unexpected—all necessary to a sense of true adventure. We rarely let them out of our sight, and then we wonder at the amount and intensity of the resulting rebellion.

But times have changed; we have other goals now. The

Russians got sputnik and suddenly we were for genius, happy or not. Conformity and being well adjusted have been very disappointing, anyway. It was leading to passive, conforming college kids with nothing on their minds but an easy job with a big pension and early marriages, and early socializing and aiming at popularity had seemed to lead toward an awful lot of much-too-early sexual experimentation and license—and as a matter of fact, we really didn't get the appreciation we had expected for trying to raise this well-adjusted crew.

At any rate, we are now in the midst of a new crusade—how quickly and expertly we can trade our children in for computers. We want them to sit quietly and memorize. This is not to be confused with thinking. In fact, children who *think* have been having a very hard time of it. They get much lower marks on multiple-choice exams than the good-memorizer nonthinkers. The thinkers tend to see too many possible answers to questions and could defend several points of view on many issues. We weed these out fast. Chances are they aren't going to make any contribution to the mechanization of man's life on earth, and we can't be bothered with drifters who may end up writing poetry or doing social work.

If you detect a note of fury, you are on the right track. I don't think anything that I have observed in our attitudes or methods in child-raising has ever made me angrier than what I see happening now in relation to the problem of academic achievement, from kindergarten right straight through graduate school. Hardly a day goes by but that I hear a new and hair-raising story. While we are busily trying not to waste time we are crippling some of our most wonderful children —or at least burdening them with fear and making them feel like complete failures, before they have lived one fifth of their lives.

Here are some of the things that have been happening:

I can start with a telephone conversation I just had with a friend whom I haven't seen for some time; we were catching up on how old our children are now and what they are doing.

Jane, eleven years old, always a good student, cheerful, self-possessed and basically optimistic about life, has been losing her hair and is now getting injections for this condition, which doctors say they don't know the cause of, but there is much evidence that tension plays a major part. Her mother said, "Jane's been placed in a very advanced class that will enter junior high school next year. She has at least two hours of homework every night." Her brother, aged ten, is in the first quartile on all his tests, but he began getting stomach aches when he was placed in the most advanced group in his school, and so the teacher agreed it might be better to put him in the second quartile. He stopped having an upset stomach, but now he feels that he is a failure, and is embarrassed to meet his friends who could "take it" in the top class. Their mother said, "The tensions and pressures and worries about marks and getting into college started at about third grade. We try to counteract it, but we really don't know which way to turn."

Phillip's parents went to a PTA meeting, where they were informed that their nine-year-old son was learning to graph his reading ability. He likes to play baseball, hates girls, is fascinated with astronomy and reads—devours—books on that subject. But his teacher is very upset because he doesn't understand how to graph his reading speed and gets all mixed up about what the dots and lines mean. An older brother, aged thirteen, curious, charming, eager to learn, has become indifferent and lazy; he refuses to do his homework, turns in sloppy work, doesn't understand directions, hates school. His mother feels he is so overwhelmed with the rigidity and narrowness of what he is allowed to learn, or supposed to learn, that all his own intellectual curiosity and excitement are being destroyed, and apathy and outright indifference are taking its place.

Wherever I go, one parent after another tells me that most evenings at home have now become nightmares. Mothers and fathers are desperately trying to understand their children's homework well enough to help them. Sometimes there is so much homework that Mother will spend several evenings every week typing out her child's report, simply so that he can get to bed before one or two in the morning. In most cases neither parent can understand such monsters as "The New Math," and since Johnny doesn't understand it either, the whole family fails.

Some schools are now instituting weekly report cards so that parents and children can be kept informed. Marks and tests are rapidly replacing study and learning experiences. We want to measure results before we produce anything.

At a time in life when children are most active, need to move around, need the stimulation of adult leadership and warm human contact, they are being made to sit for more hours than most adults and are often spending their time "relating" to machines rather than to human teachers. If you are "smart," much of the fun of learning is removed because you are always behind and can never catch up. If you are a "late bloomer," a perfectly respectable thing to have been once upon a time, you know that all is lost because your ninth-grade marks will go on your college records. And if you are just plain "dumb" in the sciences, you accept the fact that you have nothing but second-class citizenship to look forward to, forever.

An ad in a newspaper reads: "Increase Your Child's I.Q. in 30 Days." A well-known educator says about three-year-olds who can't read, "We are wasting this nation's time." Another educator says, "By the time an American child is six and in the first grade, time is already running out for him." What is this mass insanity all about? Even if you can read at three, what are you going to read—how much experience, understanding, perception can you possibly bring to reading? Suppose we can get twelve-year-olds to mouth all kinds of brilliant thoughts about profound subjects—what do they really know, what can they feel, where are the needed life experiences, the maturity, to understand what all the words mean? Where are we going in such a terrible hurry? We are going to live longer and have more leisure than any human beings ever had before. One educator, in looking at this hysteria, said, "By the age of seven, children are supposed to be fully ready to blast off into life space, whereas by the age of seventy-seven or eighty-seven they will still be in orbit." The situation is well summed up in this verse taught me recently by an irate father:

> *The golf links lie so near the school*
> *That almost every day*
> *The little children hard at work*
> *Can see the men at play.*

We seem bent on eliminating childhood. Play is certainly not to be tolerated. We seem to despise everything connected with childhood and are making every effort to see that it is overcome as quickly as possible. And this, after all the years of careful study, observation, research, which indicated so clearly that it was essential for children to go through each stage of development at the appropriate time, to master and cope with the tasks and needs of each age, in order to mature successfully.

Automation is bringing with it more and more time for leisure. Medical science is helping us to live longer so that there are more years of retirement than of childhood. Frantically, older people try to find some meaning in their lives, some inner resources to help them continue to live creatively. And yet we seem to be saying to children: imagination doesn't count, creativity is only useful if it makes you scientifically inventive, play is a waste of time, meditation, repose, relaxation, dreaming, are OUT. There is hardly a school-age child alive today who hasn't at some time in his life been described as an "underachiever," not working up to his potential. I would like to know where there is an adult who isn't an underachiever, or who lives up to his potential. I give thanks every day that I am not a child. As an adult I can be good at one thing and terrible at a lot of other things; if I am tired I can put off to another day some task or other. If I don't enjoy studying one subject, I never have to give it a thought. If I want to underachieve, no one stops me—I can dream away, I can waste time and talents of my own, and no one gives a darn. If I am successful in any area of life, I can capitalize on that and gain prestige and recognition. As long as you are not a child, you can gain fame and fortune for one little old talent—you don't have to be well rounded, you don't have to be brilliant in academic subjects, you don't have to take tests which measure nothing of any real significance about you as a human being.

I heard recently about a boy who struggled desperately in grade school and high school to get high marks—high enough to get into the Ivy League college his father had attended. In order to accomplish this feat, he would have had to have at least a 90 average, over-all, in all his subjects. He graduated from high school a complete failure, as far as he was concerned, with a 78 average. In disgrace, with his tail between his legs, he went to a Midwestern university that had to let him in if he was a resident of that state, and he became a resident by living with his aunt. At the end of one year of college he was on the Dean's list—one of our thousands of late bloomers who simply do not produce academically until they find themselves, until special interests or talents emerge. I heard about him at a dinner party, where twelve people were present. I decided to find out how many late bloomers there were in this group, which included two social workers, a college professor, two high school teachers, two psychologists, a magazine editor, one doctor, one lawyer and two businessmen. Every single one of these people was respected and successful. Not one single person in the room had any idea until college or graduate school that he would be doing the kind of work he eventually got into. Only three people present said that they had been good students all the way through school. All the others recalled periods of failure or near-failure in grade school. Four had failed two or more courses in college, and two people had to make up work by going to college during the summer. The large majority had done well in one or two subjects, but their over-all average had been B or lower.

But more important than anything else, all these people enjoyed learning, felt they were still learning, and liked to think; in fact, it was a favorite pastime. The children we are raising now are what E. B. White called "the clever generation." Not wise or profound or thoughtful—just smart; they can copy, memorize, repeat. A hopeful sign was the story I heard recently of one little girl who always put every homework assignment in quotes. Her parents and teachers told her this was incorrect, but she stuck to her guns. "These aren't my ideas," she said. "These are the teacher's ideas."

One of the chief topics of conversation with nursery school parents is whether or not their children will get into kindergarten at the beginning or end of their fifth year. The nursery school staff is begged, urged, pleaded with, to help the children who miss the right birthday by a month or two get into kindergarten a year earlier. Parents are horrified at the amount of time wasted on playing and at the awful age a child will be before he gets to college.

There are nursery schools all over that are helping to calm this panic. One in California is teaching French and geometry to nursery school children. Lots of others are seeing to it that dolls and trucks and useless toys like that are eliminated from the nursery school, to be replaced by games that teach. A recent magazine article was entitled "Why Waste Our Five-Year-Olds?" Why, indeed! They only have a life expectancy of seventy-odd more years, and not a moment must be lost in idle child's play. The perfect answer to "reading readiness" in children who are two and one-half to three was told to me by a mother who said, "My fourteen-year-old daughter is *capable* of having a baby, but that doesn't mean she's *ready!*"

A recent book reported that first graders in Russia were reading Tolstoy. Isn't that wonderful? I know some very scholarly and learned gentlemen in their fifties and sixties who are *still* finding subtleties and mysteries they feel they haven't fully comprehended in such classics.

All of this goes on in the face of fifty years of study and research about how children grow and learn, the importance of play as a tool for growth and learning, the need to cherish and preserve a love of learning, the natural curiosity and wonder of children. A research project was undertaken a few years ago where observers recorded every time a child asked a question and every time a teacher asked a question, from first grade to sixth grade. They found that in first grade, children were asking eighty-seven percent of the questions; in sixth grade, teachers were asking eighty-three percent of the questions. What happened? Where did the children's quest and curiosity go? What killed it? No doubt the kind of teaching that demanded certain answers and certain responses, that discouraged differences in interests, that scared children off.

In examining the lost ground in education—the present vilification of everything that had been proved to be sound and practical in encouraging intellectual growth in children—Dr. Harold Taylor recently commented, "People criticize educators, not for being backward, but for not being backward enough."

A contribution from *The New Yorker*, in their "No Comment" department, was as follows:

> (From a catalogue of the Wilshire Book Co., Hollywood, Cal.) The Exam Secret by Dennis B. Jackson, B.A. $1.00. Astounding study technique. Pass every examination you take. 75% less work. For adult students or children of ten. Exam nerves? Away with them . . . Hit your target every time with Mr. Jackson's examination technique. It is not those who can write well on something they know who succeed but those who can deal brilliantly with subjects of which they know nothing.

At a recent education conference I was shocked to learn that more and more children are being given tranquilizers. The educator who mentioned this said with irony, "After all, many youngsters tend to be restless and excitable. If we can give them tranquilizers we can open up their heads and pour knowledge in!"

The change for the worse in our educational goals was

clearly defined in a speech given by Walter Crewson, associate commissioner of education in New York State. He told the audience:

> The purposes of the school as outlined in the 1918 National Education Association Special Commission stated:
> Give child sense of ethics, ethical behavior in human relationships.
> Help child towards sensitivity to the responsibilities of citizenship.
> Teach child responsibility for his own health, independence in caring for self.
> Provide mastery of skills, three R's, fundamental processes.
> Learn to use leisure well.
> Encourage worthy home relationships, ability to function in family.
> It is appropriate to teach children to earn a living.
>
> A 1960 Commission stated merely that:
>
> The central purpose of the schools is to develop the rational powers of man, through basic subjects for thinking and reasoning, English, math, science, history.

This is a theory against everything we know. Children learn to reason from teachers who know how to reason *regardless of the subject.* No curriculum has a monopoly on the capacity for reasoning.

The tide will turn, but probably not soon enough to help our children much. I have been heartened by the remarkably intense interest in two recent books—*The Teacher,* by Sylvia Ashton-Warner, and *Summerhill,* by A. S. Neil. Neither of these books offer remarkably new ideas about education. In fact, the "progressive education methods" they advocate are more old-fashioned and less carefully developed and refined than what good educators know today and are capable of doing, if they had not been discouraged and abused. However, the interest indicates a basic dissatisfaction with "The Rickover Effect" in education.

I had a hard time to keep from laughing out loud when I went to a meeting recently and was told in all seriousness by an educator, "You know, we think we will experiment with heterogeneous grouping in the lower elementary grades. Something seems to be lost when children are in homogeneous classes—we seem to miss out on some talents, and children seem to need the balance of contact with differences." John Dewey and most of the progressive educators knew this fifty years ago. Who is to decide who is the more worthy human being: the fast reader or the butterfly collector, the speedy multiplier or the storyteller? Why should these children be cut off from each other? Could they live without each other? Was anything more important than appreciating differences and celebrating strengths—of all kinds, not just academic skills? Well, we have lived through the "smart" and the "dumb" groups—and there isn't a child anywhere who was ever fooled because we called them the "bluebirds" and the "redbirds"—and now, pretty soon, there will be "new" experiments with helping children to live and learn together despite their differences in talents, skills and interests.

Another possible straw in the wind is some of the research which has been going on to discover what creativity is. Business, science and government have discovered that being well adjusted and even being smart in a nice, average sort of way isn't really enough for any real progress in any field. Now it is fashionable to look for creativity, and fortunately, it is being found in strange and wonderful places—in some of those late bloomers and underachievers, as a matter of fact!

I like especially the work being done by Dr. Donald W. MacKinnon, director of the Institute of Personality Assessment and Research in San Francisco. Five hundred and thirty really topnotch leaders in many different fields were studied— the shining lights among artists, architects, mathematicians, engineers, research scientists and writers, among others; all people who represented original and creative thinking. They found that having a high I.Q. was not a consistent or reliable requirement, although all of their people were in the normal-to-bright category. In addition: "It is certain that our most creative subjects haven't been grade-getters." Most of them had a C or B average and many could not qualify for entrance to some of our graduate schools today. The most significant qualities to emerge from this study (and many others as well) were: curiosity, skepticism, independence, aesthetic sensitivity, introversion and nonconformity. Many of these people seemed to have a "sense of destiny," which tended to make them refuse to conform in their thinking.

I have pursued this one aspect of the life of school-age children because wherever I go these days, this is the issue uppermost on parents' minds. I simply don't hear as much about subjects that used to be considered of vital importance and that represented stumbling blocks for parents: sibling rivalry, sex education, family responsibilities and social relationships, for example. Those were live issues five or six years ago, but now, if survival as a parent is a problem at all, it almost invariably seems to be a great sense of distress at the pressures on children, learning problems, excessive worrying about college, a feeling of helplessness in the face of school pressures. If I meet with educators, they say the parents are putting the pressures on them; when I meet with parents, they say they are the innocent victims of a college curriculum being foisted on their grade-school-age children. I suppose this is natural enough—I guess I meet with superior parents and superior educators! But somewhere along the line, responsibility must be taken, and we cannot excuse ourselves from taking whatever action is necessary to make life and learning not merely endurable, but also pleasurable and meaningful for our children. If we are to intervene at all effectively, and begin to stem the rising tide, it had better be before high school and college.

School-age children are beginning to perceive that there is often quite a difference between what we say we believe and what we actually do. A good deal of genuine idealism gets lost at this age when the schism between belief and action is just too wide. If we want our children to grow up with meaningful values and standards, and to make the effort to live up to these, we had better give them some idea of how you do this. We have to get enough information, enough reliable reporting, to know a good deal about child nature at this age and what helps children become strong and free and learning well.

We have to let our children know where we stand. Do we respect the tasks which are set before them during these years? Do we really know what they are working at? Someone once asked a ten-year-old what kind of work he wanted to do when he was grown-up. "I thought I was working now," he replied with dignity. There are serious, earnest and difficult tasks which our children face during the elementary school years. So many skills to be mastered—all the basic equipment for every area of later learning and work. So much to learn about themselves and other people: how to make friends, how to stand up for oneself, how to join with others, how to be a teammate, the meaning of sportsmanship; physical skills of all kinds; tremendous amounts of factual information; an awareness of individual strengths and weaknesses—what one can do easily and well, what makes hard work, what kinds of things just aren't within one's scope at all; so much to learn about one's community, about one's government, about the world.

Not only have these things always been happening, but now there is the additional pressure to excel quickly and permanently on a very high level on a broad variety of subjects—and to think in terms of a far-ahead future that is really of no real concern to a young child. What eight- or twelve-year-old is really ready, or should be, to be concerned with college? It is ludicrous but true that we now insist on this kind of long-range planning—farther ahead than all the years one has already lived.

Children of this age distrust themselves enough; they don't need any help from us. Their perceptions are more sophisticated, they are so much more aware of all the accomplishments of man that they are frequently overwhelmed with a sense of hopelessness and fatigue at all that lies ahead of them. The seven-year-old walks into a public library; he can barely read fifty or one hundred words—and look what mankind has produced. How will he ever catch up? A nine-year-old works on his models with loving care—a jet plane, a rocket, a nuclear submarine—and then he thinks about "the real thing": what knowledge and skill and experience it takes to know how to make them, and he cannot believe he will ever be able to learn enough. Younger children just enjoy what they find in the world around them—TV, telephones, radios, etc.—but school-age children know these things are the result of thought and inventiveness, and they feel discouraged on all sides. They hardly need us to tell them they have a long road to go. Quite the reverse—what they need most from us is a sense of perspective, a reassurance that they have *time*, that there is no rush, that they can and will learn what they need and should not spend all their time worrying about the future. My husband decided some time ago that he wanted to study archaeology, especially in connection with ancient Greece. Slowly but surely, he has been able to become a scholar in this field. This was reassuring to our daughter who said, "Imagine, he's so *old* and he can still learn because he *wants* to!"

It is up to us to see that there is room for differences in children, that no matter what the pressures may be, the nonconformist, the offbeat, the supersensitive youngster, is helped to feel that he has a place in the world, that he is wanted, needed, admired. Because children can't really comprehend this, we have to point out the crazy inconsistency between what we expect of children and what we expect of adults. Try it out; you will find that most children are shocked if you ask them, "Does Frank Sinatra know the new math system? Could Albert Einstein write short stories? Did Marie Curie go steady? Could Eleanor Roosevelt multiply fractions?" I don't myself know the answers to any of these questions, but the point is, the questions are completely irrelevant, and children get the point. It is a good subject for conversation when Junior, biting his nails down to the knuckles in honest terror, has to face a science exam, while what he's good at is base-

ball, or a French exam, when what he really wants to learn
about is how to be a doctor. No grownup has to be good at
everything. Few of the successful grownups who are household words were "well-rounded" people. It is a lie to say that
a clever grasp of a lot of things is a sure road to success.

We can face reality ourselves and then play it straight
with our children. A lot of nice, intelligent, talented kids are
going to have learning problems they never would have had if
they had been born twenty years earlier. A lot of hard-working
kids are going to fail courses that no one would ever have
made them take, even ten years ago. They are going to have to
face the fact that no matter how well they do in school,
chances are they just cannot go to one of the more famous
prestige colleges. There just never was a time when competition was this great; the population explosion, the need for
more highly skilled people, the rapid decline of semiskilled
and unskilled jobs, require that many more of the already
greatly increased population go on to college. Some of our
children will have to take some courses over. Some will have
to study during the summers. Some will have to have tutor-
ing—not because they are any dumber than we were, but because the world presents them with tougher competition. If
we are clear about this, we can relieve a lot of unnecessary
anxiety and circumvent unnecessary feelings of failure.

We need to be clear ourselves about what we mean by "excellence." We keep hearing that word all over the place; if
you are against a killing pace of learning, if you think it might
be all right to let children learn to read at six or seven—well,
then you are anti-intellectual, you are for sloppy thinking. All
you have to do is open your mouth and ask a question about
the long-term usefulness of teaching algebra in sixth grade,
and some former Army general or college professor, who never
even talked to a child, will give you a lecture about how no
one can spell or use correct grammar in third-year college
work. We mustn't let them beat us down! The caliber of work
is just as high as it ever was, and just as many people are doing well as ever before. But more people are being educated;

people who come from families that never thought about going to school beyond the sixth grade two generations ago, are planning to get Ph.D.'s. There is a far wider and higher range of abilities in the larger college populations, and that accounts for a wider range of performance levels. If anyone tells us we don't believe in academic excellence, we can tell them we certainly do, but we also believe in *human* excellence, and that involves a belief in goodness, compassion, sympathy, responsibility in citizenship, a capacity to love, an inner core of strength, imagination, a capacity to feel and to think. These are all equally important with multiplication, reading fast, spelling correctly and understanding nuclear physics.

If our children are in a slow-learners' group, if tests scare them half to death, if they are utterly confused by a new method of teaching, we have to really mean it when we say, "You're not stupid—the world is crazy."

Speaking at a conference of the Play Schools Association, Dr. James Hymes said, "We need to accept childhood as a good and important and legitimate and worthwhile time of life." Which is really only a professor's way of saying, "Don't sit on their wings!"

❧ 7 ❧

"They Gave Me Freedom to Be a Nothing!"

Adolescence and Young Adulthood

Parental fears and anxieties reach an all-time high during their children's adolescence. These seem to be some of the areas of greatest concern: for one thing, parents say that they find it very hard to talk to their children, that an alienation seems to set in, and at a time when one might think verbal communication ought to be getting easier, it is far more difficult. Parents also say that they are frequently upset by their children's criticisms of them—that too often adolescents hit the target too well in assessing parental weaknesses and failures. Consciously or unconsciously, many parents find this age a special strain, for just as they begin to feel that their own youth and vigor is on the wane, and regretting what they have not done with their own lives, they are faced with children who have it all ahead of them, who are filled with promise. There may be jealousy of youth's vitality, its ascendant sexuality, of the opportunities in the future. Parents also feel that crucial choices and decisions must be made in the next few years and that mistakes now may be more serious or at least more significant. The psychological flight of children is accentuated and dramatized when they leave home for college, and parents are faced with an intense awareness of how their own lives will be changed. There are of course great differences between twelve- and fourteen-year-olds and between fifteen- and twenty-year-olds. But despite these differences it seems to me that a common enough thread or theme exists which is generally valid for these years of growth.

Living with adolescents can be so rough on one's ego that survival seems extremely unlikely some of the time! One of our handicaps at this stage of our children's growth is that somewhere along the line some of us got the idea that if we were good parents, our children would love us all the time. If we are *really* good parents they will more likely think that they loathe us some of the time, and it is time we began to face the fact that it is *not* necessary to be loved by our children every minute—we simply must learn to tolerate their animosity. We cringe and shake with fright at being the targets of so much disapproval and rebellion. We are "understanding parents" and that means that we deserve to be loved! Because we are the most doting and overindulgent parents in history, our children's lack of gratitude is doubly unbearable and puzzling. It seems as though the more we give and try to understand, the more they bite the outstretched hand!

In discussing the intolerability of life with a thirteen-year-old daughter, one mother explained, "It's really very simple—one of us has to move out!" Any parent who has been the victim of that special twelve- or thirteen-year-old look of disgust will understand the threat I overheard one day in a department store, of a mother to her adolescent daughter: "Don't you *dare* look at me in that tone of voice!"

But the worst part of this period is the sense of finality, especially during the later years of adolescence. Parents often feel that the "chips are down," and whatever we have or have not been able to accomplish in helping our children grow well to adulthood, we must now accept as a *fait accompli*. Before going any further, let me suggest that if you are the parent of a teen-ager and have been feeling this way, sit back and think for a moment about all the things that have happened to you since the age of twenty-one. What were the experiences that changed you? What have you learned and how did you learn it? Are you, in any way, shape or form the same person you were then? In all likelihood you are not. We can eliminate at least this one fear! The truth of the matter is that emotional growth can be far greater and more dramatic between twenty-one and sixty than before—despite what some psychiatrists may have been telling us! But there are realistic reasons for some of our concerns during the adolescent years, and again if we are not only to survive but to enjoy this stage of parenthood, we need to examine the issues that seem crucial, and find ways of coping with them.

A therapist who works with adolescents told me about a young man he was seeing. This boy, eighteen and one-half years old, was attending one of the Ivy League schools. He was a brilliant student, his academic achievements were outstanding. Why did he come to see a therapist? Because he was becoming increasingly promiscuous: "I seem to need to prove myself more and more compulsively," he explained. Recently he had become impotent: "A realization of my worst fears," he said. Several months before, having read and heard a great deal about the drug LSD being used experimentally and sometimes pseudoscientifically in a number of universities, he had decided to try it because he had been told that it produced a heightened sense of well-being, increased mental acuity, and had other interesting and unpredictable psychological effects. He and some of his friends had obtained some of the drug, and now Jerry was becoming quite terrified by hallucinations and thoughts, including "a voice that tells me to castrate myself."

In explaining his feelings about his behavior over the past few years, he said, "We're all looking for kicks—we want to do dangerous things. It makes us feel a heightened sense of being alive." Another way of "getting kicks" for Jerry and his friends was to have intercourse without use of contraception: "It's like Russian roulette," he explained.

Jerry is *not* a special case; he is not a criminal, nor is he mentally ill in any classic sense. We can't categorize him in such terms, partly because there are so many other young people like him and partly because older clinical categories simply aren't adequate to describe or account for the bizarre quality of his behavior. He has a nice, enlightened family living in a comfortable suburb. His parents are decent, intelligent, responsible people. They have always been interested in his welfare; they are understanding and friendly. Jerry has been given attention, affection, good care, rich opportunities for educational and recreational experience. With all his privileged and protected background, he says he doesn't know where he is going, who he is, what he wants from life; nothing seems to have any meaning for him. He says, "My parents are really very nice people. They haven't really demanded anything of me except to do well in school—be bright and get good marks—and that was always easy for me to do. They gave me all the freedom I would want. They gave me the freedom—to be a nothing."

Of course many of the young people who are getting into really serious troubles and are behaving in excessively destructive ways, *do* have long-term, serious emotional disorders and are in need of psychiatric help. But there are literally thousands of young people in our colleges today who simply do not fit such a category; nor can one explain their problems in terms of immaturity. All children have problems in growing up, no less at high school and college level, but the manifestations of these problems have become more serious and more dangerous. My own explanation of at least one contributing cause is that we have given them "the freedom to be a nothing."

A group of adolescents in a wealthy suburban community, ranging in age from thirteen to seventeen, had formed a ring of thieves, went into homes and robbed them of radios, TV sets, jewels and furs. It took three years for the police to solve the series of crimes. It had all begun apparently with a bored and restless teen-ager, who invited his friends to join him in what eventually led up to several hundred burglaries. Actually, they were so clever about it all that they might not have been caught even then, except that they began to get careless in a deliberate attempt to increase the suspense and excitement. When they were finally apprehended it was apparent that none of these youngsters needed any money obtained from the thefts. All of them had generous allowances; they were in search of "kicks." Most of the children were known as "clean-cut, nice children" in the community; most of them were "the high I.Q. students" in the local high school—several were considered brilliant students, who would have their pick of colleges to choose from. Most of them had cars or the use of cars. If they needed or wanted anything, all they had to do was ask their parents. During the arraignments a newspaper reported that a weeping father had said, "Many of us came from poor homes ourselves. We had to go to work when we were younger than these children. We moved to the suburbs to give our kids fresh air and plenty of space. We gave our kids everything; they didn't have to work or worry, they knew they would go to college. The houses here start at thirty thousand dollars. The men are all successful, hard-working people and they dote on their children. I guess we spoiled them. They believe in nothing and they look forward to nothing."

A recent report stated that students at an Ivy League college had stolen $200,000 worth of merchandise (3.5 percent of the total sales) from the university store in the first four years of self-service. This amount is three times as much as when the store employed a staff. Actually the students have been stealing from themselves, since the store is a co-op. It gives one pause to think of the standards that are set, the prestige involved, in being accepted at such a college.

A friend of mine went to visit one of the big Eastern colleges with her son. A new rule had recently been instituted that boys and girls could visit each other in their dormitories as long as the doors were left open. "I raced through the dorm we visited as fast as I could—I've never been so embarrassed. In room after room we could see couples in all stages of embrace. Somehow I was more shocked by their indifference to being watched than to anything else," she told me.

The Insider's Newsletter reports:

> Newest evidence that the driving pressure to succeed in school has dangerous effects on academic "failures": College psychiatrists are stepping up efforts to recognize and treat potential suicides—whose numbers have been found to jump at exam time . . . Suicide is now the number-two cause of death among students (second only to accidents) . . .

For a long time I hesitated to express my distaste and alarm when I had occasion to watch adolescents do the Twist and other rock 'n' roll dances. Usually they were ringed by a group of amused and admiring adults, who would smile benignly and try to imitate them despite the hazards to a middle-aged sacroiliac. Since I often seemed to be the only person who became depressed by the antics, I tried to keep quiet. It seemed to me that I had never seen or heard of any tribal ritual in any culture, however primitive, that was as frightening. The main theme of teen-age dancing seems to be, first of all, that the partners avoid touching each other as much as possible and *never* look at each other; each must be caught in his own mechanical, autistic movements, sexually suggestive, but absolutely alone and alienated. It is as if neither partner can reach or touch the other, they are faceless to each other, and warmth, affection or communication is not part of their experience. I finally consider myself free to admit publicly how I have felt, because of an article by Agnes de Mille which appeared in the *New York Times Magazine*. She traces and analyzes all the different dance forms throughout history and in many different cultures, and shows that always before, whatever the form may have been, contact and human interaction have been basic to the dance—as well as spontaneity, freedom and feeling. In looking at our teen-age dances she says:

> What does it mean? Quite plainly, bewilderment as to direction, as to social function, even as to sex. The children are revenging themselves against discipline, against each other, against us. They are desperate. They are untrusting. They are alone. These dances are the expression of total, persisting loneliness and desperation. They are dances of fear.

We are afraid of the pseudosophistication of our thirteen- and fourteen-year-olds. Forgetting that their academic course work at school now involves mental gymnastics we once thought more appropriate to graduate school, we are frightened by other signs of acceleration. Our present generation of teen-agers are brighter, better informed, more articulate, more knowledgeable and have more psychological insight than any previous generation. But many are also empty. They are hedonistic. There are fewer dreamers, fewer genuine rebels, fewer true adventurers.

In *Teen-Age Tyranny*, Grace and Fred Hechinger point out what many of us have slowly come to realize: that a tremendous inroad has been made by the teen-age culture on adult society. By abdicating our responsibility for setting standards, we left a void. Styles in popular music, fashions, literature and art are now frequently being set by teen-age standards. "We are growing down, instead of our children growing up."

We seem, too often, to be providing *things* for young people instead of ideas, values, purpose, and the challenges and expectations that can give them dignity. It is immoral for a sixteen-year-old to be given a Mercedes Benz, or a twelve-year-old two $25 bathing suits. Parents defend such indulgence on the grounds that we live in an affluent society and that it is silly to withhold what we can easily afford. They say it is natural to want to give to one's children. It is not natural at all. There have always been wealthy families but they have not always overindulged their children. The availability of money has never been an excuse for abdication from responsible parenthood in training the young to lead moral and significant lives.

Rather than encouraging individual growth, which takes time, self-sacrifice and frustration, we have permitted a kind of social and personal irresponsibility in our children that we would not tolerate for a moment in ourselves or in those we choose as friends.

Now we are beginning to get frightened. Over a million young people are married each year at the age of nineteen; the divorce rate is three times higher for them than for those who marry later. A quarter of a million illegitimate births are recorded each year, to say nothing of abortions, or those children (probably another ten percent) who are conceived before marriage but born in wedlock. The rate and the kind of emotional disturbances occurring in high school and college are on a rapid increase. We know we have some serious problems to face.

A college guidance counselor told me that she was appalled at the cynicism displayed by the students she talked with, but she added quickly, "It's only a cover for a sense of despair. These students are flooded by 'ontological guilt'—by that I mean, the guilt which comes from not living up to one's potentials, from not realizing one's possibilities."

A high school principal said, "These kids have been robbed of the most important gift we should give them: the right to genuine experiences, a chance to be tested, to see what their strengths are. We keep them in cotton batting until they just go berserk trying to find *some* way to grow up."

A psychologist at a college says that there are two things that college students can do for themselves: they can become pregnant (or get a girl pregnant), and they can fail in their studies. "These are things that their parents can't take away from them, or take credit for!"

"Some of the 'dropouts' may turn out to be some of the best potential in this country," a college professor said. "At least they are searching for something; they feel pain and they are struggling to grow. But," he added, "there are others who fail or who plan to leave college, and when you ask them why, they say, 'The courses don't interest me, I'm not enjoying learning.' Where did they *ever* get the idea that you are supposed to be interested in and enjoy everything you do? Much of learning is plain drudgery for anyone. They don't seem to understand being committed to work for a goal, whatever the effort involved."

A college student told me her roommate's mother had taken her daughter to be fitted for a diaphragm. "Ginny was really not at all interested at the time," she said, "but her mother told her she knew perfectly well what went on at college, and she much preferred knowing that Ginny was protected." A few weeks later Ginny met a boy from a neighboring college. My informant went on, "From what I'd seen before, I think Ginny would have enjoyed knowing this boy and would not have felt the least deprived if she didn't go to bed with him, but this time, before they had known each other three weeks, she went to a motel with him. I guess she figured she had the equipment, she ought to try it out. Anyway, they broke up very quickly, and I think none of it would have happened if Ginny's mother hadn't been trying so hard to be a modern woman."

We have, of late, sometimes been giving young people encouragement to get into trouble for which we then blame them. My husband and I recently went to visit a college that is known for harboring a very high percentage of female geniuses. We saw a notice on a bulletin board announcing a speech by a very famous gynecologist—his talk to be sponsored by a joint student-faculty committee. One of the students explained to us, "Look, most of the students here sleep with their boyfriends—why shouldn't they? No one makes it the least bit difficult; we are allowed to sign out any time we want—it would be silly for the college to pretend they didn't know. So Dr. P. was invited to talk about contraception so at least the girls can learn to be careful."

Premarital sexuality in young people is hardly a startling novelty; one could even argue convincingly that today's relationships among college-age young people are more idealistic and honest than in earlier generations. The "good-boy" and the "bad-girl" double standard has been abandoned, and except for those who would be promiscuous in any age, most young people recognize the need for some responsibility and affection in sexual relationships. But the real difference between this generation and ours is that many young people, still quite unready emotionally for sexual relations, are finding themselves catapulted into them. The titillation of the mass media, the lack of any clear limits and controls at home or at college, the focus on high marks in school as the only parental demand or expectation, have left thousands of adolescents adrift on a sea of conflicting impulses, uncertainties and self-doubts.

It is taking us a long time to realize that sexual information and exposure to sexual activity were hardly an adequate answer to the Puritan and Victorian attitudes toward sex. One of the things that has fascinated me about some of the new plays by avant-garde playwrights is that they seem to deal, over and over again, with the theme of sex without communication, sex without love. Our youth are beginning to tell us where and how society has failed them: by its emphasis on knowledge and freedom in sexual activity as ends in themselves rather than a better basis for sex-in-love than ignorance, superstition and fear. A fifty-year-old woman said recently, "The difference between our generation and theirs is that while we dreamed together, they sleep together."

Some of our youngsters are pushed into make-believe relationships in order to prove their popularity and our success in raising such desirable creatures. A report in *Time* magazine said:

In Massapequa, N. Y., Kathy came home from school and announced that she would need nylons and a garter belt to wear at her girl friend's birthday party because "all the girls" would be wearing them. Kathy is eight years old. In Los Angeles, Bill's parents gave him his first "sit-down" dinner and dance (live music) for his tenth birthday. Tuxedoed boys escorted dates who wore corsages . . . In San Francisco, Beverly, daughter of a Berkeley professor, asked her parents for a "training bra." She needed to feel a little glamorous, since she was planning to go to a drive-in movie on the back of boyfriend's bicycle. Beverly is nine, her boyfriend eleven . . . The latest social discovery of the pre-teeners, particularly in the nation's suburb-nests, is "making out," a tentative version of adolescent necking . . . Says Carlfred B. Broderick, associate professor of family relationships at Pennsylvania State University, ". . . By the time these children have reached their teens, they have pretty well covered the field, and are ready for nothing less than marriage."

With the acceleration in social relationships and the worship of the intellect, we find many of our young people unable to achieve the emotional maturity or moral strength to hold body and mind together.

We need to know this problem side of things, but of course it is only *one* side of the story. The other is (as you may have been impatiently acknowledging on your own) that for all the storm and stress, adolescence is also a marvelous time of life, and the most wonderful things happen to our children! Whatever problems there may be, either in our bungling efforts to be helpful, or in the world in which they find themselves, our children have youth and resilience on their side, and a quite unbelievable capacity to snap back, no matter how great a crisis may be. Despite bravado, they are vulnerable and achingly sensitive; though parroting the materialistic chatter of their elders, they are capable of idealism, fervor and compassion. They have been exposed to cultural and cosmopolitan experiences so early in life that it often startles and unsettles us to hear them talk. Before the age of twenty, so many of our children have traveled extensively, feel at home all over the world, have eaten the foods, talked with the people and walked the streets of strange and utterly different places than home. Easier travel, television, paperback books, local community theater, concerts, opera, have provided them with enormous riches, unknown to young people before.

What then, can we do about the problems and the potentials of our adolescents? First of all, we should learn how to TALK to them again! Stop being embarrassed and self-conscious just because *they* are; it is appropriate to be uncommunicative at seventeen not at forty-five. We shouldn't just sit back hopefully and say to ourselves, "I believe in my child"; we should tell our children what we think, what we believe to be right, and we should teach them ways to behave—and *then* we may give them many opportunities to try to test us and themselves, knowing they cannot (and really should not) be expected to accept our standards without resistance and experimentation.

At present it seems to me there is an uncomfortable estrangement between young people and adults. With so much emphasis on being pals, on being understanding, parents forget how to talk to children; they become uncertain, ill at ease, embarrassed. They are afraid to ask questions—one isn't supposed to violate a child's privacy. Well, he may not tell you what you want to know, or the truth, but there is nothing wrong in asking the questions anyway; to pretend indifference or unconcern is silly.

Sometimes communication between adults and young people breaks down because of the gap in information, understanding—the rapidly changing times that bring with them whole new worlds that we do not understand and that they feel at home in. We must be ready and willing to learn. My husband happens to be interested in subjects that are frequently exciting to young people. We find that often when we visit families with older children, the relationship is stiff and distant until he starts to talk about his work, which is highly experimental, or about the subjects that he enjoys especially —archaeology, science fiction, etc. Then they forget their discomfort and self-consciousness, and are eager and excited about expressing their opinions. All of us need to keep ourselves open to new ideas, new fields, new ways of thinking—if we want to keep in touch, if we want to help young people in their search for significance in life.

Indulgence and overprotectiveness rob our children of using their *own* wings for their own kind of flying. It seems to me legitimate to make demands on young people. A mother told me about a letter she had received from her daughter, who was a freshman at an out-of-town college. She had been there only two weeks. She hated everything about it already— the stupid people, the lack of stimulation, the dumb professors, the dull classes. "What am I doing at this horrible place?" she wrote. "What is the point of going to college—it all seems so useless and meaningless." Her parents were spending over three thousand dollars a year to send her to college; both were working hard to do it, and the financial strain was considerable.

We encourage overdependency and irresponsibility without thinking about it, sometimes stifling the healthy instinct of the young person who is trying to find significance in accepting a challenge. A friend told me that a niece at college had asked permission to spend several months living with her. My friend wrote to her niece, warning her that life might not be so simple, that her own teen-age daughter was rambunctious, and would be demanding and perhaps annoying. The student wrote back, "I am very much aware of the fact that Jill would follow me around like an affectionate puppy, and I feel I understand her very well. I wish that I had had an older sister whom I could confide in when I was her age. I think I can help her." This is the miracle of growth and sensitivity that we stifle; this is the capacity to accept the burdens of being human that we too often block from expression because we are being oversolicitous.

Another college student wanted to spend her summer working as a volunteer at a welfare agency in a big-city slum. When she heard about this opportunity she was so excited, so committed to an ideal, so eager to be of service to others. Her parents greeted her announcement with violent protests: she would be mugged, raped, or murdered; she didn't understand the dangers. When we refuse to permit our young people to have the opportunity for genuine and challenging experiences, albeit hazardous at times, we rob them of the one thing they need more than anything else: a belief in themselves, and a discovery of their own identity through meaningful and purposeful activities. We need to say to our young people what human beings seem always to have known before, but now seem to have forgotten, "Being born introduces one to the dangers of being alive, and it is the never-ending price for continuing to live."

Striving for success, working for high achievements, must always take place within a framework of values. When was the last time we told our children that more important than winning was living with yourself? A father told me that he was concerned *because* his son was very bright. "I told Eric we were not so impressed because he could get marks in the nineties with minimal effort. The test would be what he did with this gift—what kind of human being he was."

This attitude is the exact antithesis of what we have been telling our young people in recent years. The hysteria about getting into college has been so great that no place on earth (or in heaven!) could live up to such expectations. Many students feel a sharp sense of letdown when they finally get to college, and many of the first-year failures probably occur in part because of overexpectations and an unrealistic view of what to expect. Being too old and inflexible to become space-minded, what fascinated me the most each time an astronaut took off was what we learned about where they had gone to school! As soon as they were space-borne the TV camera would take us to the home town and the college campus, and in each case it turned out to be a small college I had never heard of—a point I was happy to make to any parent who would listen!

We are still saddled with attitudes toward colleges that simply are no longer at all appropriate or realistic. All our sons and daughters simply *cannot go to the twenty-five best-known colleges.* Do I make myself clear? We have too many sons and daughters, our population is too big. The small, lesser-known colleges are no longer (if they ever were) provincial, or limited in either staff or facilities. The large majority now have excellent laboratories and libraries, and many foreign students. The atmosphere is cosmopolitan, and what is most important of all (and a serious handicap at large universities) there is more opportunity for direct personal contact with teachers—the factor which is most crucial to learning.

While it is easy to say that it is the young people who are overdependent on us, it just isn't that simple. We are not only afraid of frustrating our children and therefore give in to every request, we are actually relieved when they let us do this. Many of the parents who complain bitterly because they are helping to support a married student couple, really wanted it that way; it relieved them to know their child was "settled down safely" and wouldn't be sowing any wild oats. A college student told me that when she mentioned to her grandmother that she was dating a young man whom the grandmother considered suitable as a husband, she offered to provide a diamond engagement ring and to purchase a house for them. "Such generosity, just to buy my respectability," the young woman commented wryly. The more we buy for them, the more we plan their lives, the more we support them financially, the more we feel we can control them. And perhaps, most important of all, in this climate in which we feel so culpable for our children's adjustment, it is comforting to "get them safely married," so that we can accept our own and other people's congratulations for having done such a good job of raising stable, nonrebellious, friendly children.

The psychological effect of the Peace Corps on our nation seems to me to be more significant than we can yet realize. It has been the first social reinforcement of the best that is in our young people; it accepts their idealism, courage, ingenuity, and it permits them the priceless gift of living adventurously.

I recently read a report written by a reporter who went to visit our Peace Corps volunteers in the Philippines. It was a most moving and inspiring story, and demonstrated to all doubters once and for all, it seemed to me, that given enough challenge, dared to be worthy, our children are not found wanting. This particular group had faced a number of serious difficulties; there were physical hazards, open and covert sabotaging of the projects they were working on, problems in communication that at times seemed insurmountable. The fortitude, intelligence and dedication of these volunteers should make it eminently clear what happens when we encourage our youth "to be a *something*."

If we can show more clearly that we mean it when we say Yes and when we say No, our teen-agers will have the bona-fide freedom, the emotional oxygen, to bring meaning and purpose into their lives. A friend of mine has a sixteen-year-old daughter who belongs to a youth group of their church. Edith told me that several months ago her daughter, who was chairman of activities, had been terribly upset because she couldn't find a chaperone to go on a weekend camping trip with her group. After weeks of hectic searching, Edith reluctantly consented to serve as chaperone. At first her daughter was delighted, but her gratitude was short-lived, because at the first planning meeting, Edith dropped a bombshell. "I told them that I would only come along if they accepted my rules. This was a mountain-climbing trip and we would be camping in small tents at a campground. I said that after twelve o'clock at night the boys were to go to their camping area and the girls to another. There were howls of protest, accusing me of practicing segregation, of being old-fashioned and of not having any confidence in today's youth. 'You don't trust us,' they told me. Well, I said I was sorry, those were my terms. I said I thought that sometimes grownups waited until after something happened, and then got mad; it seemed to me it was logical to make rules ahead of time. Cathy told me she was afraid I would dominate everything, and if she could have canceled the whole thing she would have, I'm sure. Well, we started out and it was obvious there was plenty of hostility toward me. The kids hardly talked to me at all, and when they did, they were very respectful and cold. One boy challenged me by saying, 'You know, rules are made to be broken.' But later I heard two girls go over to him and say, 'We gave our word.' That night I heard some girls giggling in one of the tents. They were dressed in the craziest outfits, and were putting their hair up by flashlight. I heard one girl say, 'It's a good thing she made that rule—I'd hate to have the boys see me now!' On this particular camp site, each group that uses it must contribute a minimum of one hour's work to improve the facilities. Most of the kids grumbled about it, and were sort of waiting to see what I would do if they decided to goof off. I went to work with them and they got so excited at how well it was going that after they got through leveling a road with gravel, they decided to build a new latrine. You should have seen them work! On the way home they asked me if they could plan another trip— there was so much still left to be done! Did you ever hear a better example of 'youth in search of significance'?"

Young people are like sponges, soaking up what guidance and understanding we can give them, when we are not afraid to act like adults. A father told me that one night he walked into the living room, where his son and his girl friend were necking on the couch. "Sid went right on with what he was doing, much to my surprise," he told me, "and I suddenly realized he just didn't know or have the sense to feel how inappropriate it was. I called him out into the hall, and explained, very slowly and quietly, that when an adult comes into the room, you stop what you're doing—especially if you're necking—and you stand up, introduce the girl, and in general acknowledge the presence of another person. He was genuinely grateful to me! I wondered why in hell I hadn't acted like a father more often!"

We recently went to visit some friends we hadn't seen in a long time. As soon as we walked through the door we knew something terribly disturbing had happened. Both Jack and Phyllis were white-faced and shaken. They apologized and explained that they had just learned that their nineteen-year-old son, a sophomore at college, had been arrested in a Southern state for participating in action taken by a nonviolent student group. He had been arrested while conducting Negroes to vote-registration offices. George was a brilliant student, with a bright future, but he had suddenly announced that he was leaving college for a semester, no matter what the consequences; he just felt he had to do it. Jack and Phyllis admitted having fought on the side of conservatism and safety. They had begged him not to go and had told him he would be jeopardizing his whole future. Phyllis said, "Suddenly, when I saw the look on George's face, I started to listen to what I was saying, and I was shocked! Do you remember what *we* all did in the thirties, picketing for the unions, going on peace marches—those wonderful days when we knew there were good guys and bad guys, and never hesitated for a moment to take sides! I realized that George had as much right to stand up and be counted as we had once had, and now that this has happened, all I can say is, thank God we gave him our blessing in the end."

Adolescence can be a time for greatness, and if it doesn't happen then, it may never happen. Each of us has tried to find the special way in which to become part of the mainstream of life, and our children must have this opportunity too. It is hard to let go, and yet we must. There may be danger, disappointment, disillusion and pain, but it is necessary for healthy growth, it is a bulwark against "being a nothing."

One father told me that his son had given him a renewed sense of the meaning and sacredness of life. He said, "I was so damn successful, everything seemed to fall into my lap, and before we knew what had hit us, my wife and I were part of the 'affluent society.' You know, the suburban rat race, the big house, the country club dance on Saturday night, the commuter special at seven-nineteen A.M. It sounds corny because it's been said so often, but I often got a kind of bored and

ALL
THE
YEARS

CHAPTER
❦ 8 ❦

Who's *Not* a Working Mother?

At a dinner party one evening I was seated next to a man who asked me if I worked. I asked if he meant did I have a job, and he looked at me blankly and said, "What other kind of work *is* there?" Before I had a chance to answer, he went on, "I thought you looked like a career girl—I don't know how any husband can stand it. No wife of *mine* is ever going to work!" I was about to inform this fatuous gentleman that I was sure his wife worked at least as hard as he did, but she smiled at me from across the table and I decided that if she wanted to keep her eighteen-hour-a-day job a secret, that was her business!

All mothers work, only some get paid in cold cash for part of their work and others don't. It is ironic that at a time when women are called upon to do more as homemakers than ever before, this occupation is so lacking in prestige. Women have always had to work hard, but the special burden of our times is that women have to be so many things to so many people. In past generations, women were either workers or ladies; if you were a *grande dame* you didn't lift a finger around the kitchen; if you did all your cooking, cleaning, child-rearing, you didn't have to be alluring; if you were one of the rare intellectuals or civic leaders, you just had to be smart. Women today work at being all things to all people—and that's *work* —wherever and however you do it. The so-called nonworking mother has the toughest job invented by the twentieth century. She must raise mentally healthy, socially well-adjusted children. She will be scored on how she's doing by the pediatrician, the nursery school teacher, the guidance counselor, all her children's teachers, the neighbors, relatives, friends, storekeepers, the parents of her children's friends, camp directors and counselors, any psychologists and psychiatrists she may be forced to consult along the way, and her parents and inlaws.

This "nonworking" mother is a parent all by herself. She doesn't live, as Grandma did, in a household that usually contained members of several generations, and lots of extra hands. She almost certainly doesn't have full-time help, which her mother may have had. One mother said fervently, "I'd give back my right to vote for one full-time maid!" No one thought a mother was sole possessor of the key to mental health, and so, this never crossed Mom's mind. No one expected our grandmothers to be glamorous all day and all night—slim and smiling, smelling heavenly, covered with lotions and colognes and possessing soft, kissable hands and does-she-or-doesn't-she hair. Mothers were allowed to grow old, get lines in their faces, gain a little weight, and be a little care-worn. There was a lot to do, you know, and no time for frills.

Human hands did the cleaning and laundry in the old days, but mother rarely did it alone or without help. Today, she has to be an electrician in order to keep all her gadgets working, and she has to drive a car because all her labor-saving equipment must be carried back and forth to the repair shop. In addition, since most of these "nonworking mothers" live in the suburbs these days, they need to drive because that is the only way Dad can get to the station, Junior to school five blocks away (what child worth his salt would use his legs for walking?), daughter to her dancing class, cleaning lady to the bus, son to Little League practice, Mother to her community work or the hairdresser, and baby to the doctor for shots; a mother-in-law must be met at the station, the car must be lubricated, and one must drive to the supermarket, the library and the hardware store, where the lawn mower is being repaired. Then on to the cleaner's, and don't forget to pick up the laundry at the laundromat; the man hasn't come to fix the washer yet.—A little girl won first prize at a party where everyone was supposed to come dressed up as a mother. After discarding things she knew everyone else would wear—high heels, fur jacket, etc.—she turned up dressed in a chauffeur's uniform!

My husband and I were once waiting to change planes in Rome, and got into conversation with a charming young Italian-American woman who had just been to visit her in-laws. She was telling us that she was exhausted after dealing with their envy and wonder at her "easy life." "What they don't understand," she told us, "is that in America the woman has *machines*, yes, but she is a *slave* to her machines. My sister-in-law has to do her wash in a tub. Do you think anybody worried her about 'blue-white'? My mother-in-law worked hard all her life—she looks like an old woman, all bent, and she has white hair and wrinkles. I've got machines —you think I could ever let myself get old like that? In America I'd better find a new husband if I don't look like a movie star. My other sister-in-law, she says, 'Oh, you're so lucky, you have a big car.' She doesn't understand we will pay for that car for three years, and rarely go out in it because we have to save money to pay for it! Machines—they make me a prisoner. I am not as gay and light-hearted as my husband's family. They drink the wine, they eat the spaghetti—they never worry about vitamins and staying skinny, they don't get nervous. They can have the machines!"

The "nonworking woman" can't always be sure from one day to the next whether she's even going to *have* a husband; as Margaret Mead put it a few years ago, the American wife has to be "forever choosable." Just as children are no longer an economic necessity, neither are husbands and wives. A husband doesn't need a wife to make cloth, preserve food for the winter, spin, cook, weave, etc. A wife doesn't have to depend on a husband for the raw materials of survival. If she's got young children, it's a lot easier to be supported, but she can, if she has to, earn a living. The family as an economic unit is finished. So what have we got except affection? And how ephemeral and a sometime-thing that can be! Most of us *know* we've got to stay with our kids and raise them one way or another, but the "nonworking mother" is constantly warned by the advertisements and articles she sees that if she just lets herself sigh once too often, or snap back or yell, or let one strand of hair show gray, or settle for a slightly bulging midriff—*wham!* She is told she can very well wake up in bed alone, no matter how many children she's got sleeping down the hall. From morning till night she is threatened, warned, browbeaten into buying cosmetics she doesn't need, rejuvenators that don't work, beauty secrets to hide the fact that she isn't twenty-one any more. She may live in terror of being an imperfect lover. She feels sure she will *get* it if her children feel rejected, and end up on some psychiatrist's couch if she doesn't understand and love them every day in every way. She must also be a companion to her husband, as well as lover. She must listen to him tell about his work, and help him make decisions.

Anyway, here we are, with this "nonworking mother," glamour girl, psychotherapist, playmate, chauffeur, nurse, cook, civic leader, comparison shopper and intellectual. While she's *not working* at all this, she must combine the virtues of Florence Nightingale, Eleanor Roosevelt and Tuesday Weld.

No woman worth her salt can just stay home and be a house-wife—she must be a civic leader and improve her community. She must attend PTA meetings and eventually become chairman of at least one committee, if she is ever to show her face in public. She must collect money for dozens of charitable drives and civic programs. If she doesn't, then she isn't a good wife and mother.

Because technology has made it possible for women to run a household without ever really learning very much about the old domestic arts, such as sewing and cooking, and because women have been scared by the loss of status and prestige, we have seen a strange reversal take place. With the department stores loaded with excellent ready-made drapes, women are making their own; with the stores filled with beautiful ready-made clothes, women are clogging the counters where you can buy patterns for homemade clothes. And these are not always the women who would choose these activities because they enjoy them, or who have a legitimate need to be economical.

And so we have her—"the nonworking mother." She gets up at the crack of dawn and makes an elaborate breakfast, including homemade biscuits, because family togetherness will help to make her children psychologically healthy. All her children get vitamin pills to fortify them against nutritional imbalance, and with mother's fervent prayer it will keep them healthy enough to go to school, because if they miss a day they will get so far behind in their studies that it will be her fault if Harvard turns them down for lack of academic achievement. Also, if any of her children get sick, her entire life program will come apart; she is due at a PTA executive meeting today, will lead her Brownie troop tomorrow, must help decorate her church for the teen-age party the following night, will bake a cake for the election rally of her political party, and has three appointments with the teachers of her three children. She must also go to her exercise class and have her hair re-dyed before the club dance, where her husband will want to show her off as the middle-aged woman best disguised as a sixteen-year-old. (It's a kind of masquerade party.) Then there is the card party and the theater party and the bowling party—each arranged to earn money for good causes. Somewhere in the midst of all this, Johnny has to be taken to have his braces checked, Kathy must be taken shopping for a dress to wear at her piano recital, Ben's suits must be taken to the cleaner's, and somehow or other, by the psychology of a Freud and the artfulness of a Cleopatra, he must be wheedled into going to Fathers' Night at Judy's nursery school. There are, of course, the meals to cook, the shopping to be done, and the house to be cleaned.

A mother told me, "I had a real moment of truth the other day. I'm one of those compulsive housekeepers. I can't stand disorder, I'm dusting and cleaning all day long, and I know it's making me too tired to spend time with the children and just not necessary. I was feeling depressed and grouchy the other day, so I called a friend and we made a date to go to a Wednesday matinée, something I haven't done in fifteen years at least. On Tuesday afternoon I decided to do all of Wednesday's cleaning, so I'd be all set for my day of escape. I raced around the house like crazy making everything shine, and then I started up the stairs thinking, 'If I make the beds now, I won't have to bother in the morning.' Then I realized what I was doing—I wanted to make the beds *before my family had slept in them!* It was the first time I realized what compulsive house-cleaning can do to a family. I wanted *order* more than I wanted my *family.*"

The problem for most women today is that we are so bewildered and beset by doubts about what we are supposed to be that we figure if we try to be everything, we're bound to be *something,* sooner or later.

We have had to search for a new way of looking at femininity; this quality can no longer be easily defined by what we do, how we behave, or how we look. We sometimes long nostalgically for the old days, when all seems to have been so much simpler. Being feminine meant doing those rigidly circumscribed things that men told you to do; and if you wanted

to embroider a little on that theme, you developed a tendency
to faint easily. The subtleties and complexities of our role in
today's world make our heads spin. A lady astronaut gets married and has a baby, a college president has her hair dyed,
a beautiful and exotic woman becomes her country's delegate
to the United Nations. The mother of six wears slacks and
plays baseball in her back yard, while an atomic physicist
entrances her weekend guests with gourmet cooking. The
head of a large corporation does needle point, and sweet
gentle-looking old ladies shoulder their way through the sub-
way rush hour.

We are learning that there are no longer any simple patterns or easy definitions. Each of us has to discover who and
what we are, and our own special qualities; what makes us
feel womanly. Passivity and weakness do not describe the
feminine woman; devotion to kitchen or nursery serves us no
better as a definition—where and what is the indefinable
something our feminist grandmothers were so eager to give
up and we are so anxious to recapture?

We could learn no more poignant lesson than the one most
of us will never forget—the indestructible and indomitable
courage, dignity and spirit of Mrs. Kennedy. So delicate and
lovely to look upon, so consciously concerned with beauty and
with motherhood and devotion to a husband, she was able,
when the crisis came, to measure up in every way. This
seemed to me to be the purest exemplification of womanliness; the woman who lives all that is possible within her,
naturally and spontaneously, and brings her uniqueness to
each experience, both weakness and strength, delicacy and
power—everything she is and can be.

Several years ago, my husband and I attended a large scientific conference in Europe. One of the meetings was on
chemotherapy in the treatment of cancer, and the speaker was
simply listed in the program as M. Fourghet, a French bio-
chemist of great renown. After the introduction a tiny woman
stood up. She was wearing a pink bouclé suit and a hat made

of yards and yards of pink tulle. She spoke sweetly, but before she was finished, the audience, made up mostly of her colleagues, were obviously having a very hard time keeping up with her quick calculations, her complicated charts and graphs. Since neither of us knew anything about her subject, and not very much more about her language, we listened to the comments around us when the lecture ended. Apparently, Mme. Fourghet had suggested a brilliant and profoundly exciting new approach to biochemistry.

As we left the conference hall a few minutes later, we saw that it was pouring outside. Mme. Fourghet was standing at the entrance of the building without any coat, looking for a taxi. Of course there weren't any, and since we were all going to another building a few blocks away, my husband offered Madame his suit jacket and suggested we all make a run for it. Mme. Fourghet looked up at him with genuine pleasure and gratitude. "Ah, thank you so very much, monsieur," she said softly, not hesitating for a moment to take the jacket, and out we went in the rain, my husband soaked to the skin, but ten feet tall, Mme. Fourghet leaning on him and letting him help her over the puddles. I was afraid that if we came to a really big puddle, he would spread my raincoat for Madame to walk on! When we arrived at our destination, she was all solicitude and helpless femininity—she would have been lost without my charming husband's gallantry, she told me. Then she left us to accept membership in some scientific academy—an honor never before bestowed upon a woman!

I was forced to think of what I would have said if I'd been offered the coat, and I know exactly what it would have been: "Oh no, don't be silly, you'll get soaked to the skin. I'm all right." I had learned a lesson in femininity from a tiny doll with one of the finest scientific minds in all Europe.

During the same summer we were taking a leisurely Sunday stroll through the Bois de Bologne in Paris, watching the French families rowing on the lake, taking sun baths on the grass—just like families in Central Park. At one point we

stopped to watch a tall, athletically built teen-age girl climb-
ing a tree. She looked exactly like her American counterpart;
she was wearing bluejeans and a man's shirt and sneakers.
She moved with grace and sure-footedness, and kept teasing
a younger brother to climb a tree with her. He was very slight,
much clumsier in his movements, and had a hard time keeping his glasses on as he tried to follow her. He had a radiant
smile and looked up at her with genuine affection. I thought
to myself, "She's what we would call a tomboy and he's probably a mama's boy; their parents probably wish it was the
other way around." Three women were sitting on a bench
watching the children, and I was able to catch enough of
their conversation to realize that two of them were congratu-
lating the third woman, who was apparently the mother of
the tree-climbers. "You are a fortunate woman," they said.
"Teresa has a wonderful body for having babies—she is
strong and so well co-ordinated. And Marc is so sweet and
gentle to her, he will be such a wonderful father and husband!"

Instead of going to the heart of the matter and finding ways
of being ourselves more truly and deeply, we have looked for
external ways of proving that we "identify successfully" with
being women. Because this is a false premise in the first place,
we tend to go to extremes in our search.

In the struggle for the emancipation of women, and the
right of women to be whatever they want to be, we seem to
have overstated the case. Many perfectly nice, normal,
healthy women who really don't believe for one minute that
homemaking is beneath them and who genuinely enjoy being
this exclusively, go on saying, "I am *only* a housewife," as if
that meant a kind of second-class citizenship. Being a homemaker today involves many talents, creativity and a high order
of intelligence. We need to stop derogating a way of life that
has plenty of challenge, excitement and enrichment for those
who find it appealing and fulfilling. We desperately need those
women who work so hard for better schools and communities,
who help to inform the public about important social issues.

A friend of mine was telling me about a woman whom she admires greatly. She said, "Elaine pours her femininity out in such a way that one feels the presence of womanliness as soon as one enters her house. She does it so creatively that each member of her family has his own special island of serenity. She isn't a compulsive housekeeper—what she does is bring a sense of order which is peaceful and beautiful and satisfies the diverse needs of each child and her husband. What a gift she has for living and loving!"

Writing about "The Education of a Modern Girl" in *The PTA Magazine*, Harold Taylor said:

> . . . It is a matter of teaching women that there is an open future for them which includes marriage and motherhood but is not bound by rules and specifications as to what . . . their total life should be. It is also a matter of giving the American girl a chance to become a fully educated person . . . because . . . an education that is serious and significant in the life of the person educated is never wasted . . . If her education . . . is one that helps her to develop a serious interest in ideas, an awareness of the society around her, and an understanding of herself, it does not matter which of the various fields of knowledge she enters on her way to such goals. What does matter is the conception she develops of herself, of the possibilities in life, and of the kind of person she becomes . . . The modern girl needs to learn what it means to be alive in the modern world.

No experience which enriches, which adds to one's maturity and sensitivity as a human being, is ever wasted. Knowledge, understanding, competence, experience in doing and being—whatever a woman does as she's growing up—will enhance and enrich whatever she does later on. It is nonsense to think only in terms of vocation. Let us say that an eighteen-year-old is going off to college; she has already met the boy she hopes someday to marry, and she has no great longing for any special career. She happens to love science and mathematics, but since she can't see how she will ever *use* such knowledge, she takes a business course so she can help her husband when he gets started, or she majors in home economics so she can be a better homemaker. College becomes "a waiting game" instead of life itself. If she pursued whatever most interested and excited her, she would feel a zest and excitement about learning, and her motivation for exploration would be increased and reinforced. She would feel happier, more active and more sure that whatever she was expressing, it was something of herself. Interest is the most important part of any learning, and it will help her to think, to be open to new ideas, to know how to explore, to be at one with herself. No one should deny a girl such pleasures, or make her feel that she has failed society if she doesn't become a career woman. There is no way to plan life so far ahead. We need to stop trying to anticipate the next fifty years of our lives. Living productively and creatively *right now* is the only way to plan for the future, for it means we are learning the skills of living and can adapt them to any situation or experience. There may come a time in her life when she will want to go back to school or train for a job, and who knows what crazy possibilities there are in life: the place where you may live, the people you may meet, the activities that are available, the challenges that are still unknowable. Some of the women who have trained most carefully and sensibly for a particular career end up doing something altogether different at a point in their lives where something else makes sense. A trained journalist who stopped working at twenty-five decides at thirty-nine that she's going to become a grade school teacher; she wants to work but she wants her hours to coincide with her children's days at school, and having children has made her more interested in helping children learn than in working on a newspaper. A grandmother with a college degree but no professional work experience decides that now that her own children are grown, she wants to use her years of motherhood as background for advanced academic work to become a school guidance counselor. No one can predict life; we cannot count on anything but the moment at hand, and to use it for fulfillment, for self-realization.

As women, we face a great task and challenge in deciding

for ourselves what we want to be and what we want to do—what will make us feel alive and at peace with ourselves, and what will make us feel torn and conflicted and alienated from our own inner feelings and needs. We need to feel that what we are doing is something we want to be doing, need to be doing, to feel good about ourselves.

One of the clearest ways in which a mother's discontent with herself shows in relation to her children, is when, despite ambition and drive, she subjugates her needs and centers her life around her children. She will frequently drive them unmercifully, asking them to fulfill *her* needs, not their own. One mother told me that she was just about to start her daughter on piano lessons when she changed her mind. "I decided there was just enough money for one of us to have lessons, and that I would appreciate it a lot more than she would. If she ever wants it, she'll get it for herself too, and then it will really mean something to her."

For the woman who *does* find deep satisfaction in homemaking, there are still realistic problems and pitfalls. Being a full-time homemaker tends, at least sometimes, to accentuate the differences between the roles of husband and wife. Unless she can include, as part of homemaking, a continued interest in and awareness of the larger events of the outside world, she may lose touch with the world in which her husband spends a good part of his time. Women who become too preoccupied with motherhood may find that they are too isolated and have no other avenues of interest and self-fulfillment.

However creative and intelligent one may be in one's approach to homemaking, no job in life can be exciting, stimulating and rewarding all of the time. For the housewife who feels so beset by dull routines, who feels satiated by the same demands and pressures day after day, it is important to remember that these same qualities exist in her husband's job—and in all jobs. No matter how glamorous and exciting a job may appear on the surface, it involves routine and fatigue.

A further hazard for the full-time homemaker is that her role changes as her children grow; at certain times she is needed more intensively than at others, and if she does her job well, she will become obsolescent in time! If her homemaking has included outside interests and hobbies, community service, opportunities for growing and learning through reading or taking courses, if she has continued to develop skills around her own special interests, then she can make the gradual adjustments that will be necessary.

I worked for several years with a group of women on a suburban community project. Since it was in the mental health field, some of the volunteers who were drawn to it and offered to help were women with young families who had been trained and had worked as teachers, psychologists, social workers. The large majority, however, were college graduates with little or no specialized skills. Those with professional backgrounds wanted to keep themselves informed and active enough so that someday they could go back to work; the others were looking for interests that could sustain them in the present as well as possibilities for future training. The attitudes they brought with them and the way in which they used their experiences varied greatly and affected their later decisions.

Betty had been a social worker for about two years before she started to have a family. Then she gave about one day a week to this social service agency, and was willing to do anything that we asked of her. If stuffing envelopes happened to be the most important job at hand, she did this without any feeling that it was beneath her dignity; it needed to be done, it was refreshing to be away from home, she was meeting interesting people. Her abilities were considerable and opportunities arose for real challenge as time went on; she became a board member, she was chairman of educational services, she served on conference planning committees. As her children got older, she offered to take on more and more responsibilities; finally, she became president of the board. When her children were all in high school, her experiences added up to such an impressive array that she was able to get a paid part-time job as a community organizer—exactly the sort of job she wanted.

Annette was a college graduate who had majored in education. When she offered to work as a volunteer, she made it clear that she was not interested in menial work—she was only interested in doing something that was mentally stimulating. She was not called on as frequently, because even the paid staff had to do a lot of unstimulating dirty work! As her children grew, she would try to take part-time jobs in a wide range of fields; but she was easily disappointed, excessively critical, and never stuck with anything long enough to get any training in a specific field. Her children are now in college, and while she is very disdainful of volunteer work and says she just couldn't stand going back to school, she would like to have a job that would give her some new interest in life. Her discontent is as great as her immobilization to do anything about it.

Martha, with six years of clinical psychology behind her, decided she wanted to stay home while her children were young. In addition to working as a volunteer in a mental health project, she took one course a semester in any subject that caught her fancy. "When will I ever have as good an opportunity to try a little taste of everything?" she said. One of her courses was in advertising and copywriting. When her youngest child entered grade school she decided that she liked publicity and public relations, and she got a part-time job as fund raiser for a national social service organization—combining her earlier profession with a new interest. Accepting the possibility of change and having the flexibility to meet changing circumstances seem to underlie success in finding one's place in life.

The mother who works outside the home all along the way has most of the same responsibilities and pressures as those who work at home, plus a few hundred other problems especially designed for her. I have known hundreds of career mothers and almost all of them have one common characteristic: their middle name is GUILT. The few who didn't seem to feel guilty I probably just didn't know well enough!

I am not speaking of those women who *really* have to work —the widow, the divorcée, the wife of a man with a chronic illness, the woman who must help to support aged parents or —and this is so often the case these days—the woman who really must supplement her husband's earnings, not for wild luxuries, but just for a reasonably comfortable standard of living. Many of these women have misgivings, and feel terribly harassed and unhappy when a child is sick, or they feel an overwhelming fatigue or sense of pressure. They aren't always happy with their work and some in this group would prefer to be at home. They may search their souls at intervals to be sure they really *do* have to work, but by and large they simply accept the necessity of work, know it has its problems and shortcomings, and do the best they can.

The group of women who belong to the "Guilty Club" are those who work before they have children and go on working afterward, for no other reason than that they *want* to. Because they so often feel guilty and ashamed, they may find rationalizations for their work, but beyond all the fussing, they just plain need to do what they do. The latest rationalization, and probably the most effective, is that they work because if they didn't, they would be unhappy and that would be worse for their children. Their children have nothing to do with it, really—they are just people who need more than marriage and parenthood.

I have never escaped my sense of guilt, but at least I can try to save a few others! Having a career in and by itself has nothing whatever to do with being a good mother or a bad mother. First of all, there ain't any such animals. Secondly, so many other ingredients go into the question of building a reasonably good life for children. There are mothers who stay home and devote themselves to their children and who cripple them in ways that are hair-raising. There are also mothers who stay home who are happy to be alive and to be themselves, and who can, most of the time, convey this kind of optimism and self-acceptance to their children; they bring warmth and joy to living, and their kids get infected, as they should. There are career women who should never have had children, who were pushed into it by a culture that said, "You cannot claim to be a woman unless you are a mother," which is nonsense but, nevertheless, a generally accepted myth. These women, torn and bedeviled by presssures they cannot undo, may very well contribute to their children's serious difficulties in growing. They may be magnificent workers in their own areas of excellence, and if they could have used their femininity in that area, they could have been the most womanly women imaginable, without children. Then there are women who work away from home who, despite some guilt and a great many plain, ordinary, realistic problems and burdens, have so much to give, and play so many roles well, that they love their work and do it well, and also have a ball with their kids.

Part of the problem for career women has been the easy, convenient excuses people have sought for the complicated problems that beset us and our children. The causes of delinquency, for example, are so complicated and subtle that even the most precise and conscientious expert, who may have worked and studied in this field for thirty years, is aware of how little he knows for sure. But people with power and influence who like simple ideas and like to make sensational statements to please other people who like simple answers, have found the perfect scapegoat—the working mother. Judges, FBI officials, some ministers, generals, and self-appointed guardians of The American Way of Life get the headlines every time when they offer the chance of utopian success for the human race if the mothers will just stay home. Juvenile delinquency and childhood mental disorders of any kind are NOT created by working mothers. No study, no research project, has EVER found any one-to-one relationship here. One might say that yes, John Jones is a delinquent child because his mother works—if you also add "and because his mother is an immature, unhappy, driven woman who has the full responsibility for raising five children because her husband is an alcoholic, and because she never went beyond fourth grade in school, and because she lives in a rat-infested cold-water tenement in a large, impersonal, anonymous mass of humanity that calls itself a city." One might also say that some children whose mothers work have problems. But so do just as many whose mothers don't work outside the home.

I can't imagine how you can be a full-time worker and mother without your husband's liking this idea enough to be a real partner to it. It is difficult to juggle two demanding roles, and it seems to me it would be almost insurmountable without its being something chosen genuinely by both partners. You need a husband who likes what he's doing, enjoys being what he is, and has no reason to fear or compete because you are a real live one yourself. You both must recognize there is a price to be paid for each living his life in a full and personally meaningful way—that each gains from the other's joy and riches, and each also has to accept the additional crises and burdens.

There are times when husbands must step in and take on extra chores and burdens that might not occur otherwise. However, my observation has been that just because career women *are* so dependent on the encouragement and help of their husbands, they tend to bend over backward and to try not to take advantage of them. Some women who stay at home are so filled with envy and resentment at their husbands' greater freedom that their demands are more excessive. On the credit side, a career wife can help to ease the heavy financial burdens on the head of the household. Sometimes, when both partners work, the husband feels a greater freedom to take a chance, to change jobs, to do what he likes best, even if this means less income and security for the family. Career women tend to have interesting experiences, stimulating friends, and there is frequently a level of sharing, of growing together, that is precious to both husband and wife. But none of this is really possible unless the man in the house enjoys his wife's successes, is proud of her accomplishments, is sure enough of himself not to feel competitive, does not feel that his masculinity is challenged when he puts on an apron. Most of all, he needs a sense of humor—or there would be no enduring some of the inevitable crises!

No matter how absorbing or exciting any job or profession may be, the working mother has to accept and understand that there will be times when she has to make clear choices between her roles, and that she simply can't have her cake and eat it too, all the time. There are times when doing two jobs at once is harder than at other times. I used to think this was simply a question of the age of one's children; I've learned better—age is only one consideration. It is true that while children are under six or seven, they need a great deal of care in the home. Many women will quit working for a few years, in the fond hope that as soon as the youngest is in nursery school or kindergarten, it will be relatively easy to go back to work. It is possible, but not easy, and when one is planning, provision must be made for childhood illnesses, vacations, times to visit schools, and the like. It is important to be with children at times of crisis: going to the doctor or hospital, living through such changes as moving, or facing a new experience such as nursery school. When things are going relatively smoothly, young children can enjoy being at home with good housekeepers and baby-sitters; in fact, this is often much easier with young children than school-age and teen-age youngsters. I found that my daughter welcomed baby-sitters as playmates, and seemed to resent my absences far less when she was very little than when she was ten and older. Being home when children come home from school—just being in the house—seems to mean more to older children, and working mothers tend to be unprepared for that. No matter how gifted or talented a working mother may be, she is likely to feel much better about her various roles if she can work part-time, adapting her workload to different periods of her children's growing years. Of course, not all professions permit this, but many do, and slowly but surely, many agencies and organizations, realizing the value of employing mature, experienced, stable women, are helping them to work fewer hours or to work on a part-time basis, so as to meet their special needs. If we can adapt our work to a flexible schedule, it makes us feel less pressured, more relaxed when we can be at home.

Another problem is sacrificing something to make work possible. It is almost impossible to be a compulsive housekeeper if you have a job away from home. More than any other mother, you have to keep from being brain-washed by those who would tell you that cleanliness is next to godliness, and that order and neatness are the highest goals of virtue. You have to be able to live comfortably and to refuse absolutely to spend every spare minute cleaning and organizing the household into a military camp. Something's GOT to give, and if you want to feel refreshed and playful for your children, you just can't be a perfect housekeeper.

All women have trouble keeping up with the ridiculous standards for perfection in every area that they set for themselves, and for the career woman this is hardest of all. We seem to be setting up a national competition to see who can have the most unlived-in house in America! We spend hundreds of hours every year "straightening up," putting things in an order that serves no purpose: everything in its place, no scratches, no fading, no signs of wear and tear allowed—and who live in these antiseptic mausoleums? Children and dogs, both unalterably opposed to order and firmly convinced that things are to be used, not to be put away!

I once went to a cocktail party at a very glamorous home, beautifully decorated, expensively furnished. The living room was enormous and filled with extremely modern furniture. About one third of this room was surrounded by a white picket fence—like a giant playpen! Inside were a TV set, several old reading lamps and some wonderful, overstuffed, faded, comfortable armchairs. This was "the children's corner," but the grownups were fighting to get into it and relax!

We need to live with an ability to absorb *some* chaos. There will be the morning when nine people are waiting to have an important conference with you and Junior wakes up with a cough and a high fever, and not one of your hopefully long list of good, familiar sitters is available. There will be the inevitable call from school: Junior's sprained his ankle, come and get him. There will be the day you forgot to take anything out of the freezer for dinner, so you have to go out to eat. There will be the tough days on the job when you drag yourself home to find a cranky, unhappy child, a poor report from school, or the announcement from your gem of a housekeeper that she's leaving to get married. Many times you will be tired, harassed, torn in a million directions. But if you need to do what you do, if it fulfills you in special ways, if you feel a sense of joy and satisfaction, then it's worth what you have to put up with, and it won't destroy your children. The most important legacy that any parent can give his child is to help him be himself; live out his own dreams, do those things that make one feel good to be alive.

The career mother has some sort of peculiar idea that her opposite number, the mother who works inside the home, is always available to her children, and is constantly giving of herself. There are plenty of homemakers who spend almost no time at all in an intense relationship with their children—playing, reading or talking. Because they are at home, they rarely notice or think about direct, intense experiences with children. Career mothers think about being with their children very differently, and because they do, they are likely to spend more time with children than most mothers. Aware of time limitations, they plan for special events, special ways of being together, that other mothers may not even think of. In fact, instead of neglecting our children, we sometimes watch them too much and are more oversolicitous and overprotective than other mothers. Children need and want time to feel close, time to share, to play, with parents. They also need time to be alone or to be with other children; they need to feel free of parental watching and worrying. When we are most relaxed and natural, when we use spontaneous and unexpected moments for real contact, we get and give something precious. One mother told me that she and her husband had learned that it was the unplanned, unexpected moments that had meant the most to her family—not the weekend trips that were planned, not the dates with children, but a hilarious dinner hour when one of the children had something funny to tell about a teacher, or the wild game of monopoly on a rainy Sunday, or the day the washing machine overflowed and the whole family sloshed around in the flood, or the sudden impulse to go off to a movie and have a pizza later instead of supper first. Such moments of rare companionship are infrequent in any home, but quantity has nothing to do with the meaning or significance of such times. They are the moments of affirmation, of clarifying and cementing the feelings of love and warmth and need, and they cannot be organized or planned—they are the accidents, the precious by-products of living with zest, imagination, freedom.

Unless you happen to be *very* well paid, you will probably have to assume that your career will be a luxury, at least while your children are young. Your income increases your taxes. You have no allowance for carfare, extra clothes and household help. I know one husband who said, "If my wife would only quit working, we might be able to live on our income!" It is very important to get the right kind of help, and this is usually not easy. I always tried to have at least four or five baby-sitters on call. For young children, motherly, easygoing, relaxed older women are wonderful; later on, older teen-agers who can play games are fun, but for a working mother, older women who are available during the day are important. Baby-sitters are not substitute disciplinarians—that is our job. What we need is a grandmotherly type who gives lots of love and probably is overpermissive! Children learn to differentiate between who is in charge and who is not—and parents are in charge of rules, not sitters. Whenever I interviewed somebody who was ready to train my child, or teach my child, or make her behave, I eliminated her from the list. I wanted someone who would give love and be easygoing, and let *me* take care of the restrictions and controls about such things as toilet-training or eating habits. Women who have raised their own families seemed to me to work out best. They were utterly reliable and trustworthy about taking care of a sick child, they tended to be relaxed and unworried, and understood the working mother's needs.

It is important to work for people who are willing and able to understand the emergencies that may come up, the times when mother just can't get to her place of business. Women who make that special effort to work when they have young children tend to be people who are very conscientious, and they usually make up for the time they miss on the job in efficiency and skill. More and more employers seem to be aware of that.

If Mother feels that she is depriving her children and neglecting them, or sacrificing them on the altar of her own selfish needs, she can be darn sure that she will transmit this message to her children, and they, in turn, will probably feel guilty for being the source of her misery and self-accusations. If Mother is pretty clear about the fact that she wants to be a mother and a wife, and gets great joy from this but just happens also to need other challenges and opportunities for fulfillment, she will help her children grow up feeling that they too will have the opportunity to do many things if they want to, and to find meaning in their lives in their own terms.

Many women are afraid of their talents because somewhere or other they have gotten the idea that to be competent, creative, well organized, efficient, successful, tends to decrease their femininity: if they dominate on a job, they will dominate their husbands at home; if they enjoy success, they will become unbearably competitive and tough. I have found that quite the reverse is true. I have been terribly lucky in that, through my work, I have met some of the most able and successful career women, and have known some of them as close personal friends. Many of them have jobs of great responsibility and challenge. I have found that they are almost all as much or more dependent on their husbands than the women I know who work within the home and who would appear to be more dependent, if one looks only at the surface. Many of them say that while they frequently appear to be self-confident, knowledgeable and independent in their work, they would "fall apart completely" without their husband's encouragement, love and support. Many of them are actually unsure, shy, need lots of bolstering, have great waves of self-doubt and fears of failure.

A woman I know who has an extremely important government post, but who can also be clinging and helpless in her private life, said to me, "I finally am beginning to figure it out; whenever you are more of *anything,* you are more of *everything!* The more talented and able a woman is, the more she seems to have the capacity for dependence, for love, for being needful of masculine support. The wider the range of experience, the more the capacity for feeling one way, the more the capacity to feel another way. The more self-determined one can feel, the more dependent one can also feel."

Even when a career woman stays at home for a period of months or years, she is thinking, growing, changing. Whatever we do at any point in our lives affects us forever after. Staying at home with young children is not a lapse of nothingness, a waiting game. It is a time for learning about oneself, for reading, for marveling at the miracle of a child's growth, of being at one with nature, with the deep natural rhythms of life. Looking back, I can see that I felt an unnecessary sense of urgency about working when my daughter was young—I was learning so much and didn't even know it. I thought I was stagnating for lack of adult conversation, for stimulation of outside interests. If I had relaxed more, I would have realized how much there was to learn, to feel, to experience, in thinking my own thoughts, in walking next to a young child and seeing how she looked at the world, of watching her discoveries. I painted with her and played with clay, and built sand castles—and all of this enriched me without my being aware that being close to childhood, to something young and growing, was a way of discovering the capacities of growth within myself.

What we do with the time we have in life reflects our basic attitudes, and they are what count. Do we do whatever we do with a sense of purpose and hope, and an acceptance that discomfort, pain and frustration are real and part of living? If we do, we are helping our children live with the impossible problems of life. Our work—whatever that work may be—must be an answer to our deepest sense of being alive and at home in the world, and when we work at being what we *must* be and using what we have within us, guilt can begin to abate, it ceases to exhaust us wastefully. I know one mother who is a living breathing dynamo. She is so creative in so many areas, so competent, so alive, that she would explode if she tried to limit herself to the job of wife and mother. She runs a business that would exhaust and overwhelm most people, and along with that, is able to work intensively with several community agencies; has a tasteful lovely home; enjoys reading, theater, music; seems to expand the more she does. When her first child was about three years old she took him to a psychologist because he seemed unhappy. Being conscientious and aware—and guilty—she worried because he was shy, had some bad dreams and seemed to cling to her. The psychologist told her that there was nothing seriously wrong, but that Bobby resented his mother's going to business. The psychologist suggested that he see Bobby three more times, and that Mother give up her work. This dynamic, forceful, energetic and talented woman suddenly came to when she faced this threat to her own life, her need for challenge and stimulation. She said to the psychologist, "You see him *six* times, and I'll keep my job!" She was right for herself. Her children had problems growing up just like any child anywhere. Problems are part of life, and we learn to surmount them as we accept being human, and grow in strength and courage and initiative. Her two children are now almost grown, and they are alive, each in his own way, each with his own choices, needs and drives to work out, to try to solve, and then to go on to the next challenge. The fact that mother was true to herself has been a legacy of strength.

There are times when children need real help, when life overwhelms them, when we really have to offer, freely and genuinely, the aid and comfort at our disposal, and sometimes this will mean postponing a need of our own. This is part of being mature. We all want to give clearly and unequivocally when someone young and vulnerable cries for help. All parents face such crises, and whatever the nature of their work or whatever they may be doing with their own lives, they will have to make sacrifices and accept discomfort, anxiety, a readiness to do what must be done. I recently heard a doctor say that "all ethics have their origin in the mother's instinct to protect her young," and I think there is much truth in that. The best way to protect one's young is to nurture what is young and alive in oneself.

What makes a woman feel like a woman is to feel like a *person*. Each woman has to struggle to find what that will mean to her—and until she begins to operate on this basis, she cannot truly nurture her young.

Oh Dad, Poor Dad,
If You're Hanging in the Closet
It's Your Own Darn Fault

Contrary to some public opinion, fathers are parents too and have their own special survival problems! But I find myself thoroughly annoyed and impatient with so many voices being heard in the land which weep for the "feminized man"— the articles one reads so often these days with such titles as "The Downfall of Masculinity," "The Decline of the American Male."

In the course of my career I have met many competent, talented, able women. I have rarely met a woman who did not want, at times, to be dominated by a man, who never longed to be dependent, needful, clinging and helpless. And yet women have been so thoroughly frightened by the voices of

doom that they feel an overwhelming sense of guilt: they are
too domineering, their husbands feel threatened by their aggressiveness. However, no man can be psychologically cas-
trated without his co-operation! I will admit that there are
enough extremely unhappy women around to make the struggle for manhood quite a contest in some cases, but that is far
from the whole story. Whenever rapid changes occur in the social roles of men and women, these changes are accompanied
by self-consciousness, anxiety, discomfort and uncertainty.
The revolution in the lives of women has brought with it all
kinds of analyses, warnings, many easy formulas for what is
right and wrong in male-female relations. As women began to
take their place beside men in every social role, a dramatic and
unsettling shift had to take place, and we find ourselves right
smack in the middle of it right now. What is happening to
men and women is having a direct and vital bearing on children, and if we want to help our children grow up to the full
enjoyment of being men and women, we must come to terms
with our own attitudes and feelings.

We seem to have a great nostalgia for the good old days—
"when men were men"—or so we think. I think we have
greatly romanticized this picture. It was so much easier for a
man to *look* masculine when women were subservient. A man
didn't have to be a real man at all, and he could fool everybody, including himself. When he was supposed to make all
the decisions, be the big boss, set the pattern for all sexual activity, he could do all this without really having to be much of
a man. He played a role, and no one ever really knew or
thought about what he was or felt beneath the surface of
that role. In fact, I would speculate that the less masculine a
man was, the more comfortably he could live in that earlier
time. It seems, for example, that today, the more uncertain a
man is that he is all male, the more likely he is to try to per-
form what he conceives to be the male role: he orders his wife
around, proudly announces that no wife of his is going to
work, uses autocratic discipline with his children, and in
many cases boasts of his sexual exploits of an extracurricular

nature. He would rather die than diaper or burp a baby, because such acts increase his own uncertainty about himself.

We are sometimes told that what confuses us in our male-female roles is that men are now asked to share more directly in the domestic life of the family. It is not the sharing of what were once "womanly activities" that makes for the "sexual ambiguity" that men are so afraid of. It is that our internal fears and uncertainties make us cling to appearances, to external roles, that really have no useful purpose or meaning any more. Women want to be free to be themselves and to be successful and active and creative. But they also want to be cared for, protected and loved. They don't want men to be afraid of female competence, but simply to accept it as one side of their qualities, to be enjoyed and shared without any question of who is better or worse, who is passive or aggressive. Women want men just to be themselves, to respond openly and honestly, to fail and succeed, to be passive and aggressive, to be direct and powerful and protective when that is appropriate and needed and mutually satisfying. Women will have to help men understand that they do not want to be overwhelming and frightening, that they would much rather be loved by an imperfect man than be rejected by a man trying to achieve an impossible perfection.

Where men feel they have lost control of their own destinies, when they feel irrevocably trapped and hen-pecked, they have usually asked for it. I have never yet met a reasonably happy, competent, fulfilled woman who wanted to wear anyone's pants but her own. Many of these women are yearning, aching, for their men to feel less threatened by them, more able to enjoy their mutual and separate roles. As I meet and talk with women—all kinds, living all kinds of lives, doing all kinds of things—my impression is that although assuming a certain basic self-acceptance and enjoyment of being women, the large majority want men to be in charge in many, many ways.

There *are* women who are so discontented and unhappy with themselves that they need to destroy anyone who seems to be better off than they are—and that will include children, whatever their sex, as well as husbands. In many of these destructive relationships, a man will permit his wife to nag, harangue and control so that he can hate her with a clear conscience! The problem of the truly hostile, aggressive and driving female is the problem of anyone, male or female, who tries to destroy others because of a basic discontent and feelings of worthlessness within himself. It is a conflict of human beings in torment, not a battle of the sexes.

The emancipation of the American woman rendered a lot of myths obsolete. When it became reasonable and proper for a woman to seek sexual fulfillment, we saw a fascinating revolution take place. In the nineteen-twenties and thirties psychiatrists and writers on matters of sex were concerned with frigidity in women; by the nineteen-forties and fifties there was a noticeable shift, and the focus was now frequently on impotence in men. Men were being challenged to become perfect lovers, to satisfy their wives, to learn the art of lovemaking. This was frightening, because it was bound to reveal the fact that there is a great variety in the sexual needs of men. It is said of the Victorian age that men went to prostitutes to satisfy their animal appetites, which they had to hold in check with their pure and decent wives. In more recent times, men have probably turned to prostitutes for that quick, uncomplicated "roll in the hay," in which they do not feel challenged to satisfy anyone but themselves!

It is true that emancipation makes us feel drunk with power for a while, and undoubtedly the liberated woman did make demands and did have expectations for fulfillment that could not be brought about and that were quite demeaning and terrifying to the male who for centuries had been able to maintain his own myth of great sexual prowess. Now, with more open and honest and equal relations between men and women, and with the ending of the novelty of female sexuality, we can begin to hope for a new kind of relationship, in which both men and women can feel freer to be themselves:

freer to experience a greater variety in their sexual relations; each playing aggressive or passive roles at different times; each free to reject the advances of the other. Men can be too tired and not at all inclined sometimes; women can feel free to show their sexuality without feeling they are threatening a man—we can reach a point where, without feeling demeaned or lessened in any way, a man can gratify the sexual needs of a woman in other ways than intercourse, and where a woman can sometimes passively accept the quick lust of a man, without always demanding her own gratification. Such partners, who work at being themselves and who enjoy sharing and giving of themselves, need not play the game of "new positions," but of *new moods*—the vast and wonderful variety of feelings that can be expressed in a hundred different ways, without that sense of threat hanging over their heads. Women don't *have* to be passionate lovers all the time, just because it is now permissible. They don't *have* to be aroused and made love to artfully and tenderly all the time, just because that's nice sometimes. Men don't *have* to be magnificently romantic all the time; they can also take their pleasures, with a woman who loves enough not to demand something for herself all the time. And a man doesn't have to prove his love and responsiveness by always performing like a tiger. Sex can be cozy and quiet, hilariously funny and a lot of other things, we are beginning to admit.

The shifting roles of men and women can offer greater enrichment than ever before, not necessarily greater problems and dangers. If men and women bring what they are, with the infinite variety of their changing needs, to each other, they can find greater fulfillment than either or both have ever known before. We are still thinking in old-fashioned terms if we worry about male superiority. The superiority of a social role had nothing whatever to do with a man's real feelings. Plenty of men have always felt areas of inferiority to certain women some of the time. It just didn't show because a façade was maintained by both sexes. Now the façade is gone and at first we were all scared, men and women alike. A man who feels like a man *is* a man, and a woman who feels like a woman *is* one, and what they actually do, wear, work at, are interested in, has little to do with it. The basic, biological difference will always (I sincerely hope!) make them respond and behave differently, whatever they may be doing. The sexual function is different, the glands are different, the ways of responding to the external environment just have to be different, because their bodies are different. It seems likely that these physical and deeply psychological differences at the very heart and core of man and woman will remain indefinitely, and will continue to make them need and want each other. The expression of these differences and the fulfillment of these needs are now open to all of us, and if we can lose our self-consciousness and defensiveness, what unknown wonders may yet await our discovery!

A negative approach to the complexity of today's relationships between men and women was exemplified by the psychiatrist who decided that the whole trouble with today's marriages was the loss of the older and clearer roles of men and women. He advised his men patients to take up "manly sports," such as hunting and fishing, and to be "very tough" with their wives, because women "like it that way." He encouraged his patients who were discontented housewives to go on having babies, to renounce all intellectual or professional pursuits, because a woman's fulfillment is still just where it always was. This is a great oversimplification of our dilemma.

Men and women need each other as friends, lovers and companions in an infinite variety of unexpected combinations and refractions, without fear or threat, but simply by being alive and at peace with themselves and each other.

I do not think there was any story about President Kennedy that was more touching or true as a measure of the man than when he interrupted a serious and important meeting in his office to wipe his little boy's nose! So confident of self, so alive to the world, and at home in it, so fully and deeply a *man*, he did not feel it was beneath his manhood to be a warm and loving parent, doing "woman's work."

· · ·

The problem for the man who feels trapped, who feels that he is nothing more than a provider, who is having more and more frequent fantasies of deserting this sinking ship of family life, is not to protect his masculinity by disappearing into a closet, but by fighting for his life *with* his family. His wife needs help too, and he can be the force that gets the family going again, that insists that help be sought.

Here is a composite picture of a man hanging in a closet: he wasn't absolutely sure what he wanted to be when he got out of college, and he began to feel pretty panicky when his parents and teachers began chewing their fingernails over his indecision. At one point he had the feeling that what he loved best was reading, and he liked the idea of being an English teacher but he wasn't absolutely sure, and so, when he met his future wife six months before getting his B.A. degree and her father offered him a place near the top in his advertising agency, he figured he had it made. He could earn more in the first year than he could after ten years of teaching and two graduate degrees. It seemed perfectly logical to let his parents-in-law "loan" him the money for a suburban house when his wife got pregnant—after all, he *was* a member of the firm; it was all in the family. It was a big house, and his father-in-law wanted to show off what he had bought, so mama-in-law brought in the decorators. He has the feeling he is walking into a hotel each night, where the décor bears no relation to what he would consider either comfortable or pleasant to look at. He has almost lost touch with his wife, who seems harassed and driven, and as uncertain about what is happening to her as he is about himself. Every workday he maneuvers the problems of a car pool or catches an early commuter train, hoping fervently he doesn't meet anyone he's supposed to cultivate, which seems unbearable and indecent before ten in the morning. All day long he pretends that his work is worthwhile, and he convinces everyone but himself. The fatigue of discontent is worse than any other kind, so he's really bushed when he arrives back in suburbia at seven or seven-thirty. In

order to bring some sense of purpose into his life, he has vol-
unteered to be a board member on one or two local charitable organizations, and with some pushing from his in-laws,
who say the advertising business begins when you leave the
office and can meet people, he is also active in his church or
temple (which has often become a place for making connec-
tions—with one's business associates instead of with one's
God). So one or two weekday evenings are usually devoted to
meetings and civic duty. If he is really in trouble, he may
also be a "den father" or a coach for the Little League, and
his wife assures him—if he hasn't heard it directly at a PTA
meeting—that the experts all agree that children need time to
play with Daddy, or they will be neurotic, insecure and may
become delinquent. So Daddy becomes the friendly chauffeur
on weekends, as a way to be close to his children. Friday
night he drives them to parties, bowling, ice-skating; Saturday
morning he either goes to football practice with his son at the
school or he drives his daughter to a music, dancing or art
class. Dinner parties on Saturday night in suburbia tend to be
a little hectic these days, because somewhere between nine
and eleven, half the men in the group have to leave to pick up
and deliver a child who is out somewhere in the suburban
wilderness.

This sounds terribly superficial and stereotyped. The sad
part is that it isn't. The price of the material comfort achieved
is a high one, whether this was made the easy or any other
way. The rich who seem to be happy in the suburbs are
those who are rich incidentally, doing something they would
do even if they weren't paid for it. The unhappy people seem
to be the ones who are caught in a web of their own making,
and do not feel sure enough of themselves to change anything.

And this, it seems to me, is where a lot of men (and
women) get stuck in a psychological closet that suffocates
them, because they think they have to change *everything* in
order to change *anything*. I talked recently with a father who
was visiting his child's nursery school, and who told me,
after listening to the children discuss what they would like to

be when they grew up, that he wished he had studied medicine instead of law. Very defensively he added, "But don't you tell me that it's never too late to start over; that's a damn lie." There are some men and women who, even after being well settled in life, have a clear and firm conviction of a new place they must get to, and it has been done; men have given up great economic security in order to return to school and to prepare themselves for new jobs—or have left one comfortable and secure area and started on a shoestring, a wild gamble, in something else. We all know and look on with admiration when people really have the guts, the courage and the will to find the right path for themselves. But that isn't always possible or sensible or necessary. Many men who say they are discontented, feel driven and alienated, unable to enjoy their children, too tired to enjoy their wives, are really doing what they want to do; or they are comfortable enough to be too lazy to change it. Nothing really stands in their way except their own lack of genuine concern. The society we live in now offers every possible kind of avenue for creative fulfillment: the adult education courses that are offered, the variety of civic volunteer jobs, the available range of reading, recreational activities, are simply fantastic. It is possible to plan, to put first things first, to reorganize one's time and activities, to substitute meaningful and satisfying activities for the other kind. It is possible to be a real person, a man with pride, conviction, a role of great importance to one's children, even in the suburban "rat race."

I know one man who wanted to be an opera singer, but his voice just missed being quite great enough for the big league. He became a businessman, and very carefully selected those enterprises that would leave him as unencumbered as possible. For example, he chose to live in a suburb that was really a small city, surrounded by other large suburbs and small cities. He bought and sold businesses successfully until he had just what he needed to live comfortably—some apartment houses, a garage, a laundromat. He was a good businessman, the best he could be, and he gave his job everything when he worked at it. He also organized a local symphony, a community concert series, and he works with the board of education on a project to bring more classical-music experiences to school children—and most important of all, he is a man of integrity, a man who says what he believes and stands behind it, so that he brings to his two sons the greatest gift any father can give his children—character. He lives on a street that has slowly become interracial in the last five years. He is largely responsible for the sensible, nonhysterical attitude of his neighbors, both Negro and white, who are working together to see that the neighborhood stays interracial and does not become another Negro ghetto. Because he was able to look at the realities in his life, and plan effectively, he enjoys himself thoroughly and feels truly at one with himself.

One can work at a job that is far from satisfying and still have a good life. One can always search for meaning and values, wherever one lives and whatever one's circumstances. Courage is classless. The large majority of women and children who live with these fathers and husbands will feel good about seeing a man search for himself and demand the right to be what he must be, do what he must do. Such a man brings marvelous qualities into his home; he is an example for his children and can offer the same kind of self-fulfillment possibilities to his wife. If *he* feels good, usually everybody feels good.

The role of men as fathers has undergone tremendous change in the last thirty or forty years. The democratization of family life, the change from rural to urban living, the shifting roles of women, the greater isolation and autonomy of the individual family unit, and the child-centeredness of family life have all contributed to this change. The change was speeded up and reinforced by the return of our soldier population after the Second World War and the G.I. Bill of Rights, which sent thousands of married men back to school. Living in barracks on college campuses, many young families had to supplement their available funds by the wife's working while her husband went to school. If there were young children, Father was often left in charge to cram for exams while waiting for the laundry at the laundromat or while baby-sitting. A scene I will never forget is coming home from work late one evening and finding my husband and six-month-old baby both lying asleep on the floor, next to the typewriter and the textbooks my husband had been reading! A lot of our teen-age and college-age children spent their infancy listening to Father memorize his lessons out loud—a modern-day version of the lullaby!

Fathers were as much affected by the child-raising revolution as mothers, although they tended to resist it more ferociously. More fathers said, "What was good enough for me . . ." or "My parents spanked me and it didn't do me a bit of harm," than mothers. I was always more scared of going to a parents' meeting where the fathers would be present, because while the large majority of mothers were eager to learn new ways, many fathers hated all child experts on sight —especially female ones! I really never blamed them. After a long hard day at the office they were dragged by their conscientious wives to listen to lectures on the new and often confusing and strange theories of child-raising. Men seemed to be much more threatened by changes in discipline than women —there was more fear of losing control and authority. They were being asked to accept a new and different frame of reference about father-child relationships, and usually did not have either the interest or motivation to go into this, since it played little or no part in their status feelings as fathers.

The reluctance of fathers to buy all the latest theories may be one of their greatest potential contributions to family life! As I look back now and think of all the things I was absolutely sure about fifteen years ago, and how my own thinking has changed, I can appreciate the healthy skepticism of the fathers who didn't want to listen to me!

Mothers and experts often found it wasn't easy, but by dint of hard work they did manage to make a generation of fathers almost as guilty and anxious as they were! A psychiatrist told me recently that many of the fathers he sees feel uneasy with infants and are dreadfully ashamed of this. Our society has proclaimed that children need to be loved by both parents, that fathers are important to babies, that wives need to be encouraged and supported by Daddy's devotion to the baby. Some men simply do not know what to do with a baby. They can't say anything sensible to a baby. They can't discuss baseball or the stock market with a baby. They can't play games. They feel that all they can do is make idiots of themselves by talking baby talk or changing a diaper or wiping away the sour milk—and it's about as much fun as latrine detail in the Army. On the other hand, some men discovered in this age of flexibility and enlightenment that they were naturals with little babies, and loved taking care of them. For such fathers, the freedom to enjoy this early period of development has been a good thing. But many fathers feel guilty and troubled, because they figure there must be something terribly wrong with them if they don't have those great stirrings of fatherly pride and love, which they are assured they should be feeling. One father told me with guilty discomfort that he guessed he had been very rejecting because his first child was a girl. He had wanted a son first, and he didn't really even talk to his daughter until she was almost three years old. Well, she wasn't talking much before that either! And even if he had had a son first he might have felt the same disinterest until baby turned into a human being!

With all the instructions we've been giving fathers about all they must do for their children in order that the children may feel secure and be neurosis-free, it has taken great ingenuity for fathers to squirm out of it! We were visiting some friends one evening, and the four-year-old son reminded his father, who was happily relaxing with a highball, that it was bedtime and "you know you always have to tell me a story when I go to bed." Daddy pulled himself wearily out of his comfortable sprawl, but his face cheered up as he walked toward the hall. "Okay, Danny, listen—I'm going to tell you a *long* story while we're walking upstairs." A recent cartoon showed a suburban household with three children creating bedlam indoors on a rainy day, and Father is walking away from the house with his briefcase while his wife calls from an upstairs window, "Come back here, it's Sunday and you *know* it!" A father confessed to me recently that breakfast had become so unbearable at his house, with the three-year-old spilling honey and orange juice all over and the two-year-old bellowing for food, that he had gotten into the habit of leaving for his bus early, enjoying the quiet and solitude on the corner while he waited for ten or fifteen minutes. "Don't know what I'll do when the weather gets really cold," he said ruefully.

The suburban father has it made if he can handle his guilt and survive his wife's complaints. It is necessary to leave very early, and if you are lucky and have a very demanding job, the kids will be in bed by the time you get home. I have a strong feeling that as mothers and experts have stressed the father's role more, and as children have become more and more bratty for lack of an available and self-assured father who can set them straight, more fathers are working longer hours! I suspect that the shorter work week, which the unions are seeking, may not be so popular after a while, when husbands discover that their wives are taking full advantage of their availability for shopping, chauffeuring and disciplining. For every father that just loves to romp with his kids, there seem to be three or four reluctant and unwilling playmates. I remember going to a nursery school meeting, and being very much impressed with the turnout. There were almost as many fathers as mothers, and almost the entire school population seemed to be represented. However, before I could flatter myself that they had come out of an uncontrollable desire to hear my words of wisdom, one father put a damper on my delusions of grandeur. He explained, "You see, this is a co-operative nursery school and we never have enough money. We decided to put a special tax on parents who didn't come to meetings, one dollar per person per meeting. We haven't made much money, but we get a great turnout now!"

Fathers were greatly relieved a few years ago by Robert Paul Smith's book, *Where did you Go? Out. What did you Do? Nothing.* It began to get them off the hook, and the great palship with the children became suspect. Many fathers had a strong propensity for being fathers, not pals, and had been too ashamed to admit it. Now they were being offered encouragement; it wasn't even good for children not to have a time and a place to be alone with their own kind. There are undoubtedly thousands of fathers who, loving baseball, have taken to the Little League like ducks to water, and there is a place for some supervision and participation in the recreational life of our children, of course, but this was not for all fathers.

Fathers should be themselves, first of all. It is not necessary to pretend, for children are too smart anyway. There are so many ways in which a father can be paternal to his children, without formulas and prescriptions. A grim determination to serve leads to nothing but embarrassment, discomfort, self-consciousness, on the part of both father and child.

A number of years ago a friend of mine told me this story: she and her husband and fourteen-year-old son were sitting in the living room after supper. Father was sitting in a comfortable chair, about to read the paper, Mother and son had started to talk about a trial that was in the headlines at that time, involving a ring of gamblers, and "call girls." David's interest and willingness to talk about this pleased his mother because she felt it gave her an opportunity to bring up a number of things she had wanted to talk to him about. She had felt ill at ease and had been very aware of his embarrassment in talking about girls and dates, and sex, and several times she had suggested that her husband talk to David, but he had kept postponing it. As David and his mother got into a discussion of prostitution, its meaning and consequences, the various attitudes and values involved in one's personal view of sexual activity, etc., Father seemed to sink deeper and deeper into his chair and to be literally buried in the paper. When

David seemed to be satisfied with the discussion and started
to leave to go to do his homework, his father called after him
timidly, "Some day you and I must have a talk, David!"

"It may be a good idea, theoretically, for fathers to talk to
their sons," my friend said, "but what are you supposed to do
if he won't take over? Here he let me do all the work while he
hid behind that paper, and then he says he's going to talk to
David some other time. *This* was the time."

Maybe it was and maybe it wasn't. It is, in any event, a
good example of the danger of oversimplifying a father's relationship to his children. Maybe this particular father needed
to work a little harder at overcoming his own uneasy embarrassment in order to help his son feel freer to talk with him—
but not necessarily. If a son feels at ease about discussing
something with his mother, it is foolish to be self-conscious
and artificial and insist that something else is more appropriate. It is possible that David feels extremely close to his father in ways that are very deep and important, but which are
less verbal than his relationship with his mother. Maybe they
feel a deep kinship that goes far beyond the necessity for
words; maybe he knows he can get information and opinions
more readily from his mother, and that as far as the way he
feels deep inside about girls and women, living with his father
has taught him some precious and delicate things that don't
ever have to be put into words; maybe he remembers the way
his father held his mother when his younger sister was killed
in a car accident; maybe he remembers the way his father
looked at his mother when she was all dressed up in evening clothes and looked so pretty. Or he knows how his father
talks to his secretary, when he visits his office—how he gives
instructions quietly, respectfully, how he praises warmly, how
he seems to enjoy talking to women friends and relatives. It
would be nonsense to say that because a father can't do one
kind of thing with his child, he isn't doing something good
and real. In other words, one act, one look at behavior, doesn't
disclose what a father is to his children, and because women
tend, on the whole, to be more emotional and more articu-

late about their emotions, they and their husbands have to be careful not to undervalue other kinds of communication.

I think children have the feeling that fathers are really for "when the chips are down." Children who actually spend very little time with their fathers when they are young seem to have that feeling too. Even if Mother thinks she has been forced to be the disciplinarian, the manager, the one always on call, she will often be surprised to discover that in a real emergency her children will expect Father to take over. This is a quality of fatherhood that may not show up in a spectacular way, but it is of crucial importance.

Women have a tendency to identify strongly with a child's feelings and experiences and may often get overinvolved emotionally, unable to really help, because they are reacting so intensely. Fathers seem more able to be somewhat objective, to get at the major issues more clearly and to respond with less feeling and more thoughtfulness. This often makes it appear that mothers are closer to their children, but it isn't necessarily so. I remember one mother who told me she was beside herself with grief when her daughter wasn't invited to the Junior Prom. "I couldn't control myself," she told me, "I went into Julie's room and I cried too, I kept telling her I knew just how awful she felt. When Abe came home and heard the news, and saw us both carrying on, he was furious with me. He told me it was normal for Julie to think this was the end of the world, but it certainly didn't help, for me to act as if I agreed with her. He sat down very calmly and talked to Julie about how silly it was to look at this as if she had failed in some way. For one thing, there weren't enough boys; for another, she just wasn't the type that would be attracted to boys her own age—she was more mature and would have more fun socially in college. He put the whole thing in perspective."

Many men who don't say too much or who don't play with their children in the ways prescribed by TV, women's magazines and some experts, let their children know very clearly that they are there. Another mother told me that her husband was really quite shy with their fourteen-year-old daughter and just not the sort of person who could make small talk about clothes and parties and dates. Mother was worried about this; her daughter, she supposed, felt that her father was not interested in her. Dena was invited to a party at her school, and she and Mother went out to buy her a new dress. Two days before the party, Dena reported that the boy had changed his mind: he had told her he didn't want to go with her and was taking someone else. When the father heard this he was outraged. Quietly but firmly he said that fourteen-year-old boys just didn't understand about obligations and responsibilities, and he had to learn that he could not be so rude and hurtful. Despite Dena's wails of protest, he called Ted's father and said, "I understand our youngsters are going to the school party together Friday night. I thought I'd see if we could share the chauffeuring. I'll be glad to pick them up if you are planning to take them." With quiet dignity and authority he had moved into a situation where values were involved, and where the man in the family had to protect the young and the helpless. A shamefaced Ted arrived with a corsage on Friday, and became so engrossed in talking about his interest in space travel with Dena's father that it was clearly evident Ted was relieved that a father had set him straight!

Many fathers just aren't the baby-talk kind, nor are they ever really able to be their children's pals. But this does not mean they aren't respected or that their children feel neglected because Mother is around more and is more immediately involved in the day to day business of living. If mothers who worry could listen to their children away from home, they would be surprised at how often Father is quoted—and mostly about major issues, matters of values and standards, a philosophy of life.

This doesn't mean that fathers don't have to make some effort to meet their children halfway. Some fathers are much more at ease with babies, others really begin to enjoy fatherhood when their children reach an age of reason, and if there is a basic sense of concern and caring, this will surmount the difficulties of communication at various stages of growth. But it does help if fathers try to find their own way of relating, whatever form that may take, so that contact is established and so that deeper, unsaid feelings can come through.

One father said that he just doesn't feel comfortable making table conversation with his son, but they both talk very easily to each other while driving in the car. Another father says he makes contact best when he can swim or ice-skate or ski with his children. Another, bookish gentleman just cannot honestly share his son's enthusiasm for baseball, but they love to watch quiz shows together, where his son is pretty impressed with his erudition. Fathers usually tell their children how they feel about them less directly than mothers. They do it by working for them, by showing their concern for all children in their civic activities, in their political and religious beliefs and actions, which tell their children how they feel about people.

What children need most from their father is for him to be himself: enjoying being a man, responding and reacting as the head of a household, passing on those traditions, values and standards that he wants for his children, serving as a connecting link to the larger world, offering protection and guidance. The form this takes is utterly different for each father, if he is honest and spontaneous about it. I know one father who simply could not stand reading the children's books his daughter presented him with. Instead, he took her on his lap at bedtime, and in soft and dulcet tones read her the *Wall Street Journal,* killing two birds with one stone. Daughter was delighted to be sitting on Daddy's lap, nestled warm and snug and safe, and with due apologies to its editors, this material put her to sleep faster and more easily than anything else he could have read. I know another father who loved all the games his children played: he liked to join them in mud puddles, he made sand castles, he splashed in the water, he ran and jumped and climbed; when his children were young, they all had a ball. When his children reached adolescence, he was tongue-tied, couldn't think of anything to say. His fifteen-year-old son took pity on him and said, "It's all right; you don't have to make fatherly speeches to me. Just come to the baseball game with me."

Children need fathers who are natural and relaxed with them, fathers who accept their own limitations as well as the child's. A father who feels ridiculous playing house with a four-year-old may have a glorious time playing chess with a twelve-year-old. Fathers who go to pieces with a sick child may love to take hikes and go camping with a healthy child; fathers who hate "Mother Goose" may love to read Emily Dickinson and Robert Frost to a teen-ager.

Fathers need to find their own ways of communicating with children, without interference from mothers, who sometimes get so agitated and concerned because their husband's ways are different from their own. Too often Father lets Mother come between him and his own special way of reaching his child, and he needs to feel assured that his way will be all right, and he must do it his way.

One couple had a fourteen-year-old daughter, and Jean was greatly concerned because her husband did not seem to be able to achieve a warm, outgoing relationship with Nancy. She nagged him about it, and would tell him, "You ought to ask her questions and show you're interested in her." He usually got angry and more uncommunicative than before. Jean was called out of town when an aunt had suddenly died, and she worried all week about how awful it must be at home, with nobody saying anything. When she got home she found that Nancy and Daddy had gone to a movie one night, had invented a new dish involving scrambled eggs and raw apple, and Nancy was typing some business reports for her father. It occurred to her that she had tried to impose her more verbal, direct communication on two people who had their own, different, just as valid ways, and left to their own devices they had managed just fine.

. . .

The man who says he is run by his wife and children has usually let that happen by default. I have rarely met a mother who wanted to do the whole job. Some mothers have been somewhat overbearing and overanxious and do interfere too much, but by and large they want their children to feel that Father is the head of the house. Too often, because it may be easier, or because father is absorbed in his work and outside interests, he lets mother become the arbiter of justice, the organizer of action and policy. There is, for example, the story of the little boy who called home from a friend's house. His father answered the telephone and the boy asked if he could speak to his mother. When she came to the phone he said, "Tell Daddy to come pick me up."

If fathers want to be in charge, it takes time and effort and contact—but not necessarily in playing games or in being together a great deal. It takes *quality* time for quality communication, which is something natural and real, not phony. Children need to know what their fathers do, what they believe, what they expect of themselves. In nursery school one day I saw a young man of four playing in the doll corner. He was playing that he was the daddy and had just come home from work. He turned to his make-believe wife and children and said, "I am sick and tired of the whole business." This young man is certainly getting an impression of his father's world, but there may be some question about its being the impression his father hoped for!

There are fathers who feel demeaned, unappreciated or not respected by their children if the child sees him wearing an apron, helping with the dishes, doing a load of laundry or even cooking a simple meal on a night when mother has to go to a meeting. The only way a child will get the idea that such activities are unmanly is if father thinks so. A father who feels sure of himself, at home with himself, can do any job and not feel frightened or threatened by it. Children are smarter than we are about such things. A mother told me recently that her husband had lost a very high-paying executive job with a firm that went out of business. Such jobs are very hard to replace, their way of living demanded a very high income and it took months and months for her husband to find the right place. During this time she went to work full-time. She and her husband worried in advance about how the children would react to this. They relaxed when they discovered that while the children still turned to her with bruises, both physical and psychological, their school work and requests for permission to do something still remained clearly her husband's province. In an article by Dorothy Barclay in the *New York Times Magazine*, April 28, 1957, entitled "Trousered Mothers and Dishwashing Dads," she reports on the experts' views: ". . . They held it more important that each individual . . . regardless of sex . . . have . . . the freedom to become his or her own best self."

Boys and girls need fathers equally: a boy to discover how he can be a man in his feelings; a girl to enjoy being a girl with a man. A thirteen-year-old boy decided that he wanted to take three or four friends to a baseball game, and Dad was elected to go along. Dad was a botanist, who did not know the difference between baseball and football, and the only reason he knew who Jackie Robinson was, was because he'd heard him give a talk on race relations. He went under great pain and protest—and returned to admit shamefacedly that he'd had a marvelous time, it was a fascinating game and the boys were a lot of fun. Sometimes we have to permit ourselves to be open to new experiences before we decide what ways we have for sharing.

I have never yet met a teen-age boy or girl who didn't really want Father to represent law and order. They might fight it hard, but want it all the same. In our reluctance to interfere we have often left our children helpless and confused. Father seems to represent something very special for most children in this connection. One father felt very strongly that some television programs were just too bad to be watched at all, too filled with sadism and naked horror. He and his daughter had fought bitterly over this; she would nag and nag and fight back, and try to break him down, but if he meant business and stuck to it, she would eventually give in. His wife often wondered if he wasn't making an awful fuss about a very minor issue, until one day the daughter went to visit a friend for the weekend. On Friday night she called home twice to ask if she could watch two different programs. Father said Yes to one and No to the other, and of course she got mad about the one he said No to. But why did she call in the first place? Father never would have known if she'd watched both of them. It has been a source of comfort and joy to many teen-age girls when Father has taken over the controls about other, "really important things, like make-up and dating" as well.

I am more and more impressed, as I watch children and talk with parents, by the fact that a child's image of himself as either a succeeding or a failing person seems to reflect what Father thinks of himself and of his child. Recently a father was telling me how mad he got when his three-year-old daughter defied him. He would say, very reasonably and sweetly, "Now you can play with this, but you mustn't touch that," and invariably his little angel would do exactly the opposite. He started to tell me that this was why he felt she needed much sterner discipline. I asked why. He replied, much to his own surprise, judging from the startled look on his face, "Because, damn it all, I don't want her to turn into an ornery character like me!" When we discussed his so-called orneriness, he changed his tune. He was an independent thinker, a nonconformist, he chose his own way in life—all this said with pride and conviction. What his little girl needed most from him was to know that being like Daddy was not really a bad way at all—it had good things in it.

Quiet, softspoken, sweet men can raise quiet, softspoken, sweet boys that become real men just like themselves if they have accepted and found lovable these qualities in themselves. A man who says red-bloodedly, "I'll make a man out of my son if it kills us both," as he pulls out the boxing gloves,

hasn't made a man out of himself, so he probably isn't going
to have much more success with his son. Some real men like
physical combat and challenge, other real men hate it. Some
boys compete with their bodies, others with their tongues and
their minds. A father who can say with genuine conviction to
a daughter, "Sure, you want to be a physicist, go right ahead.
You'll be the prettiest and cutest physicist anybody ever
saw," is helping his daughter enjoy being a person and a girl.
The doctor who told his truly brilliant college daughter,
"Don't be a doctor; I hate career women; they make their
husbands feel inferior," was keeping her from accepting her
femininity. If she is cut off from being herself, from following her interests and talents, being a woman will become a
burden instead of a joy. When I met this confused but charming young woman, I said I thought she could be a wonderful
doctor and would bring her warmth and understanding and
gentleness to a profession that can always use more of these
qualities. She smiled and said, "When my father says No, I
don't want to be a wife and mother. When you say Yes, the
first thing I think of is yes, I want to be a doctor, but I also
want to be loved as a woman."

A group of fourteen-year-old girls were discussing their feelings about boys, dating, sex and marriage. One youngster said
thoughtfully, "The best way for a girl to wait until she really
falls in love is if her father showed her a lot of respect." Fathers set the stage for good feelings about oneself.

When a youngster boasts, "My father can lick your father,"
it is not really a declaration of war, but rather an expression
of faith and trust: "If it ever should be necessary for my
health, safety or general welfare, my father would lick your
father." That is really what fathers are for.

The most frequent explanation for the cry of doom about
the survival of manhood in our society is that there are no
more frontiers to explore, no more ramparts to scale, no new
worlds to conquer, and these are what make men feel like
men.

There are more frontiers, ramparts and new worlds than

ever; enough for every man now alive or born hence. But they are *different* from the older, simpler kinds. Instead of hunting wild animals, we have other monsters to slay: hatred, prejudice, stupidity, poverty, enslavement. Instead of conquering the land and the sea, we have the universe of space. Instead of protecting one's own little band or tribe, we have the opportunity and the possibility of saving all humanity. Instead of discovering the wheel or developing a language, we have the most undiscovered world of all, about which we are still ignorant—the mind of man.

There is an old joke about the husband who said, "My wife and I have a very democratic relationship. She makes all the minor decisions, such as where we live, where the children will go to school, what clothes to buy, et cetera. I make all the important decisions, like should we recognize Red China, should we remain active in NATO, how to get a civil rights bill through Congress."

Actually, that old joke isn't so funny! Women *are* more concerned with the details of domesticity; men *are* the ones who must take a stand on moral issues and must create the moral climate in which families can live in dignity and peace. Although men may not literally have to "keep the home fires burning," they are still keepers of the flame; torchbearers of morality; keepers of the faith of our time. Men may no longer be knights in shining armor, but after all, that was the easy road to heroism: you fought with your sword and your lance against your enemies. Now men must fight with thoughts and words and ideas, not only *against* things, but also *for* things as significant as liberty, decency and democracy. If that isn't a call to masculinity, what *is?*

✿ 10 ✿

Marriage Is a *Pas de Deux*

During all the busy years of parenthood we may sometimes forget that it all started with a marriage of two people and will someday return to that.

My husband and I were sitting in deck chairs on an ocean liner, watching the New York skyline recede. I noticed a couple near us, leaning against the railing. The man was tall and rangy, with iron-gray hair; the woman quite a bit shorter, rounder, with a young and vivacious face surrounded by white hair in a feather-cut. Something about them fascinated and attracted me to them. At first I couldn't figure out what it was. The man had a pair of field glasses slung on a strap over his shoulder, and every once in a while he would hand them to his wife without her asking for them. Sometimes they each seemed to be lost in their separate thoughts; at other times, with or without words, there seemed to be a kind of communion in their movements and manner. I guessed that they were in their middle sixties. Slowly I began to realize that completely unconsciously and naturally they seemed to move in a kind of rhythm with each other, and it occurred to my romantic mind that this was a kind of *pas de deux*, a dance of marriage. Their years of living as partners gave them an indefinable but lovely quality, and I found myself wondering what those years had been like, what joys and sorrows, what frustrations and fulfillments, had led to this moment. I felt a renewed sense of perspective for all the years of one's marriage and parenthood, and the infinite range of delights and dilemmas that come to make up one's adult life.

We have all been made acutely aware of the "ages and stages" theory of child development. We need an "ages and stages" theory for grownups! It is silly to think that after adolescence, life just stops in its tracks. The difference between a young woman on her first job and the same woman as a grandmother of seventy is just as great and dramatic as between the infant and the adolescent. As long as one doesn't overdo it, there is good sense in looking ahead and being somewhat prepared for some of the normal and natural changes that are part of life, to be able to meet them with some information and understanding and without fear.

Our roles go on changing dynamically and radically all the way through our adult lives. First there may be the adjustment of living away from home, earning one's own livelihood. Then the more complicated adjustment of learning to live as a marriage partner. The adjustment to parenthood happens in its own ages and stages, since we know that being the mother or father of an infant is nothing at all like being the parent of a sixteen-year-old. There is the adjustment to one child, then perhaps to several young children; the years of great concentration and energy focused on child-raising; the gradual change until the nest is empty once more; the new adjustment to being a married couple alone again. And then, of course, the adjustment to being a parent-in-law, a grandparent, becoming widowed and being alone; of aging, and the physical changes that go with it; retirement, and the shift this creates in one's social role.

Several years ago the Manhattan Society for Mental Health offered a service to community agencies working with the aged. A series of mental health discussion groups were organized, following very much the same sort of pattern as the child study or parent-education discussion groups most of us have heard about or attended as parents. A group (fifteen to twenty-five or thereabout) of elderly people would meet for one or two hours a week, for ten to twelve weeks, to discuss the emotional adjustments necessary in the later years of life. It was soon apparent that many of the feelings of distress that were expressed reflected a lack of preparation, of any awareness ahead of time of what the special qualities or characteristics of the later years might be, and that the inability to deal effectively with life often reflected this sense of shock, surprise, failure to master one's own life. One of the ingredients that can make living more than mere survival is the capacity to change and to grow, to welcome new experiences, to seek the new and to use it for one's own growth—until the day we die.

One of the most difficult tasks in marriage is to keep alive the glow that started it. In a play called *Anniversary Waltz*, by Jerome Chodorov and Joseph Fields, the father, who has two growing youngsters and is beset by the demands of parenthood, says:

> But my God, Millie. Before you're married, everything seems so simple. You're in love and that's it. You take your girl dancing . . . you don't know it but over that lovely girl's shoulder is the Sunshine Diaper Service . . . And instead of "I love you," pretty soon you're looking into your loved one's eyes and saying, "The baby didn't throw up again, darling?" I tell you, Millie, by the time you get that wonderful girl . . . away from the children, your father-in-law, the PTA, the A&P, Dr. Spock and Dr. Gesell . . . by the time you close the door to the bedroom at night, you're just too exhausted to give a damn . . . Love is one thing, and marriage and children are another . . . They're ships that pass in the night . . . one ship is you and

your loved one, sending out an S O S and the other ship is full of children—firing on the life boats.

Along the same line, there is the story of the couple who were approached by a police officer when found necking in a parked car on a college campus. The embarrassed man in the car said, "Sorry, officer, we're parents of a freshman we just brought here and this is the first privacy we've had in eighteen years!"

During the first years of marriage, a couple usually have the time and the opportunity to work out their problems and enrich their relationship in relative privacy. Then a baby arrives and his needs must supersede much of the time. One couple told me that they had expected to lose a lot of their privacy while their children were little, but it came as quite a shock when they realized that the older their children became, the less time they could have alone together in the evenings. "The children's bedtime got to be later and later, and we had to help them with homework. They wanted our attention and it really was the only time we could talk to them."

As their children reach adolescence, many parents have told me they feel a new self-consciousness, even behind closed bedroom doors. They feel embarrassed about locking the door ("*that's* a public announcement if I ever saw one," a father said) and if they don't lock the door, they are afraid that one of the children will just walk in. Smiling sheepishly, one mother said, "Even if they knock—well, it's a very embarrassing scramble!" A father said, ". . . and for healthy married people, necking in the car at a drive-in movie somehow doesn't answer the problem!"

Finding opportunities for expressing love and affection is one of the difficulties that comes with parenthood, quite obviously, but a more basic consideration is how any couple is going to accept and (sometimes!) surmount the normal realities of a long life together. A cartoon depicted a husband and wife watching television, and the caption underneath read, "I agree it's the same thing night after night—but what isn't?" I once heard an argument between a middle-aged couple, in

202 / HOW TO SURVIVE PARENTHOOD

which the wife was nagging her husband to take her out more,
to "make her feel like a woman." His reply was, "I'm not
your twenty-five-year-old boy friend any more, I've been on
my feet for eight hours, I've got a backache, and it can't be
Romeo and Juliet around here all the time!"

No one can maintain romance at a burning pitch all the
time, and the very best of lives include dull routine. During
the middle years of child-raising especially, husbands and
wives become more and more separated in their daily activities, and there are inevitably periods when they almost never
see each other except when they are tired. But if we accept the
fact that our role as parents will become far less time-
consuming and central to our lives when our children are
grown-up, then it seems logical to work at marriage even during the years when parenthood is most demanding. And not
only so that there will be something good left for the later
years, but even more because marriage is the very heart and
breath of parenthood and family life, and has its own rights,
needs and values. What can we teach our children about family life if we are not enjoying our lives as husbands and wives?

A friend told me that she realized she and her husband
were in a rut when their two teen-age sons presented them
with theater tickets for their anniversary with a card that
read: "All work and no fun mean Mom and Pop are pretty
dumb!"

In each marriage one or the other partner usually seems
more able to take the initiative in finding ways from time to
time to keep the romance alive and glowing. It doesn't really
matter which one does it, as long as someone does! This is
especially true in marriages I know where the wife would
love to take the initiative, and could but won't; spiting herself,
she waits for her husband to do it, and they both lose out.

Because of the problem of real privacy, getting away alone is
frequently one of the important ways to keep love alive. A
forty-eight-hour weekend can be a honeymoon—if both partners *really* leave the children behind, both literally and figura-
tively. A woman once told me that her husband had arranged

a surprise for her—a week-long cruise. When the time came to leave, her mother was with the children but her youngest daughter had the measles. "I went with Dick because I just felt I couldn't disappoint him— but I ruined the whole thing for him because I was worried about Joanie. I should have told him the truth and we could have gone another time."

The day I got married, a marvelous great-aunt, who had had a glamorous and exciting life, took me aside and said she had some advice for me. She told me that she had been married for forty years, and there were times when she still felt like a bride. She and her husband had a secret code—when parenthood and work and the tedium of life seemed to be getting the best of them, Uncle Harry would call her up from the office and say he had to go out of town on business the following weekend. She would say that was fine, she had been planning to go away by herself for a short rest anyway and had arranged to have the children visit her parents. My uncle would say goodbye to her Friday morning and go off to work. At about six that night Aunt Catherine would be sitting in the lounge of the Algonquin Hotel. Uncle Harry would happen to drop in for a drink, and he would try to pick up Aunt Catherine. He would tell her that his wife was away for the weekend and he wondered if she'd have dinner with a lonely man. The pickup was the beginning of an "illicit weekend" at the hotel! She told me, "Find your own way—maybe you think this was silly and old-fashioned—but find *your* way to keep love alive—and take my word for it, there are times when that isn't easy later on. But keep your sense of humor about life— you can't always do what you want, and you have to accept disappointment too. One day Uncle Harry decided to make his own arrangements for us to go away together. He called his unmarried sister and arranged for her to come and stay with the children, he bought some flowers and candy, and came home to tell me the news—we were going to a lovely country inn for a few days—and he walked in and found me crying in the kitchen. Our maid had left, I had burned the stew, and

Eddie had the measles, but he gave me the flowers and candy, and we waited for another time."

It was good advice and I never forgot it. But when we try to "turn off reality" and responsibility we must be prepared to know that sometimes it will click and sometimes it won't; if there is humor and affection, one can survive the times it doesn't work out. This kind of maintaining romance is more sensible and possible than the kind advertised on TV. It is NOT possible to wax the kitchen floor in high heels and an Italian knit suit. It is NOT possible to look glamorous and sexy every night—or even most nights—after changing diapers, making formulas, wiping runny noses, going to PTA meetings, shopping in a supermarket, putting up the drapes. It is pure unmitigated propaganda that men are only attracted to beautifully coiffed, stylish, girdled, untired women. Of course there are gay times when husbands and wives want to be glamorous and attractive for each other, but at the end of the day husbands are usually tired too—life at work is full of similar problems and pressures. It is actually a pleasure to come home and be comfortable with someone who is also tired, to take your shoes off, open your tie or put on a torn and much-loved sweater or a ragged old bathrobe, and with your feet up on the coffee table, drink a glass of beer with a comfortable companion. Wives are sometimes horrified and mortally wounded to discover that when a husband strays, it is frequently NOT to a raving beauty, but to a comfortable, relaxed, womanly type!

Sometimes our problems in combining marriage and parenthood successfully have to do with individual tendencies to go to one extreme or the other. Agnes is a magnificent cook and homemaker—there really is nothing she can't do around the house and she loves every minute of it. Her absorption is such that she feels no need to spend time alone with her husband, and slowly but surely their marriage has eroded. They spend all their vacations on camping trips with their children and have lost contact with each other in every area of living except in their role as parents. Frank has fallen in love with someone in his office, is filled with guilt, doesn't want a divorce because of the children and thinks there must be something wrong with him; after all, Agnes is such a fine woman—how could he have done such a thing to their marriage? Agnes lives in blissful ignorance and complacency, viewing herself as a perfect little housewife.

Charlotte is the exact opposite. At thirty-seven she dresses like a teen-ager and has maintained a childlike romanticism. She demands a great deal of attention from her husband, wants to go out several nights a week and is devastated if he isn't always attentive and gallant. She is a very poor housekeeper, extravagant, disorganized, helpless. When her husband reaches a point of saturation and exhaustion, he stays late at the office or has dinner with some of his female coworkers who are refreshingly independent and stimulating company.

Maturity in marriage challenges both partners to live with the inevitable boredom and frustrations of life, meeting their responsibilities with as much good sense and good humor as they can, knowing that there will be times of stress and discontent, but knowing also that with some imagination and ingenuity, it is possible to rekindle feelings of tenderness and passion. The goal we have set ourselves is a difficult one, for in a modern American marriage, we ask to be all things to each other.

If our kind of marriage is to work, we must all, in our own individual and spontaneous ways, find a means to fulfill all the realistic and responsible roles expected of us—and remain lovers as well! On a return ocean voyage, coming back into New York harbor, when I was again "people-watching," I overheard a conversation between a middle-aged couple. They were standing at the railing holding hands and looking at each other lovingly. They seemed to be saying goodbye to each other, and I was surprised because all during the trip I had assumed they were married. I heard the man say, "This was a glorious affair. I hope we can meet occasionally in the city, if you can get away during the winter, but I'll surely see you again next summer," and the woman replied, "It *was* wonderful—I hope your wife won't be impossible to go back to—just remember I'll be back." And down the gangplank they went— to be greeted by three children shouting "Mommy! Daddy! Here we are!" It was one of the most romantic scenes I have ever witnessed! Some couples keep the glow alive more quietly; some do it by fighting! Some need a great deal of time alone together, others don't. But we all need to find our own special way.

Someone once said, "All weddings are happy; it's the living together afterward that causes all the trouble." Well, troubles we all have, no doubt about that, but it is the troubles that can't seem to be handled that most affect the lives of our children. Having met and talked with many divorced parents, I have arrived at the conclusion that one important way to survive parenthood is to stay married!

Children need both their parents, and parents need each other to raise children. Marriage happens, however, to be the most difficult and challenging of all human relationships, as well as the most worthwhile and potentially satisfying, and it takes a great deal of effort, imagination, patience, flexibility, compassion—and just plain old-fashioned maturity and high moral convictions to make it work. I have been quite frankly horrified by the number of divorces that occur, and am convinced that a very high percentage of them need never have happened. Neither party ends up being that much better off, and the children are rarely better off. There are of course some thoroughly intolerable situations where it actually takes courage and self-respect for one partner or the other to insist on ending the marriage in order that the children survive at all. But I am more and more convinced that these situations are the exception, and that a great many divorces are an excuse for immaturity, selfishness, a refusal to face the tough real issues of life. It takes "two to tangle," and I find that when divorced people tell me about how everything was the other one's fault, I am not at all convinced. The immaturity and inability to face up to life may be reflected more distinctly in one or the other, but many marriages survive the imbalance and differences of the partners, and catastrophe is seldom so one-sided.

Most marriages are far from perfect. I don't know anyone who hasn't thought about divorce at some time or other. It is nonsense to say that children are always better off living with one parent than living in a house where there is tension. *Every* house has some tension. *Every* couple has moments of absolutely despising each other. *Every* marriage does both good and bad things to and for the individuals involved. But it is still the best arrangement we have been able to devise for the raising of children, and with all its imperfections, we really ought to try a lot harder to make it work. The fact that so many people don't is the reflection of a kind of mental laziness or immaturity—an attitude that says, "I expect marriage to be all fun, and if it isn't I'm going to get out of it." The satisfying life is the life in which one is able to transcend what is difficult and painful. The greatest sense of self-fulfillment and of pride comes from surmounting obstacles.

I have seen the destructiveness of separation and divorce on children. One senses the stress, the turmoil and the confusion they feel. New fears emerge, feelings of unworthiness, conflict over loyalties. One cannot help but feel that children are the ultimate victims of divorce. Of course there are divorces that represent responsible concern for children, that are protective. Sometimes one has no other choice. Other times there is a choice—between working hard at saving the marriage or getting out when the going gets difficult.

In each separation or divorce, one or both partners feels that life is intolerable and something better is in store for them. This is infrequently true. One divorcée with two teen-age children told me, "I was a fool. I was so sure I'd marry again right away. Instead I've spent ten years raising my children alone, unable to find any man who would be so much easier to love or live with than the one I had. It wouldn't have been perfect—in some ways we might each have had to live our separate lives—but we certainly could have stayed married, and now I know this would have been much better for the children. It was lazy and stupid of me to think I just couldn't do anything constructive about our troubles."

All other things being equal, children can tolerate the arguments, misunderstandings, the plain old-fashioned fights that occur in every marriage. A marriage relationship has to be seriously disturbed, it seems to me, to cause more damage to children than divorce. The lack of continuity in a relationship with both parents, the inevitable struggle not to be caught up in taking sides, the conflict in loyalties, the uncertainties about the future, the homesickness for whichever parent is absent most of the time, the artificiality of the visits with the other parent—these cause as much, if not frequently more, stress and strain than a somewhat shaky but permanent home. We are inclined to approve of divorce because it will hurt our children if we try to maintain a relationship that isn't real or honest. All marriages are a mixture of many conflicting feelings, and who is to measure what is "true" or "false" in the ebb and flow of a relationship? By and large, children of divorce suffer deeply, and in addition to their own emotional scars, they are inadvertently being taught an object lesson: if you don't succeed, don't try.

A marriage specialist, Dr. David Mace, once described marriage as a condition similar to that of a family of porcupines on a cold night; if they get too near each other, they will be pricked by the quills, but if they move too far away from each other, they get too cold! An awareness of the quills that come with continued and intense contact can sometimes help one to maintain that balance which provides more warmth than discomfort.

One of our more common kinds of trouble in today's marriages is infidelity. Greater social freedoms produce more opportunities. Boredom helps. Lack of personal fulfillment and the wish to live more fully may precipitate infidelity. An inability to tolerate frustration, lack of self-direction and long-range goals frequently seem to play a part. One can always hope that as more people discover the pleasures and the practical safety of fantasied infidelities—really a very fine sport!—there may be less need for acting-out in a way that under most circumstances is likely to place a marriage in considerable jeopardy! But it seems to me that we must face the fact that there are times and places where extramarital relationships are chosen with maturity and dignity, and may under very special circumstances even enhance a marriage relationship. At the very least, not all such situations need destroy a marriage.

Some people marry when they are very young and cannot possibly have any clear sense of where they are going. If they are extraordinarily lucky, both partners in a marriage mature together, or if they don't, they are still held together by strong ties of mutual attraction, dependency and love. Some people grow so much or so little that by the time they reach middle age they are almost strangers to their younger selves. It is conceivable that an earlier balance achieved in a basically sound marriage is now much harder to maintain, and that mutual needs have shifted so that the ties that bind are weakened. There may be times in the course of such marriages when the partners find themselves seeking and finding a deeply needed fulfillment outside of the marriage relationship, and what frequently surprises them is that very often the marriage is improved and strengthened. This only seems to occur where the individuals involved are exceedingly mature, responsible, and gifted within themselves and in living with others. For it means that they are able to maintain two deeply significant relationships without exploiting or destroying either of the other two people directly involved. Although it is rare, it happens often enough to warrant a candid evaluation, for it seems to me that because immaturity is so often associated with infidelity, we fail to see those situations that involve genuine growth and sensitivity. The danger is that divorce becomes too easy an answer in all cases.

Two college classmates who hadn't seen each other for fifteen years met on a plane trip. During the trip one of the women, who looked haggard and despairing, confessed that her twenty-five-year-marriage had recently ended, that she and her husband had separated and that divorce was probably her next step. "Do you want a divorce?" the other asked. Polly looked shocked. "What else can I do?" she said. "After twenty-five years of marriage and with two grown children, Les had an affair with a young girl. Am I supposed to pat him on the head and say, 'There, there, that's all right, just come home whenever you're ready'?" As they talked, Sarah helped Polly realize that she and Les were both being destroyed by their separation, that their marriage had survived many storms well and was basically of great importance and satisfaction to them both. This was the husband's first and only escapade, and it had ended as abruptly as it had started, with Les in anguish at the price. Sarah found herself reacting very emotionally; she begged Polly to try to realize that her decision to get a divorce could be more destructive and immoral than the infidelity, that she and her husband might face years of lonely desperation as the price of her pride. Polly became very thoughtful. In a puzzled voice she said, "Sarah, something has happened—you've changed. You wouldn't have given me such advice a few years ago." Sarah smiled and said, "You're right; I *have* changed. My husband died two years ago."

Must it take such a crisis for us to have the perspective to see the real issues in a marriage that has lost its way for any reason? An acceptance of human frailty and an awareness of the hollowness of pride as a value in itself can restore and renew many relationships.

Another frequent source of bitterness and imminent disaster in marriage occurs in relation to in-laws. By and large, feelings about one's in-laws frequently reflect feelings about one's marriage. When we are feeling good about a spouse's talents, charms, gifts and winsome ways, his or her parents look pretty good to us, even if they are not always easy to get along with. When we are preoccupied with our partner's fail-

ings, flaws and weaknesses, even the most considerate and
kindly in-laws may look like monsters! We tend to project our
marital insecurities, uncertainties and frustrations onto our
in-laws, and they, in turn, are likely to do the same thing with
us.

A friend who has been married for about twenty years told
me that her mother-in-law had suggested that her husband
take a very good job in another city and come home to visit
for a weekend every month. "Weren't you *furious?*" I asked.
"She was implying that you and Jeff can live apart, that it
wouldn't make any difference." My friend laughed. She said,
"If this had happened when we were first married, I would
have carried on like a maniac. I would have screamed at Jeff
to defend my honor. In the beginning of a marriage you're so
unsure of it yourself that you can't endure any attack from the
outside. But if you don't have an inner confidence in your marriage after twenty years, you never will. Now I know that Jeff
would consider this as outrageous a way to live as I do, so I
don't have to fight with anyone to maintain my sense of security."

When a young couple overreact to open or implied criticisms, it is often because they themselves are unsure and bewildered about the issues involved.

In the same way the need to interfere, to force one's own
child to take sides against his or her spouse, the need to be
destructive and hurtful in one's criticisms, often reflect the unhappiness and dissatisfaction in the parent's life. A man once
told me, "It never fails; when Betty and I are getting along
wonderfully, I know for sure my mother will tell me she's terribly worried about us! Her own life has been so empty and
lonely since my father died—she feeds on suffering instead of
finding new ways to live a little herself."

One of the major problems that arise between the generations is the wish to deny all the complexities and sensitivities
in the relationship. For most people it is almost impossible
to be pals with parents or in-laws. One simply can't pretend
that parents are ever completely able to see their children as

grownups, or that children ever get over feeling somewhat "infantilized" by parents. The relationship is a difficult one and it demands sensitivity, politeness and self-imposed controls on giving advice too freely or interfering too much. A woman of seventy said, "My daughter looked at me as if I was a scarlet woman when I let my granddaughter teach me the Twist; to her, I've got to be an old lady." A woman of forty-five said, "I have four children, I have lived through a serious illness and my husband's unemployment, and I am now state president of the PTA. Five minutes with my mother, and I feel like an incompetent five-year-old."

There are such potential assets for children in having real experiences with grandparents that it behooves us to try to come to terms with differences where they exist. Grandparents contribute a deep sense of the continuing cycle of life, the never-ending human condition from birth to death. They can give our children a sense of the past, a feeling of tradition, and a sense of rootedness in life. We used to have a theory that parents could give their children unconditional love; they can't, because parents have to raise children to be civilized people. But *grandparents* who do not have this responsibility *can* give a close approximation of unconditional love and should be permitted to do so! We worry too much about "consistent discipline," about confusing our children because we may expect them to do one thing and their grandparents let them "get away with murder" on the same issues. How wonderful! There are so few opportunities in life when one can receive with no strings attached—just for love. Our children are much clearer than we are about this: they know perfectly well that home laws are different from grandparent laws, and they have no difficulty whatsoever adapting themselves to what is appropriate in each situation!

Being able to have a warm and satisfying relationship with parents and parents-in-law means that we are mature and civilized people who can solve our marriage problems where they belong—within a marriage. It means that we are able to enjoy that necessary link with our own past and future, and it means offering our children a kind of love that is unique and special. It is not always easy for the generations to meet together in understanding and mutual acceptance, but if marriage is worth working at, so is this part of it.

Another frequent source of marital difficulty is our tendency to postpone or deny ourselves those things we need to sustain us for some distant plan or goal. It is fine to have such goals, but not at the expense of today's sufficiency, and not out of a misguided belief that we can really control the future. One of the ways in which we express the unrealistic and immature hope that life can be orderly, controlled and predictable is the manner in which we plan for the future at the expense of the present. It is very admirable to plan wisely, to have money for the education of one's children and for retirement. Each of us has to try to do what will make us feel at ease and comfortable with ourselves, and whatever our natural inclination may be, it is certainly sensible to provide some safeguards if—and what a big if it is—there is also a balancing pleasure in being alive today and in living now. We know many people who are inclined to be hoarders. They are scrimping and saving and counting every penny they spend, and you would think, to hear them, that they are poverty-stricken. And then you are shocked to discover that what they have salted away in stocks, bonds, annuities and savings could support them in comfort for years. These same people seem to me to be getting the least out of life, too often. Every move they make is calculated, there is nothing spontaneous in their lives and they live in a kind of self-righteous misery, enjoying nothing except their sacrifices to the gods of the future.

I hasten to add, before I am stoned in the streets, that I have nothing against a financial bulwark against such occasional disasters as an accident, illness or untimely death. What bothers me is that often the safety-security margin for the unknown future is ten times as wide as what one is willing to provide for the immediate experience of living. I suppose some insurance companies have been able to play on our fears as well as our wish for predictability. Many of us have become so alienated from one another, so limited in our capacity to genuinely trust and to give to one another, that it seems far more logical to seek the help of an insurance policy than a friend or relative—we trust policies more than we trust ourselves.

My husband and I have operated on the principle that beyond a certain minimum guarantee of safety, the best insurance policy for our old age is lots of marvelous memories! When we deny ourselves the enjoyment of the present in a bargain with the future we are pretending that one can buy a plan for an orderly life. One sees this most frequently these days in parents who deny themselves vacations, recreation, any of the luxuries that make living more fun, because a large portion of their income must be saved for their children's college education—an undeniably expensive proposition. Many students have worked their way through college, at least contributed toward it; chances are that such students are likely to have a better sense of what they are doing in college, what its purposes and goals are. Actually, not all children should go to college right after high school; some should not go at all; some should get vocational training instead. Whatever they do, often our need to wrap them in cotton batting at a time when they should be searching their own souls for purposes and plans, does not help them find out what will matter to them most.

There are different ways of planning ahead; one way is to try to anticipate and arrange one's life to such an extent that the present loses significance. Another way to be ready for what is ahead is to be as thoroughly alive as one can be and to keep oneself capable of the kind of flexibility that changes in our lives may require.

It was the wedding day of the youngest daughter in a family; now the nest would really be empty. After the bride and groom and wedding guests had all departed, her mother wept as she emptied ash trays, cleaned the silverware and put her house back in order. "What shall I do with my life now?" she

wailed. "My life is over, my children are gone—what will become of me?" Her husband answered quietly, "Why don't you
try being married?"

Vital to our survival is the capacity to change, to adapt ourselves to each stage of life and to live it fully. A friend wrote
to me: "I've been feeling quite depressed lately—don't know
if it was the fatal fortieth birthday or the decision to give up
my old job and try something different. Maybe everything together. It was really the crisis of finding out that each of us is
really alone, no matter how much we may love or be loved. I
am my own woman, nobody else's—and in a way I release the
people I love to be themselves when I say that. But it is terribly painful, all the same. One day I looked at Jeff and Cyn-
thia and realized they are almost grown. In five years they will
both be at college, in ten they will be married, probably—I
might even be a grandmother! I guess I knew I must find a job
that was no longer just secondary in my life—a little extra
cash, a little diversion from housekeeping. All of a sudden I
looked around and I couldn't own anyone's soul but my own
and I had to face this. These are the years when Sam is most
absorbed in his work and most fulfilled by it—his vintage
years. I have to start building a life of inner meaning and satisfaction. Then I'll have something to give to others without
being so dependent on them that I choke them. I realized
that one simply can't ask what I've been asking of another
human being. I'm beginning to understand one is really alone
—that removes the burden of the impossible and the release
can be wonderful for everyone."

And the changes go on . . .

What seems to be the difference between those who enjoy
life in the later years (and who are genuinely enjoyed by others) and those who make life miserable for themselves and
everyone around them? Health seems to be a relatively minor
factor, for I have seen people severely handicapped by illness
and crippling pain lead lives of great beauty and deep satisfaction. As one woman of eighty, suffering from terrible ar-

thritic pain, said, "I manage to live on a different plateau, away from the pain." Being healthy certainly does help, but it is not the crucial issue; that seems to be the ability to accept change and to use it wisely. And right after that, the capacity to enjoy one's own inner life, not to need constant reassurance from others, not to need constant activity, busyness—the frantic search for a substitute for inner life. This quality of self-containment seems to bring with it, strangely enough, the capacity to give oneself really unselfishly to others, with a genuine enjoyment of giving because one is so interested in what other people say and feel and need and do. Probably no one ever exemplified this better than Eleanor Roosevelt. Closer to home I have known a few rare and wonderful women who had something of the same quality. There is a lady in New York called "Nanny" who is ninety-four years old. She works in an office every day as a board member of an educational organization. Her vision is very poor, and she is lame. She travels all over the country to visit grandchildren and great-grandchildren. In the city she travels by bus, and recently stood up so that a crippled man could have a seat. The bus driver, seeing this, stopped the bus and said, "I am not moving this bus until someone has the strength to stand and let this little lady sit." She lives fearlessly, and with joy and trust. A salesman recently visited her. He was selling those one-way "peepholes" for apartment-house doors and tried to sell one to Nanny. He warned her that it was very dangerous for a tiny, defenseless old lady to live alone and let anyone enter her apartment. If she had a peephole door, she would be able to let in only people she knew. Nanny's reply was, "Young man, we have had a very pleasant conversation and I think you are nice. If I had one of your one-way viewers and had seen you in it, I wouldn't have let you in, and where would you be if no one wanted to let you in?" This is a woman who is more alive and has more zest for living than almost any of the women I know in their thirties and forties. She adapts to the times she lives in as they change. She is always willing to try new things, listen to new ideas, she sees advantages in new

experiences and ways of doing things. It is her flexibility and
her acceptance of life that keep her young.

Another young lady of ninety-two, who is a patron of the
arts, is sponsoring a one-man show for a promising young
painter. Her problem at the moment is: will she need a new
corset for the revealing gold-knit dress she has bought for the
opening, or will the old one do? When she settles that problem, she can get on with a dinner party she's planning for
about twenty people. She does all her own shopping and cooking. She is also crippled by arthritis and almost entirely deaf.

What is it that happens to one person which stops him
dead in his tracks, makes him seem old and crotchety and a
nuisance to children and grandchildren—while someone else
the same age goes on having a ball?

Mrs. M. and Mrs. E. are both in their middle sixties. Both
have grown children and grandchildren, both of their husbands are still working. Mr. M. manufactures children's coats,
and Mr. E. is a high school art teacher, who will be forced to
retire in a year or two. Mrs. M.'s children do not enjoy visiting
her, and dread her visits to them, in different parts of the
country. To be perfectly candid about it, she's a pest! She is
always complaining about her health, always has all sorts of
ailments that she discusses at great length; she worries terribly about her children and gets emotionally involved in every
crisis in their lives. When her children left home, she focused
her entire life on her apartment. Nothing is ever allowed to be
out of place; every blemish must be removed at once. We were
once at a dinner party at her home, and Mrs. M. suddenly
gave a gasp of horror in the middle of the conversation, then
caught herself and apologized: she had seen a slight irregu-
larity in the paint on the opposite wall from where she sat—
none of us could find what she was talking about. She visits a
few relatives occasionally, supervises the cleaning and cooking, and once in a while goes out to the theater or a concert,
but not very often. She is exhausted and busy—just straightening the house and supervising the maid takes almost all
morning. Mr. M. comes home as late as he can from his

business and then quietly drinks all evening—if he can sneak it down without his wife catching him. This is their favorite evening activity: seeing which one can outsmart the other.

Mrs. E. used to be Mrs. M.'s best friend. They had their children about the same time, they were intelligent, conscientious parents, they went to child study meetings, sent their children to the new experimental progressive schools that were very popular at that time, did all kinds of interesting things with their children. For Mrs. M. the children became the be-all and end-all of her life. In discussing the tragedy of her later years, her daughter said to me, "The real tragedy was that she accomplished her task too well. The very thing she raised her children for—to grow up and be independent people, to be themselves—was the source of her self-destruction. It is terrible to be needed so desperately by others."

Mrs. E. is so busy with her own life that her grown children find it difficult to get her to visit them. By the time her children were in high school, she began building up her own interests outside her home. She took courses at several museums, studied painting, and slowly but surely moved toward becoming a designer. She and her husband have planned that when he retires, they will move to a small seaside town in Maine, where they have a small house that they use during the summers. The house was rebuilt so that it would have two separate entrances. Thus, when their children visit, their comings and goings never disturb the grandparents, nor do they have to get caught up in each other's life any more than they want. As a result of this system, they have wonderful times together. Mrs. E. let go when it was time to let go, and worked on building her own life and resources. Her children like to be with her, and when they are not with her, they don't feel at all guilty. Their mother doesn't need them for fulfillment and happiness—she has her own life. When children feel guilty because they simply cannot find any way of ever satisfying parents' wishes for love and attention, the relationship gets distorted and painful. The E.'s were able to move to each new stage of life, making demands on themselves first and foremost, to move with intelligence and imagination, and finding in each period of life something good, something special, about it. Mr. M. lives in terror and dread of retirement. Mrs. M.'s life came to an end when her children left home; Mr. M.'s life will end when his work ends. Neither one was adaptable or flexible enough to play different roles at different times of life. Parenthood in the later years simply cannot resemble parenthood in the beginning. Children must move from total dependency to a point where they can assume adult responsibilities and make their own lives. Parents must, if they want to enjoy parenthood of grownups, move from accepting the total dependency of the infant to a relationship of equals: adults who all face life's challenges and problems, and who must ultimately arrive at individual solutions. Parents who continue to develop and change all through their lives, and who recognize and acknowledge their changing role as parents, can be loved and admired by grown children. Respect comes when it is most deserved. Where parents feel that their grown children don't respect them, they had better look at what they are doing with their lives, to be worthy of respect.

Another woman talks incessantly about what her life might have been: she was talented and beautiful and she could have done a million things, but she had children and raised them, and "now it's all over." At sixty-four she sits and complains endlessly about her poor health, her lost youth, the neglect of her children. She is a pain in the neck to be with, and so a vicious cycle starts: self-pity and laziness, which lead to the contempt of others, which leads to more self-contempt, etc. She has neither the guts nor the fortitude nor the courage and patience to really take a fresh look and do things with her life. Much older and far more physically handicapped women are leading fruitful, useful lives.

You know, it's just possible that we and our grown-up children won't like each other very much or have many interests in common! It happens far more often than anyone seems willing to admit, and maintaining this well-kept secret puts a strain on everyone involved. Sometimes one has to accept a limited relationship of respect and affection, even though it cannot provide intense satisfactions. Sometimes, if our grown children are very different from us, it may indicate how well we have succeeded in letting them be themselves, in not trying to make them carbon copies of ourselves. A college professor once told me, "Yes, Marilyn is married. She lives out West. Walter, her husband, drives a truck." He smiled. "He's a *good* truck driver, and a good man, and we were glad Marilyn didn't choose the life of the intellect just because that suited her mother and me." Some of our children will just not be "our type"—they may rebel against us, or they may have personalities and interests that are just completely different. Even in the very best of parent-child adult relationships, expecting constant rewards in the form of gratitude and appreciation are just exactly what make them hard to come by. Such feelings must be freely given, and they can't be if they are constantly demanded.

We need to plan for our later years so that we can be relatively independent both economically and psychologically. But this goes two ways: we must also plan to avoid encouraging our children to remain dependent on us. This is not to suggest that adult children should not have a mature sense of responsibility toward older parents—we hope they *will*—but it comes naturally when we ourselves have self-respect and autonomy and have given the same to them.

There can be a time of closeness and genuine enjoyment between the generations, but it can come only with an acceptance of the changed roles and also with an ability to live comfortably with imperfection: we must not judge our own success or failure as reflected in the lives of our children—a burden that is completely impossible for them to handle. Success or failure, the meaningful life, rests on what one does with one's *own* abilities, talents, inner resources, and must never be measured in terms of the accomplishment of raising children.

.   .   .

I had a rare privilege recently—I saw a young couple fall in love! I had known them and their families since Ted and Louise were babies, and on a hunch I invited them to come for dinner together. The static electricity in the air was violent from the moment they looked at each other, but what really moved me was the change that took place in both of them. When they met, each was drowning in his own uncertainty, his own self-conscious shyness, his fear of his own vulnerability. By the end of the evening they had forgotten themselves in wanting to protect each other. Each had sensed the other's needs, and reaching out with compassion, forgot himself. That is how the *pas de deux* of marriage starts. Each of the dancers is given full range for his capacities; nothing is circumscribed, there is an increase in the expression of potential for both. Each one enhances the power and the beauty of the other, without being diminished by it. The partners are equal in importance and value, but entirely different in role and purpose. Each has his own special moments of glory while the other remains momentarily in the wings. There are moments of great passion and exultation as well as periods of rest, which may be tedious, monotonous, repetitious; these are the necessary counterbalance to the greatness, and help to sharpen and accentuate it. At times the unity of the partners seems to make them complete and they move as one; at other times they are truly alone in an inner core of self. There is a fundamental trust between them, without which the ballerina could not leap with gaiety and joy into her partner's arms, or fall as he catches her.

When a *pas de deux* is truly exquisite, the artistry of each is deeply felt and exulted in by the other, and what the audience perceives as lovely movement is really the full expression of self, through love.

The Promise of Being Human

I have the same feeling now that I often have when a parent-education discussion-group series draws to an end. Even if we have had eight or ten or twelve sessions together, I always have a sense of frustration at all that could not be accomplished. I have a childlike optimism when we begin: finally, at long last, *this* time we are really going to cover in depth all the questions and concerns of the group members, and we are going to gain some of the as-yet-indefinable but perfect clarity that is teasing us, just out of reach. Of course it never happens —and it hasn't happened here either. When I started this book I wanted to say everything I have ever thought about parents and children. I hoped for the revelation of some great truth, just as most of us do when we set out to find relief from our uncertainties.

Now I find myself thinking of the mothers and fathers who often come up to me at the end of a series of meetings and say, "We came in the hope that you would give us some nice simple answers, but even though you didn't really do that, for some reason we feel better." Since *I* usually feel better then, too, I think I know what they mean. It isn't that we have found any formulas or final answers for the terribly complicated and difficult questions that face us all in our living with other people; it is that there has been a reaffirmation and a strengthening of old answers, a renewed feeling of vitality and a reinforcement of our strengths, and the healing comfort of sharing something of ourselves with others; in giving and getting human compassion.

The exploration of ideas and information, and the willingness to use these resources to strengthen oneself and enhance one's experiences in living, make us all feel proud to be human, proud to be ourselves. We feel a renewed value in ourselves, a new optimism about our ability to accept challenge and meet it creatively and with courage.

Just spilling out our feelings, and the renewed awareness it brings of how close we all are in the universality of our needs, confusions and imperfections, helps sometimes. In one of my child study groups, the mothers met once a month in each other's homes. At one point we had to change the meeting date to one week later because of the Christmas holidays, so there were five weeks between meetings instead of four. One mother arrived breathlessly and said, "Never do this to me again! I can be a reasonable, understanding mother for four weeks, but five is just TOO MUCH!" At a school where we were having weekly meetings a mother reported that she had a cold and hadn't planned to come this particular week, but her ten-year-old son had insisted. "He told me he didn't know what happened at these mothers'-meetings every Tuesday afternoon, but that I was so nice to him for two or three days afterward that he didn't want me to miss a single session!"

Sometimes the simplest exchange of information can make such a difference. A colleague told me that she met a woman who had been in one of her groups about five years earlier. This mother talked about her recollection of these meetings so glowingly that my friend was overcome with self-satisfaction. "Yes," she was told, "you never knew it, but you changed my whole life." Having not learned when to let well enough alone, the expert asked what she had done to account for such a dramatic change. The mother replied, "Well, I told you that my husband was very grouchy when he came home from work, and wanted to have his supper right away, just when I was busy with the children—I guess they were about three and five then—and the early evening was bedlam no matter how I tried to organize things. You suggested that if the table was set he would feel reassured that things were just about ready, and he wouldn't be so upset. I laid the table while the children were napping or out playing, and just seeing everything neat and ready, he didn't seem so upset about waiting a few minutes. You have no idea what a difference that made!"

I've noticed that very often parents will report at a first or second meeting that they would like to talk to their children about some vital issue, but that no opportunity ever seems to present itself in a natural way. Sometimes this may be a wish to impart some sex information; it came up many times in groups of adoptive parents around telling children they were adopted. Parents complained, "I just can't find a way to bring it up," or "What can I do—Mike just doesn't seem the least bit interested." Then, after we have been meeting for a while, parents will come in saying, "I have no idea how or why—I guess it's just a crazy coincidence, but guess what my child asked me last night!" Without ever knowing just how it happens, without listing any formulas or prescriptions, learning and thinking together often create a readiness in ourselves that we don't even see and can't measure; but we know it must be there because things begin to happen in a new and different way.

What I am really saying is that the absence of answers is no measure of growth. Often quite the reverse is true—the increase in questions may be an indication of great strides, for it indicates that life is being examined, and as Socrates said,

"The unexamined life is not worth living." The process of learning is an end in itself, for when we learn we are alive, we are open to new possibilities, we find new dimensions within ourselves that give us a sense of greater stature, a pride in ourselves.

In my work with parents I hope to provide some background information which can give parents a wider range of choices. I hope that we can all widen our own perspectives and become more sensitized to more possibilities. I hope that through meeting and thinking together each person will find something new about himself, some new strength, some new interest or talent or deeper dimension—and it happens to me all the time.

I would not like to feel that I had suggested anywhere in this book that our problems can always be solved by suggestions from others, discussion, getting information or in exploring our own feelings. There are times when we simply can't do it alone. There are times in our lives when we can profit from the special kind of help involved in counseling and psychotherapy. Often this can be the most profound acceptance of one's human vulnerability as well as one's search for significance in life.

Sometimes we seek help around some very specific stumbling block, in which case we may want some direct counseling and advice. At other times we begin to perceive a pattern of failure and discontent so distressing that we know we must really work very hard to effect a change. Some adults who do not seem seriously disturbed, who function fairly well in their daily lives, will want psychotherapy because they are people who have unusual depth and potential, and who realize they are not living up to it; they could "get along" without psychotherapy but they want much more out of life than that.

Whatever one's reasons and needs, help is available—excellent help if we know what to look for. But that's a big "if," for the field of psychotherapy is a confusing one today. Major changes have been taking place in a field that is still in its revolutionary beginnings. Social change has been so rapid that

the insights and techniques of psychotherapy even ten or
twenty years ago are inadequate for dealing with today's problems.

As in the development of most sciences, the earliest research involved the careful study of pathology; it was necessary to study the mentally ill before one could develop practical procedures for cure or for prevention. This early concern
with clinical pathology tended to focus our attention on what
was unhealthy in the personality, and only in more recent
years has psychotherapy turned its interest intensively to what
are the healthy strengths, the forces for growth, in the individual's make-up.

Because maladjustment was the real challenge at first, there
was a false overvaluation of adjustment and we found that we
tended to encourage an adjustment which avoided crises, pain
and discomfort, and fostered conformity. We are now realizing
that this was an empty and unreal goal, that there is much
more to good mental health than mere adjustment. One psychiatrist commented ruefully, "Some of my patients are much
more interesting at the beginning of therapy than at the end!
I help them to accept the world as it is—and you have to be
pretty dull to do that." This view denies the validity of pain
as a worthwhile price for being a live person. An opposite
view is that of a wise and sensitive therapist who said, "There
is nothing really wrong with being neurotic—it's just a question of where the neurosis is located. If it is in front of the
person and is choking him to death, I try to help him push it
around to the back, where it can serve as an outboard motor!"

We live in a time of anonymity and bigness, of technological advance, of large and crowded cities, of feeling helpless
and insignificant. We have lived through the horrors of Nazism and the concentration camps it produced, through two
terrible wars and scores of small ones, through the development of the atomic bomb with its capacity to destroy human
life on earth. We are filled with doubts and find ourselves responsible for our own destinies in a world that presents us

with fearful choices. Rather than suffering primarily from a repressed unconscious, today's patients come to psychotherapy asking, "Who am I? What does life mean to me? Where am I going? What do I want?"

In the light of these developments many people are very much confused by the different kinds of treatment available to them, and the different philosophies represented. In order to be able to make one's own evaluations, it may be helpful to know about some of the major changes that seem to be going on today:

1. Earlier theories held that man was entirely ruled by unconscious drives. The newer view is that although unconscious needs and wishes certainly play a role in decision-making, they are not the only factors involved. Rational, intellectual, thinking man participates. Spiritual and moral values also influence decisions consciously.

2. In orthodox analysis, it was considered desirable that all major decisions be postponed during the course of treatment. The newer approach suggests that psychotherapy must be part of the concurrent life of the patient—an added dimension to growth.

3. The psychotherapist, who used to maintain careful neutrality, who served as a sounding board for one's own thoughts, is now becoming a participating member of a decision-making partnership. He brings objectivity and breadth of vision to the exploration of a choice, but he does not withhold his own views. Psychoanalysts were once not supposed to voice approval or disapproval, until recent years when there has been a great deal of discussion about the role of the therapist in relation to moral and ethical standards. A patient was very shocked when her therapist insisted that she should not do something quite hurtful to a relative. "What kind of a psychiatrist are you, anyway?" she asked. "I thought you were supposed to understand my feelings and help me express myself." The therapist replied, "That's just what I'm

doing—helping you express the part of you that is thoughtful and compassionate."

4. In the past very little that a patient said was likely to be accepted at face value; if he said he loved his mother, he was just hiding his hatred; if he was late for one appointment, he was resisting; if he was neat and orderly, he was compulsive. We are discovering that not every expression or event has to have a hidden meaning. Furthermore, the credulity of the patient is as much deserving of respect as the therapist's.

One of the confusing elements in seeking help is knowing which professional discipline to turn to: psychology, psychiatry, social work or counseling. The decision depends partly on community resources and partly on the nature of the problem. Ordinarily the possible distinctions and factors affecting one's choice can be discussed with a qualified referral service, such as the health department or a mental health association. Whatever professional title a person may have, the most important thing is still his professional integrity, his philosophy of life, whether or not you like him as a person. We want a qualified person, of course, and each of these professions has associations that set standards for their members. Many states have also set up certification and licensing not only for medical personnel but for anyone practicing psychotherapy. When we are considering the possibility of getting help we have a right to information that can increase our powers of selectivity; we need criteria for evaluating any new experience. Sound information frees the individual to trust his judgment, to accept the validity of his own intuitive reactions.

Basically what one must look for in this important choice is an artistic human being—and this is a difficult quality to describe. Such a person is able to relate warmly and well to other people. He obviously seems to be enjoying his life and his work. He has many interests, is curious, flexible, ready to learn and to experiment. He says what he honestly thinks and one feels that he is not holding back, maneuvering or manipulating the discussion in a self-conscious or stereotyped way. He talks a little about himself; he expresses his likes and dislikes; one feels that he is friendly, wise and compassionate.

A friend described his therapist as "someone who is unashamedly glad to be alive." Another friend said, "She *likes* me! She makes me feel lovable!" These are important ingredients in the artistry of psychotherapy.

Psychotherapy can be one of the greatest and most rewarding adventures, it can bring with it the deepest feelings of personal worth, of purpose and richness in living. It doesn't mean that one's life situation will change dramatically or suddenly; it doesn't mean that life will become a bed of roses. It does mean that one can develop new capacities and strengths with which to meet the natural vicissitudes of living; that one may gain a sense of inner peace through greater self-acceptance, through a more realistic perspective on one's relationships and experiences. The large majority of former patients still face conflicts, fail in meeting challenges, have difficulties in work and family relationships. But they also feel more self-confident about solving their problems, they are strengthened by a deeper understanding of themselves and others, and perhaps most important of all, they are using their talents, their energies, in a freer and more fruitful way.

The theme throughout this book can hardly be credited as new or startling. But in a sentence, it is the simple, old-fashioned notion, "To thine own self be true . . ." Some of you may be disappointed and angry. You've spent a lot of time reading, and what have you got for your effort? I know how you feel; it happens to me all the time, and to the parents I meet with. We all hope for new answers to old questions. Where did we ever get the idea that there *could* be simple answers to the problems and opportunities of life? Why should human relationships—the most complex, subtle, delicate, crucial aspect of life on earth—be easy to figure out? And how could any of us be smart enough to solve the problems of the minds and hearts of human beings, when no one has come near accomplishing this in five thousand years of recorded human history?

For, really and truly, there is no single task in life that demands more hard work, more courage, more sensitivity, more imagination and thoughtfulness, than trying to understand and know oneself and to use the rich potentials one discovers for living creatively with others. None of us ever succeeds. Many of us need all kinds of help along the way. It is a lifetime process to search for meaning in one's life, to explore and discover one's identity, to develop a sense of meaning that can bring with it a commitment to that life and give it significance.

Every time a parent takes another step toward developing the best in himself, he increases his enjoyment of, and his talent for, parenthood. It is the toughest work in the world. A sense of personal identity grows as one accepts the responsibility for living up to one's deepest convictions. This means living significantly, so that one's life counts. It means demanding righteousness, accepting pain, believing in possibilities that no one can ever promise to make come true. In discussing the qualities of maturity, Dr. Blaine McLaughlin, Director of Psychiatry at the Women's Medical College of Pennsylvania, said, "To grow up in life means learning to live with impossible problems."

Values are never clear and absolute, and we are constantly having to struggle between opposing values. How often do we not find some really clever rationalization for not living up to a principle, an expectation? Because issues are complex, how often do we not evade making some kind of commitment, limited and imperfect though it may be? And it is in the heart of this struggle that our sense of personal survival exists.

Several years ago, when our daughter was eleven, she wanted to go to a social dancing class. Naturally, "everyone else is going"—did you ever hear it any other way? I made some calls to other parents and discovered that for once this estimate was not an exaggeration. What was my decision to be? I was and am unalterably opposed to many of the boy-girl social absurdities that we foist on our pre-puberal children. I also believe that children cannot be expected to carry social burdens that they are not ready for, or that they had no part in creating. If I was a red-blooded American mother and said, "No, you can't go, because I am opposed," would I be living by my values, or making my child do the dirty work for me? I would demand a strength and courage from her that would be intolerable at her age and level of vulnerability to the opinions of her peers. I decided that of greater value was compassion for the hopes and hurts of eleven-year-old girls, and while I made my standards perfectly clear to my daughter, I would not deprive her of belonging. Right after this decision had been made, and there was hysterical joy abroad in our home, I learned that a Negro child in her class was not going to the dancing class. Now we were on different ground. This was no minor value—this involved the foundation of my own and my husband's lives—a firm and aggressive belief in the equal rights and dignity of all human beings. We told our daughter that if her classmate was left out, she could not attend the dancing class under any circumstances. Interestingly enough, where there had been hysteria about not going because we just didn't believe in the program, there was none now. I knew there was pain and anguish in the possibility of not going, but there was also a basic sense of justice, and a pride in our stand.

Every day we face these issues in our own lives and in our children's, and it is a constant struggle to make the right decisions.

We know a couple who have been political rebels since their college days, during the Depression. Now their brilliant college-age daughter wants to work for one of the integrationist organizations. A beautiful and sensitive young woman, she has gone to jail twice, and they know the experience of what she is living through will be with her always. What values are involved for them, and which ones take precedence over the others?

Another family was warned that their son would be expelled from college if he continued in his political activities. He was editor of the college paper, and had been writing "inflammatory editorials" denouncing the faculty and trustees for not permitting an avowed communist to speak to the students, as a breach of the right to free speech and the freedom of assembly. What happens when we have told our children what we consider to be the fundamental rules of an ethical and moral life, and then by default accept the defilement of these standards every day of our lives, in small ways and large, by excusing our friends, by compromising, by exempting ourselves or our children?

A high school student was offered a summer job working for a business associate of his father's. In the course of filing some papers he came across some notations which indicated that his employer had filed a false income tax statement. In righteous indignation the young man informed his parents that he wanted to report this to the proper authorities. His parents were deeply troubled. They knew and admired the employer, who was in many ways a decent and kind person. On the other hand, they had tried to instill a respect for law in their son. How do you inspire righteous indignation and courage to act, and also help a young person understand all the potential consequences of an act—how do you yourself weigh the human hurts that are involved in such a choice? This is the tough work of being truly alive and involved— and it is the only road to the self and then to the capacity for joy and satisfaction in parenthood.

It is the *struggle* which is honorable. Everyone lives with confusion, uncertainty, anxiety, guilt, doubts and fears. But we feel alive, we feel proud, when we face these conflicts and challenges—there is an affirmation of life and its meaning in the search, the quest.

·   ·   ·

One of the major and unnecessary causes of emotional exhaustion is the tremendous amount of energy we put into maintaining the myth that we are all happy, that happiness is the only thing that counts and that material success is the source of our happiness. I often wish the Declaration of Independence offered us the "pursuit of fulfillment" rather than "of happiness," which seems to me to become a more and more useless and misleading goal. Many people said that they felt a sense of relief during the mourning period after President Kennedy's death, because it was, for a brief time, all right to cry in public, to express grief openly, to show one's pain and anguish for the human condition. The shame was gone, there was a kind of honesty and integrity in admitting together that death and tragedy and terrible grief are still as much a part of life as they have ever been, and that there is significance in meeting these with courage and dignity. We play the "happiness game," we all pretend that it's true, we work at the pretense that life is gay. Well, it isn't. All of science, all of modern knowledge and technology, all the current tendency to evade the issues of living and dying, don't really do one bit of good. Life goes on presenting us with its uncertainties, its shocks, its events that we cannot control or change. Happiness is not an end in itself. Nor can we find it, looking for solutions to insoluble problems. I sometimes suspect that what people call happiness is simply the absence of feeling. Joy, on the other hand, is something quite different: the piercing, unforgettable moment that gives height and depth to our existence, and that includes, as its necessary counterpart, pain and grief. Joy comes for a moment, unexpectedly, with great intensity and buoyancy, giving us for a moment a quality of indestructibility. Max Lerner once wrote that what he wished for his children was not happiness but occasionally "the stab of joy."

Our preoccupation with happiness seems to be related to the popular myth that we can arrange our lives! How furious and outraged we are when our best laid plans run off course! We make such an investment in orderliness—how dare life challenge us by indifference to our plans! Well, we live in a disorderly universe, and the sooner we relearn that, the better. There is no harm in trying to plan sensibly as long as we have a genuine acceptance of the unpredictability of life, and don't invest our present in our future, leaving nothing for here and now. I think that our attempts at living in the future may account for a high percentage of our discontent.

We can't predict the future; we are not omnipotent; we can't control our children or their lives. We can just live and do, bringing to it whatever best we can search out in ourselves—and we don't know everything; we can't control everything; we are not responsible for everything. Our technological age makes us lose sight of these comforting and essential limitations!

An awareness of the unpredictability of life is not, however, an excuse for weakness! We are challenged to make sense out of our *lives*, not of arbitrary events.

How desperately our children want us to have pride and dignity in our lives and to live with purpose! Over and over again we see it in the way children react when we really begin to set some standards and to demand something more of them and of ourselves. Whenever I have eavesdropped on a conversation among children (of any age), sooner or later I hear the theme, the central core of what gives them a base, a sense of being rooted in life—and that is their redefining and restating of what their parents believe and don't believe, what they permit and what they don't permit.

Children are positively gluttons for values! I have never yet seen or heard of a child who did not respond with enthusiasm to an explanation of why something was either good or bad, right or wrong. He might be mad for a minute if this interferes with his enjoyment of life; but just watch young children more closely, see what happens when you express righteous indignation about some social injustice, or when you explain the reasons for living by certain principles. Children seem to turn into human sponges in their eagerness to absorb this essential nutrient—morality.

We seem to have gotten the strange notion that standing up for what we believe should be easy and pleasant. Why should it? First of all, just searching for one's own values is a life-and-death struggle, especially because each of us is really on our own in finding the answers. Such issues were once determined almost entirely by the external force of one's religious heritage and association, and the rules and regulations imposed from above. Democracy and a revolution in religious and philosophical thought have changed all that. With rare exceptions, and even with strong identification with a religious group, most of us are still called upon to discover our own meanings. Church membership does not disguise the fact that agnosticism is the mood and temper of our times, and a liberal relativism has almost completely replaced the acid, fear-inspiring, hell-fire-and-brimstone religions. And so we must, if life is to have meaning, find a path for ourselves. But that is only the beginning of the struggle. Once having found a frame of reference, how do we live up to it? To make it work at all, we have to fight for what we believe—and that means being *against* something as well as *for* something. We have to fight against social injustice, for social progress; against enslavement, for freedom; against anger, for compassion and brotherhood; against ignorance, for enlightenment—in whatever terms we see these issues. Individual man has always, and still does, stand alone against some vested interests or other, in every aspect of life. He feels alone and afraid. And there are so many escape clauses! It is so easy for us, right now, to avoid taking a stand; so many of us are protected from the full impact of social issues, if we want to be. If you are in the path of a hurricane, then you have to take action; the true heroes in life are those who can take action without the hurricane. As Thoreau said, "We should be ready for all issues, not daring to die, but daring to live." And a Polish writer is quoted as saying, "He who swims against the current must not expect it to change direction."

Giving the graduation address at a girls' school in 1937, Mrs. Eleanor Roosevelt told them, "Most people die of boredom. I wish for you the ability to be curious and the unselfishness to think of others, which will in the end bring greater interest to your own lives. I wish for you always the ability to feel the flow of new ideas, so that you will never be old, never bored."

We need to trust life more and to be able to accept our own and our children's failures and limitations. If we can truly believe that mistakes and failures offer opportunities for learning, we won't be paralyzed by the inevitable failures that occur. A minister told me that a family had come to him in great distress because their seventeen-year-old son had accepted responsibility for the pregnancy of his sixteen-year-old "steady." The parents, who considered themselves understanding and loving, were greatly shocked and desperate for guidance in helping their son meet this crisis. The minister said, "What impressed me in this case, as it has in many others, was that even though the problem might be very serious and disturbing, it seemed to bring the family members closer together in ways they had never dreamed possible before. I've tried to analyze what seemed to make the difference, and I think it is that under such crucial and intense circumstances, all pretense is forgotten, all shyness and pride disappear. Parents begin to act just the way they feel; they show their distress and are honest often for the first time in saying, 'You are a child and we will defend you and protect you no matter what it takes.' The whole family talks openly and directly with each other in a way they never have before. There is no more hesitancy and shyness about discussing every aspect of sexuality, love, the problems and possibilities inherent in male and female relationships." One father had said to him, after dealing with such a serious problem, "You will probably think I'm crazy—it was a ghastly thing to live through—but I find I can't really be sorry it happened. No matter how great the scars for all of us, what we have *learned!* We reached each other in a way that we never had before—we touched each other's lives without pretense, without caution, without shyness or uncertainty. What this brought to our family was something so wonderful and strong that it will mean something to us long after the pain is gone. We are close in a way we never were before; it's a kind of primitive, instinctual experience, and all the veneer of civilization was swept away. Do you think I'm crazy if I say I'm glad it happened?"

This is the kind of experience that no one recommends, heaven knows, but it has implications for all the lesser crises and failures and mistakes that we and our children make. We would get so much more out of our relationships with those close to us if we could abandon our defenses and meet each other halfway, completely open and without pretense—and not have to wait for some disaster to rip down the barriers for us.

The only way to survive parenthood is to survive *life*; to become a parent just because that is part of life, without bargains, without claims. If you do a thing, you should do it because you *want* to, and this applies to parenthood perhaps most of all. If you want to put love, effort, concern, energy and time into being a parent, do it for *yourself*, not in order to claim a reward from your children or to prove your worth to yourself or anyone else. Someone once told me, "When you become a parent, you are a vessel of life," and nothing I've heard before or since seems to me to say it better. Parenthood is an affirmation of being human, of being alive. It is a creative process for oneself, like painting a picture, designing a house or making a dress. It does something for *you*. If we can really believe and live by that principle, fewer children would become defensive enough to say, "I didn't ask to be born," for they would not feel called upon to prove themselves worthy of our act.

And to sum up, finally:

The main task of parenthood is to be oneself, to work at self-discovery. Being a poor parent comes from having poor feelings about oneself: areas of unfulfillment, unfinished business of growing up, hating parts of oneself. A magnificent play by Arthur Laurents, "Clearing in the Woods," describes the struggle that can lead to fulfillment as a person (and as a parent). The heroine is so filled with self-hate that she is finally driven to attempting suicide. But at the final moment of decision she chooses life, because she discovers that somewhere, deep within herself, she has compassion and concern for herself. In finally facing herself, she meets herself as a child in various stages of growing up, and as she gets to know the problems and feelings of herself at different ages, she learns to understand, to feel compassion, to love herself. Her greatest affirmation and maturation comes when she opens her arms to the little girl she once was, who she thought she despised and who she thought was ugly and unlovable.

A therapist once described to me a technique he had used to help his patients begin to accept all the parts of themselves they had rejected. One patient, Jenny, whose mother had died when she was five, and who had had a stormy and difficult childhood, had become a nursery school teacher. She was able to pour a great deal of warmth and affection into her work with other children, but was filled with hate for herself. One day the therapist asked her to recall a time when she was very young, a time that was especially sad and difficult. Jenny described a time when she had been naughty and had been spanked and sent to her room. She was lying on her bed crying. The therapist asked the patient, "If you could go back there now, as an adult, what would you do if you walked into that room?" "I'd beat her and beat her," Jenny said with fury —and then, shocked at her words, added, "Oh my God, the poor little thing!" She began to see that when she could love that part of herself, the little girl she had thought was so bad, she would be able to love others in a new way. Learning to live with oneself, and enjoy this inner companion, is the first step toward living with children, for our children arouse in us the feelings we have about ourselves. We can accept and enjoy what we have liked in ourselves; we reject and destroy what we have misunderstood and hated in ourselves.

. . .

A friend wrote to me about the tragic death of a young woman she cared about deeply. She described her terrible sense of loss, her despair and anger at the exigencies of fate. But then she added, "Damn it, though—through all the 'existential absurdity,' the fact of life and the promise of being human still seems to be enough."

Bibliography

This is a suggested reading list, not a comprehensive bibliography. Anyone who wants reading material on marriage, parenthood and family life can find lists available from many sources. One of the best resources is a very carefully selected and well-thought-out listing of a wide range of subjects made available by the Child Study Association of America, 9 E. 89 Street, New York, under the supervision of Mrs. Mildred Rabinow. A comprehensive listing of the best books in the field of parent-child relations costs 60¢, and there is a yearly supplement, which costs 50¢. Public libraries; mental health associations; *Parents' Magazine*, published by The Parents' Institute, 52 Vanderbilt Ave., New York 17; *The PTA Magazine*, official magazine of the National Congress of Parents and Teachers, 700 N. Rush Street, Chicago, Ill.; as well as the Children's Bureau in Washington, D.C., help to keep us abreast of new materials that are available.

The present list represents a few of the books and pamphlets that have made some special difference to me; they are resources that I feel have helped me to grow, to gain new insights, to keep me alert. They represent a point of view that I find especially helpful and meaningful and that I'd like to share with you.

Barclay, Dorothy. *Understanding the City Child: A Book for Parents.* Franklin Watts, 1959, N. Y.

Fraiberg, Selma. *The Magic Years.* Charles Scribner's Sons, 1959, N.Y.

Friedenberg, Edgar Z. *The Vanishing Adolescent.* Beacon Press, 1959, Boston.

Grossman, Jean Schick. *You Don't Have to Be Perfect.* New York State Mental Health Association, 105 E. 22 St., N. Y. (20¢)

Grossman, Jean S. and Max. *Ethical Values in Family Life.* New York Society for Ethical Culture, 2 W. 64 St., N. Y. (35¢)

Gruenberg, Sidonie M. and Krech, Hilda S. *The Best of Both Worlds: Housewife and Woman.* Dolphin Books, 1964, N.Y.

Halsey, Margaret. *The Folks at Home.* Simon & Schuster, 1952, N.Y.

Hechinger, Grace and Fred M. *Teen-Age Tyranny*. William Morrow & Co., 1963, N.Y.

Hunt, Morton. *Her Infinite Variety: The American Woman as Lover, Mate and Rival*. Harper & Row, 1962, N.Y.

Hymes, James L., Jr. *A Child Development Point of View*. Prentice-Hall, 1955, N.Y.

Hymes, James L., Jr. *Understanding Your Child*. Prentice-Hall, 1952, N.Y.

Jenkins, Gladys Gardner. *What Is Success? What Do We Value?* Association for Family Living, 32 W. Randolph St., Chicago 1, Ill. (25¢).

Keliher, Alice, et al. *Don't Push Me!* The Association for Childhood Education Int'l., 3615 Wisconsin Ave. N.W., Washington 16, D.C. (75¢).

Maslow, Abraham H. *Towards a Psychology of Being*. Van Nostrand, 1962, N.Y.

May, Rollo. *Man's Search for Himself*. W. W. Norton & Company, 1953, N.Y.

Murphy, Lois. *The Widening World of Childhood*. Basic Books, 1962, N.Y.

Neisser, Edith. *How to Be a Good Mother-in-Law and Grandmother*. Public Affairs Pamphlets, 22 E. 38 St., N.Y. 16. (25¢)

Rainer, Jerome and Julia. *Sexual Pleasure in Marriage*. Permabooks, 1962, N.Y.

Redl, Fritz. *Understanding Children's Behavior*. Teachers' College, Bureau of Publications, Columbia University, 1957, N. Y.

Thomas, Alexander, M.D., Birch, Herbert, M.D., Chess, Stella, M.D., et al. *Behavioral Individuality in Early Childhood*. New York University Press, 1963.

Wheelis, Allen. *The Quest for Identity*. W. W. Norton & Company, 1958, N.Y.

About the Author

E D A J. L ᴇ S H A N, a graduate of Columbia and Clark universities, is one of this country's foremost authorities on problems of family living. She has been nursery-school teacher and director, child welfare worker, diagnostician and play therapist, a director of education, a consultant to *Parents' Magazine,* and is currently Education Consultant, Manhattan Society for Mental Health, and Consulting Psychologist, Colonial Nursery School of New Rochelle.

She has written and published widely—in *Parents' Magazine, Childcraft Encyclopedia, National Parent-Teachers Magazine,* the *New York Times Sunday Magazine* (four appearances), *Journal of Marriage and Family Living, Journal of Psychiatry, Journal of Occupational Therapy, Book of Knowledge,* and others. She has written pamphlets for Public Affairs Pamphlets on such topics as "You and Your Adopted Child," "The Only Child," and contributed an essay to *Encyclopedia of Child Care and Guidance.*